MACCABEE,
CHRISTIANS, AND QUMRAN

A NEW HYPOTHESIS OF QUMRAN ORIGINS

BY

ROBERT H. EISENMAN

Grave Distractions Publications
Nashville, TN

STUDIA POST-BIBLICA

INSTITUTA A P. A. H. DE BOER

ADIUVANTIBUS
L.R.A. VAN ROMPAY ET J. SMIT SIBINGA

EDIDIT
J. C. H. LEBRAM

VOLUMEN TRICESIMUM QUINTUM

MACCABEES, ZADOKITES, CHRISTIANS, AND QUMRAN

A NEW HYPOTHESIS OF QUMRAN ORIGINS

Grave Distractions Publications
Nashville, Tennessee
www.gravedistractions.com
© 1986, 2013 Robert Eisenman

2nd Edition
ISBN-13: 978-0-9890293-1-5

In Publication Data
Eisenman, Robert
Categories:
1.Religion 2. Biblical Studies 3. Exegesis and Hermeneutics

Publisher's Note
This edition is a faithful reissue of Robert Eisenman's classic work. The content of this text is identical to the original, however minor changes have been made to the original text's layout and syntax. The goal in presenting this work is to convey the original information in an updated format.

Printed in the United States

Judas, called Maccabaeus, with some nine others, withdrew into the wilderness, and lived like wild animals in the hills with his companions, eating nothing but wild plants to avoid contracting defilement. (2 Macc 5:27).

The disciples said to Jesus: "We know that you will depart from us. Who is he who shall be our leader?" Jesus said to them: "In the place where you find yourselves, go to James the Righteous One, for whose sake Heaven and Earth came into existence". (Gos Th 12).

Noah was a Righteous One. Assuredly so after the supernal pattern. It is written, "The Righteous One is the foundation of the world", and the Earth is established thereon, for this is the Pillar that upholds the world. So Noah was called "Righteous" below ... and acted so as to be a true copy of the supernal ideal ... an embodiment of the world's Covenant of Peace. (Zohar 59b on "Noah").

When God desires to give healing to the Earth, He smites one Righteous One ... with suffering ... to make atonement ... and sometimes all his days are passed in suffering to Protect the People. (ibid., 218a-b on "Phineas").

CONTENTS

ABBREVIATIONS

ANF	The Anti-Nicene Fathers
Ant.	Josephus, *Antiquities of the Jews* (*Antiquitates Iudaeorum*)
1 Apoc Ja	First Apocalypse of James
2 Apoc Ja	Second Apocalypse of James
Apost. Const.	*Apostolic Constitutions*
APOT	*Apocrypha and Pseudepigrapha of the Old Testament,* edited by R. H. Charles
ARN	*Abot de Rabbi Nathan*
BASOR	*Bulletin of the American Schools of Oriental Research*
CBQ	*Catholic Biblical Quarterly*
CD	Cairo *Genizah:* Zadokite Document
Comm. in Matt.	Origen, *Commentarium in Evangelium Mattheum*
Dc Mens et Pond	Epiphanius, *De Mensuris et Ponderibus*
Dial.	Justin Martyr, *Dialogue with Trypho*
E. H.	Eusebius, *Ecclesiastical History*
Gos Th	Gospel of Thomas
Haeres.	Epiphanius, *Adversus Haereses*
Hist. Nat.	Pliny, *Natural History* (*Naturalis Historia*)
IEJ	*Israel Exploration Journal*
In Flare.	Philo, *In Flaccum*
JBL	*Journal of Biblical Literature*
JJS	*Journal of Jewish Studies*
JTS	*Journal of Theological Studies*
Mur	Wadi MurabbaCat Cave I
NTS	*New Testament Studies*
PEQ	*Palestine Exploration Quarterly*
Quod Omnis	Philo,Quod Omnis *Probus Liber Sit*
Qumran	*Revue Qumran*
RB	*Revue biblique*
Rec	Pseudoclementine Recognitions
REJ	*Revue des dudesjuives*
SBL	Society of Biblical Literature
Test. L.	Testament of Levi
TZ	*Theologische Zeitschrifi*
Vir. ill.	Jerome, *Lives of Illustrious Men* (*De Viris Illustribus*)
Vita	Josephus, *Life of Flavius Josephus*
V. T.	*Vetus Testamentum*
War	Josephus, *The Jewish* War (*Bdlum Iudairum*)

INTRODUCTION

Various preconceptions have dominated Qumran research. These, in turn, have blurred the significance of documents of the most incalculable historical value, so that only 35 years after their discovery, they have become objects of only passing interest to many scholars. Primarily, these preconceptions stem from an animus towards and derogation of the Maccabean family and the additional underlying motive (albeit at times unconscious) of trying to distance the materials in question as far as possible from Christianity's formative years in Palestine. These preconceptions subtly deform archaeological and palaeographic studies as well, so that scholars end up with "results" that are psychologically and spiritually more in keeping with their original assumptions and beliefs. In turn, these are used to render solutions, based on the clear thrust of internal data and the reality of the historical *sitz-im-leben*, stillborn.

Though Josephus is properly recognized as the important source he is, his associations with both the "Essene" and "Zealot" movements (and what we shall refer to as "the Messianic"), and his canny evasions resulting from these, are in large measure ignored. It is forgotten, too, that apart from the period 55-75 CE, when he was a mature observer, he too was working from sources: sources he sometimes either treated too hastily or did not fully understand himself; and his confusions compound our own. For example, he takes notices (probably from different sources) about Herod's regard for both "Pharisees" and "Essenes" and sets them side-by-side without realizing his sources were themselves most likely talking about the same group. This confusion of "Pharisee" and "Essene" terminologies is also at the root of the contradictory notices about "Hassidaeans" in 2 Macc and 1 Macc as both the supporters of Judas *par excellence* and his betrayers. Elsewhere, Josephus contradicts himself in what he says about James' nemesis, the high priest Ananus, heaping praise on him in the *War*, while abusing him in the *Antiquities* and the *Vita*. In fact, many startling omissions in the *War* are made good in this way in the *Antiquities* and the *Vita*. Compounding this particular confusion, early Church accounts insist that Josephus connected James' death with the fall of Jerusalem, which is precisely what he tells us about Ananus' in the extant copy of the *War*.

The inability to come to grips with a whole new vocabulary in Hebrew also prevented many scholars from seeing through to the real implications of the materials before them. In particular, it proved difficult to recognize the Hebrew originals of familiar expressions known only through Greek, Latin, and more modern translations.

e.g., *Derech* ("the Way"), *Tamim* or *Tom* ("Perfection"). *Da^cat* ("Knowledge"—"Gnosis" in some traditions), *^camal/ma^casim* ("works"), *yazdik/yizadek* ("justify" or "be justified"), *Yom* or *Beit ha-Mishpat* ("the Last Judgment"), etc. Perhaps because of a dearth of really credible translations, specialists also found it difficult to come to grips with the use of interchangeable metaphor where the names of numerous familiar groups were concerned, e.g., "Essenes" (*Hassidim*), Zadokites (*Zaddikim*), Ebionites (*Ebionim*), Nazoraeans (*Nozrim*), "the Meek" (*^cAnavim*), "the Saints" (*Kedoshim*), "Zealots" (*Kanna'im*), etc. This is compounded by the basically secretive nature of the tradition, which itself was connected with an ongoing "hidden" tradition, and in turn, accounts for the seemingly dizzying multiplication of sects and groups, when in fact one has to do essentially with one "Essene" or "Zealot"-type orientation. Part of the problem, too, stems from the inability to recognize subversive groups in what on the surface, anyhow, appeared to be harmless "ascetics". Here, Josephus is more forthcoming, albeit still using his familiar circumlocutions, when he tells us that "the imposters and deceivers" (*i.e.*, whom we shall call our "Zadokite" leaders) were scheming to bring about *both* "innovations" (*i.e.*, religious reform) *and* "change in Government".

One must be prepared to put aside all preconceptions stemming from one's own terms-of-reference, usually either the viewpoints of Rabbinic Judaism or "Christianity" as it has devolved upon us, since the tradition under consideration is implacably hostile to both. For example, the authenticity of the Letter of James has been consistently undermined from Eusebius' time to Luther's; but aside from some polishing and minimal ideological tinting, it fits perfectly into the materials of concern to us in this study. Exhibiting that studied reticence in identifying its antagonists which is usually the result of fear of powerful, hostile forces; its "not one jot or tittle" approach to *Torah,* its constant stress on "keeping (not "breaking") the Law", and its antagonism to "fornication" (cf. Ja 2:8ff., the formulations of which appear to predate and underlie Mt 5:17ff.) all have their parallels in Qumran usage. Its application of "tongue" imagery, extant at Qumran, to describe a troublesome internal adversary, is also generically parallel to the "lying", "spouting", and insolent "scoffing" allusions there. Elsewhere, the interpolation in Paul's presentation of the order of resurrection appearances in 1 Co 15.4ff. is widely assumed to involve the reference to "James and all the apostles". However, we prefer to turn this around, considering it rather to consist of the improbable "Cephas and the twelve" (there were only eleven at the time). Neither can the historical *sitz-im-leben* of the Qumran tradition be reconstructed solely on the basis of traditions to which Rabbinic Judaism is the heir. In fact, in this period both it and "Gentile Christianity" exhibit a telltale pattern of deference to Herodian religious requirements and political designs.

Some words should be said about our reference in passing to *Zohar* tradition, correspondences to which are pointed out in the footnotes. It should be noted that I confine myself to the "Noah" and "Phineas" sections only, where allusions relevant to James' person are found. Though I prefer to stand aside on the question of the Second Temple or medieval origins of *Zohar* tradition (cf. Paul on Mosaic "splendor"; 2 Co 3:8ff.), the appropriateness of these allusions to the materials under consideration should give those who dogmatically adhere to the latter position something to consider; certainly these references have nothing whatever to do with thirteenth century Spain. Correspondences are also pointed out in the footnotes to Karaite traditions and *selected* use is made of materials in the Slavonic Josephus. Anyone who would object to recourse to such parallels should realize that Gospel and Rabbinic traditions are not much better attested to and all such materials, anyhow, must be treated *equally* according to the *same* criteria. Here, attention to work done in traditions in the Islamic field of a *completely disinterested kind* might prove helpful. Its results illustrate that traditions of the most surprising content, considered poorly authenticated for some reason, or "divergent", by majority opinion, often turn out to carry the earliest strata of historical data. Where the documents at Qumran are concerned, of course, we are in possession fortunately of contemporary accounts in large measure unaffected by the distortions of tradition-manufacture and the retrospective imposition of a later historical consensus.

Another serious problem in Qumran textual studies is the inability to come to grips with literary genre and literary device; in particular, the Hebrew love of word-play. This is true, for instance, of the Qumran exegesis of the crucial "Zadokite Statement" of Ez 44:15 (which is very definitely *eschatological*, as is that of Hab 2:4), the use of the term "the Many" in Qumran community organization and (together with both "*'amal*" and "*Da'at*") in "justification"-theorizing going back to Is 53:11 usage (the currency of which is attested to by Paul in 1 Co 15:4 above), and figurative allusion to the central priestly triad as "the

Holy of Holies" in a general context of Is 40:3 "making a Way in the wilderness" and Ps 118:22 "cornerstone" imagery.

Two basic Hebrew concepts, *Hesed* and *Zedek* ("Piety" and "Righteousness"), run through all descriptions of opposition groups in this period. Justin Martyr identifies these as the twin components of the "all Righteousness" doctrine. Putting them side-by-side with the elemental Noahic proscriptions on "idolatry, fornication, and manslaughter" (also at the root of James' "Jerusalem Council" directives), he shows how this duality was expressed in the two scriptural commandments of "loving God" *(Hesed)* and "loving one's neighbor" *(Zedek;* cf. Mt 22:34ff. and Mk 12:28ff.). Starting with the description of the *Anshei-Hesed/ Zaddikim* in Hebrew Ecclesiasticus and Josephus' parallel note about Simeon the *Zaddik* in the *Antiquities,* this dichotomy is the common thread running through all Josephus' descriptions of "Essenes", his description of John the Baptist's wilderness activities, and all early Church accounts of James; and comprises the essential basis of what we shall describe as "the Zadokite Hassidaean" movement. Where James and "the Essenes" were concerned (and probably Jesus as well), the "Righteousness" commandment (cf. Ja 2:8 on "the Supreme Law of Scripture") underwent the additional fundamental metamorphosis into a demand for economic equality, which is at the root of "the Poor" terminologies and "the hostility towards the Rich" so closely connected with all these Essene-like or "Jewish Christian" personalities.

Another important theme in this period is the "hidden" ideology we have alluded to above. This is linked in our literature to "hiding in *caves"* and taken all the way back via *Zohar* tradition to the first *Zaddik* Noah's paradigmatic experience of "being hidden" (by God) in the ark to escape the destruction that was being unleashed. It finds additional expression in a strong *redivivus* tradition adhering to these "Noahic" priest-Zaddiks, which, in turn, is closely associated with another element in the "Noahic" tradition, *rain-making.* An additional echo of all of these motifs is to be found in the Talmud in the *redivivus* and "hidden" traditions circulating about Honi, the circle-drawing *Zaddik,* not to mention in Josephus' "magician" and "imposter" accusations.

Not only does the *ARN* associate rain-making (not insignificantly under the heading of "Simeon the *Zaddik")* with proper (i.e., "Zadokite") "Temple service", but in the War Scroll eschatological "rain" imagery is definitively connected to the exegesis of "the Star" prophecy. This is expressed in terms of "the Messiah" coming to give "Judgment" *(Mishpat)* and the coming of "the Heavenly Host" to "rain judgment" from the clouds "on all the sons of men". The connection of both of these allusions with the well-known Messiah "coming on the clouds of Heaven" imagery should be clear (cf. also Paul in 1 Thess 3:13-4:17 and Jude 14f.). This is precisely the proclamation early Church tradition attributes to James (to whom the rain-making tradition also adhered) and it is repeated in the letter conserved under his name, which itself culminates in Messianic "rain" imagery, and in the process, specifically refers to one of the key rain-making forerunners in the *redivivus* tradition, Elijah.

Two titles. *Zaddik* and *Oblias* (or "Protection of the People"; the last paralleled in Qumran "Shield"/*Maʿoz* and "Fortress"/*Migdal*/imagery), were applied as if integrally to James' being; and it is specifically acknowledged that Qumran-style scriptural exegesis was carried on with regard to his person (as at Qumran, the passage in question. Is 3:10, is a *zaddik*-passage of the kind applied to the events of the life of the Righteous Teacher; cf. Hab 2:4, Ps 37, etc.). Also, two adversaries can be readily identified with regard to his life. These, in turn, precisely parallel the two nemeses of the Righteous Teacher, one an establishment high priest outside the movement called "Wicked" and the other, a "treacherous" individual within the movement who follows a more antinomian approach to the Law (including "denying the Law in the midst of the whole congregation"), "leads Many astray" (in contradistinction to the more proper "justification" activity of "making Many Righteous"), and is variously dubbed "the Liar", "the Pourer out of Lying", "the Scoffer" or "Boaster". Tradition, too, actually places James with *all his community* in the Jericho area in the early 40's, corresponding to an impressive rise in Qumran coin distribution under Agrippa I (Rec 1.71, a notice which can hardly be ascribed to historical interpolation).

It should be appreciated that according to the scheme of the Zadokite Document, the Messianic "Root" has already been killed, and that, therefore, dwelling too much on the person of "the Messiah" (who even for Gospel artificers and their modern-day form-critical and redactionist inheritors is a figure shrouded in mystery) will not prove very productive. This was the defect of J. Teicher's fantastic theorizing, which did more to discredit work on this subject than advance it, itself prefigured in the earlier and *more solid* work done on the Zadokite Document by G. Margoliouth. However, the Zadokite Document does conclude with the unmistakable evocation of a "Messianic" *return* (repeated three times). The language it uses precisely corresponds to James' several like-minded proclamations noted above and Paul in 1 Thess 3:13. A proper grasp of the Hebrew usage, "*ʿamod*", which does not only mean "coming" as per most translations, but also "standing up", as per the original reference in Ezekiel, would clarify these matters.

Finally, it should be appreciated that Qumran exegetical interpretation raises the clear presumption of a first century provenance for most Qumran sectarian materials. This is as true of the exegesis of Hab 2:4 (including the notice about "the delay of the *Parousia*" which precedes it), as it is for the citation of "the Star" prophecy (which Josephus definitively connects with the uprising against Rome and which all available evidence attests was "in the air" from the 40's to the 60's CE and beyond) upwards of three times in the extant corpus—once in connection with the Messianic "rain" imagery described above: the reference to "the True Prophet" proof-text (Deut 18:15) well-known in Jewish Christian tradition; and the application of "Lebanon" imagery to the fall of the Temple, which *ARN* definitively ties to the fall of the Temple in 70 CE

In addition, there is the implied presence of the terminology of Is 53:11 in the very structure of Qumran organization itself. as well as in Qumran eschatological exegesis of Ez 44:15 and Hab 2:4, and the fairly large collection of Qumran allusions, including "the Way" (which Luke identifies as an alternative name for first century "Christianity" in Palestine), "the Poor", "the Meek", *Yom ha-Mishpat* (cf. Jude 6). "works", "the *kez ha-aharon*" (cf. Heb 9:27), etc., all with a fairly well attested first century provenance.

Then what principally holds researchers back from arriving at such conclusions? Aside from a strong psychological and spiritual predisposition not to arrive at such results, the answer is to be found in the supposedly secure "results" palaeographers and archaeologists have claimed for themselves. Here, a small group of specialists, largely working together, developed a consensus which was used to press the provenance of the most important Qumran sectarian texts back into the first (and sometimes even the *second*) century BCE In *lieu* of clear historical insight or a firm textual grasp, preconceptions and reconstructions, such as they were, were stated as facts, and these results, which were used 'to corroborate each other, in turn became *new* assumptions, that were used to draw away a whole generation of students unwilling (or simply unable) to question the work of their mentors. The archaeological evidence they used was mainly based on a questionable treatment of coin data; while the flaws in palaeography (a subject notorious for its imprecision) were mainly connected with F. M. Cross' and S. Birnbaum's assumptions of a "rapid", *straight-line* development of scripts. In fact, where palaeographic sequences are concerned and the rather simplistic straight-line functions developed to describe these, the situation is probably far more uneven and complex than either scholar originally envisioned; and historical and textual studies will be able to do much to clarify these, not *vice versa*. Despite the fact that a majority of concerned persons do not appear to have seriously examined the various positions of those principally responsible for this consensus or their methodologies, this consensus has been allowed to stand.. Therefore, I have felt obliged to treat and criticize their arguments and conclusions in detail, particularly in the footnotes. (These footnotes contain much substantive material and supplementary documentation generally. The reader is nevertheless urged to study them carefully.)

In providing an alternative historical and textual framework in which to fit the most important Qumran sectarian documents, it is hoped that most of the preconceptions that have dominated Qumran research for so long will fade away, and that new ideas will be brought into play and previously unused sources given their proper scope. When this is done, individual beings, the facts of whose lives tradition has distorted beyond recognition, or who have been consigned to historical oblivion, spring immediately to life and a whole block of associated historical fabrications and accusations evaporate.

I wish to express my appreciation to Robert Morgan of Oxford University, Luigi Cirillo of the University of Calabria, William Farmer of Southern Methodist University, and Morton Smith of Columbia University, all of whom took the time either to listen to some of the arguments expressed, offer suggestions, or read through parts of the manuscript. My expression of thanks to them in no way implies their agreement with any of the ideas expressed, which are solely my own. Also, I wish to thank the President, the Board of Trustees, and the Office of Research of California State University Long Beach for generously encouraging and supporting the research that went into this study. Finally, I dedicate this work to my wife and to my children without whose patience and forbearance it could never have been accomplished.

Chapter One

QUMRAN RESEARCH

Over and over again in Qumran research one comes upon the assertion that one or another of the Maccabee family had some connection with "the Wicked Priest" and/or "the Spouter of Lies". Furthermore, it is claimed that the Maccabee family, including even Mattathias or Judas, "usurped" the high priesthood from an earlier, purer line known as the "Zadokite".[1] These ideas have on the whole dominated Dead Sea Scroll research, but they are at variance with the evidence found at Qumran itself including material in the Book of Enoch, Daniel, and the Testament of Levi. They display a curious insensitivity to the true meanings and origins of the Sadducee, Zealot, and "Christian" (or what in Palestine probably should be called "Messianic") movements.[2]

Josephus is usually taken at face value with little attempt to analyze the data he provides beyond a superficial comparison of it with other known facts. Where religious movements were concerned, however, he was a self-serving and inadequate observer. Like the final redactors of the Gospels (whose contemporary he was), he was at pains to avoid certain potentially incriminating facts: in his case, his own association with the "Zealot" and/or "Messianic" movements.[3] The curious lack of reference to the Christian movement in his works is passed over by a scholar as eminent in

---

[1] See F. M. Cross, *The Ancient Library of Qumran*, New York, 1961, pp. 127-160 for perhaps the classic discussion of this problem; for his use of the word "usurpation", see pp. 135 and 140; G. Vermes, *The Dead Sea Scrolls in English*, London, 1962, pp. 62ff,; J. T. Milik, *Dix ans de dicouvertes dans le Désert de Juda*, Paris, 1957, Chapter 3 (Eng. tr., *Ten Years of Discovery in the Wilderness of Judea*), London, 1959, pp. 44-98. etc. F. F. Bruce in *Second Thoughts on the Dead Sea Scrolls*, Exeter, 1956, p. 100, perhaps sums up the prevailing view admirably with the words "... in the eyes of the Qumran community every ruler of the Hasmonean dynasty, not being a member of the house of Zadok, held the high-priestly office illegitimately and was *ex officio* a Wicked Priest."

[2] For these purposes, it is often overlooked that the "Christians" were not and could not have been called "Christians" in Palestine if the testimony of Luke in Acts is to be credited: "It was at Antioch that the disciples were first called 'Christians' "(Acts 11:26). Epiphanius, for whatever his testimony is worth (and in this instance I see no reason to quarrel with him, since, however he garbles the traditions he presents. there is often a credible core to them) thinks that "before the Christians began to be called 'Christians' at Antioch", they were called at least in Palestine "Jessaeans", by which apart from his facile derivation of this term, he clearly intends "Essenes"; *Haeres*. 29.1. He repeats this in 29.4 in no uncertain terms: "therefore either by that Jesse or from Jesus Christ our Lord we call them by the name of 'Jessaeans', because their teaching arises from Jesus and they became his disciples..."

[3] It should be remembered that Josephus advertises himself in the *Jewish War* as military commander of Galilee under the insurgent government in Jerusalem, though in the *Vita*

the field as M. L'Abbé J. T. Milik with the words: "... we should remember that Josephus hardly mentions John the Baptist and Jesus; *his interest lay in other things*" (italics mine).[4] The same writer, whose work is one of the foundation pieces of Qumran research, pokes fun at Dupont-Sommer's outrage over his suggestion to identify the "heroic and holy" Mattathias with "the Man of Belial", and defends his own position as follows: "Whatever may have been the attitude of the Asidaeans ... to Mattathias", their successors "could easily include in their disapproval the ancestors of the ruling dynasty. *This Semitic custom needs no comment*" (*italics* again mine).[5] Milik's response is biased and based on an inability to come to grips with the true nature of the documents under consideration, and by implication, that of the movement upon which Christianity is predicated. In this instance, Dupont-Sommer's righteous indignation is justified, though his passion is on firmer ground than his scholarship, as his identifications in the beginning at least were only little better than Milik's (and for that matter Cross', whom Milik includes with himself).[6] Not only are these kinds of assumptions derogatory to the Maccabees who

---

his role seems more that of a priestly commissar. Depending on his audience and purposes Josephus is always altering his facts in this way. Since the uprising was actually begun by young priests who stopped sacrificing on behalf of the Romans, Josephus is compromised by this association as well. S. G. F. Brandon, *Jesus and the Zealots,* New York, 1967, pp. 114-41, covers the role of the lower priesthood in the war against Rome in some detail. Several other curious matters must be explained with regard to Josephus. The first has to do with his trip to Rome in order to obtain the release of two priestly prisoners. Here he seems very quickly to gain entrance into the imperial family itself. As well, he makes the contacts on this trip that are to prove so useful to him in his later betrayal of the "Zealot" cause. His knowledge of the importance of the "Messianic" prophecy in the atmosphere of the times is made clear in his use of it to flatter Vespasian, not to mention his inadvertent revelation of it as the basis of the uprising against Rome; cf. *War* 6.6.4. A second interlude in Josephus' life which needs explanation is his novitiate period with the mysterious "*Banus*" in the wilderness; *Vita* 2. Who *Banus* was and what role he played in ensuing events remain a mystery. *N.b.,* however, the parallel themes of "bathing", wearing only "linen" (cf. "clothing that grew on trees" for *Banta),* and vegetarianism (*Banus,* Rechabite-like, ate "food growing of itself") in descriptions of *Banus'* contemporary James; cf. below, pp. 49 and 53.

[4]Milik, p. 74.

[5]*Ibid.,* pp. 63f. His actual words are: "Dupont-Sommer practically accuses us of blasphemy in proposing this slander."

[6]His understanding that the sect would be violently opposed to the machinations of the Phariseeizing Hyrcanus II, who in effect invites the Romans into the country, and his grasp of the significance of a *Zaddik-type* like Honi the Circle-Drawer, whose life and death prefigure those of the above-mentioned *Zaddik-type* James the Just. are very close to the mark; A. Dupont-Sommer, *Nouveaux apercus sur les Manuscrits de la Mer Morte* Paris. 1953, pp. 33-61. Actually, he adopts the suggestion of R. Goosens that Onias the Just was the founder of

with perhaps the single exception of Alexander Jannaeus were held in the highest esteem by the common people (including Christians), as we shall show;[7] they are self-serving and should never have so easily passed the tests of critical scholarship, so that now twenty years later one finds them dutifully recited by most students and textbooks in the field.

One should perhaps quote finally from the concluding sentence of Milik's book: "... although Essenism bore in itself more than one element that one way or other fertilized the soil from which Christianity was to spring, it is nevertheless evident that the latter religion represents something completely new which can *only be adequately explained by the person of Jesus himself*" (italics mine).[8] It is perhaps unfair to single out one author in this way, but his remarks are representative of a wide segment of Qumran scholarship. Granting even that these last might have been included to a certain extent to satisfy Church authorities, they are still illustrative of the crux of the problem.

It is difficult to acknowledge that there is a relationship between Judas Maccabee and the priesthood growing out of his activities, and Jesus and the priesthood growing out of his.[9] But on closer examination, why this

---

the community and therefore Hyrcanus. the enemy, in "Onias le Juste. Le Messie de la Nouvelle Alliance, lapidé à Jérusalem en 65 av. JC", .*Nouvelle Cleo*, vii, 1950. pp. 336-53. Cross, who rightly criticizes Dupont-Sommer on his misuse of the Testament of Levi, on the other hand, cannot in any way understand why Dupont-Sommer should prefer to include Aristobulus in his list of "saviors" while leaving off Hyrcanus II and makes what can only be considered an uninformed remark in saving, the "Essene author" of the Testament presumably "was unaware that Judas never functioned as high priest"; cf. his comments, pp. 158ff.

[7]See below, p. 40, W. R. Farmer in *Maccabees, Zealots, and Josephus*. New York, 1957, pp. 28f. has observed the proliferation of Maccabean names by the time of Jesus and these are particularly in evidence in the Gospels themselves among the ᶜ*am* (probably equivalent to the ᶜ*am ha-arez* in the Talmud and the ᶜ*am* that James protects through his Righteousness; cf. Eusebius, *E.H.* 2.23.8).

[8]*Op. cit.,* p. 143. *N. b.* how this attitude is reflected in a preceding statement: "One has the impression that there is a perpetual increase in Essene influence on the early Church. In the generation of *our Lord and of his first disciples* there are *hardly any similarities.* In the earliest phase of the Church in Palestine, as we find it in Acts, institutional parallels become more frequent. Slightly later we find in one part of the Church Essene influence almost taking over and submerging the *authentically Christian* doctrinal element; indeed, it may be considered responsible for the break between the Judaeo-Christians and the *Great Church*" (italics mine), pp. 142f. "Essene", as Milik uses the term here, is synonymous with "Jewish Christian".

[9]Unlike Cross and most other observers I take Josephus literally when he tells us Judas Maccabee was *elected* to the high priesthood, *i.e.,* "The people bestowed the high priesthood on Judas"; *Ant.* 12.10.6. He repeats his reference to "the high priesthood" of Judas in two other places. Indeed, even in 1 Macc Judas presides over the cleansing of the Temple in Ezra-like

should be is itself puzzling. The events surrounding the appearance of Judas form the background of every sectarian movement in the Second Temple period including that coalescing about Jesus and to a lesser extent John the Baptist. Both Judas and Jesus are referred to or treated in the extant texts as *Zaddiks* (as was Jesus' brother James, his successor and heir in the priesthood he represented);[10] both are priests "after the Most High God", as the Maccabees styled themselves, and if R. H. Charles is right, of "the order of Melchizedek";[11] both seem to be ascetics of some kind possibly abjuring marriage;[12] both are probably "zealous for the Law" (witnesses to the contrary in the New Testament notwithstanding);[13] both come from large families of five brothers and are succeeded by their brothers;[14] both seem to be

---

fashion. However, most observers cleave to the incomplete testimony of the *Jewish War* where Judas' priesthood is concerned and often underrate native procedures such as election. I take all couplings of putative *Zaddikim* with their natural constituency, "the people", as significant and worth cataloguing.

[10]Judas' role as one of "the ten *Zaddikim*" is evoked by 2 Macc 5:27. Jesus is specifically referred to as "*zaddik*" in Acts 3:14, 7:52, and 22:15; Pilate and his wife both refer to him as such in Mt 27:19ff. without the theological implications of Luke. His father Joseph is so designated in Mt 1:19. In Herod's description of John in Mk 6:20 the term "pious", *i.e.*, "*hassid*", accompanies the usage; cf. *Ant.* 18.5.2. In transliterating *hassid*/Hassidaean, I prefer the double "s" to conserve the parallel with *zaddik*.

[11]Of the numerous references to this in Charles' works, see for instance *APOT*, ii, pp. 9, 32, 61, 309, and 418 with reference to Jub 13:25, 32:1, As. Mos. 6:1-2, Test. L. 8:14-15. He rightly points out the crucial position of John Hyrcanus in this and the reference to such in *Ant.* 16.6.2. Fitzmyer discusses the matter in " 'Now this Melchizedek ...' (Heb 7:1)", *Essays on the Semitic Background of the New Testament,* Montana, 1974, p. 235, unfortunately without citing his source, Charles.

[12]Though Judas is referred to in 2 Macc 14:25 as having "married and settled down", there is never any mention of children, which would have been important genealogically speaking, and the reference has more the character of a narrative device. In any event, Judas soon resumes his warrior ways.

[13]The claim is specifically raised on behalf of Jesus in Jn 2:17 in reference to the temple-cleansing incident; Judas' similar zeal is not in question.

[14]See Mt 13:55, Mk 6:3, Ga 1:19, 1 Co 9:5 etc. The problem of Jesus' brothers bedevils apostle lists and resurrection appearances. We take the Emmaus road appearance in Lu 24:13-35 involving "Cleopas" as being the lost one regarding Jesus' family members and the analogue of Paul's "Damascus Road" experience. The reference to "Simon", preceded by allusion to "True Prophet" ideology and "Nazoraean" terminology, we take to refer to Simeon bar Cleophas. Cf. Origen in *Contra Celsum* 2.62 and Jerome's report in *Vir. ill.* 2 of a first appearance to James including the common theme of "breaking bread". Unlike v. Harnack, we consider the interpolation in Paul's 1 Co 15:5ff. resurrection-appearance sequence to comprise the orthodox "Cephas and the Twelve" (patently impossible), not "James then all the

acknowledged as "messiahs" by their enthusiastic followers;[15] and both purify the Temple in some way.[16] While the Maccabean movement emerged in response to the destruction and corruption of the previous priesthood represented by Simeon the Just and his son, Onias, and the forcible imposition of Hellenistic civilization; the events and sentiments culminating in the Messiahship of Jesus came to fruition as a response to the destruction of the Maccabean priesthood by the "Herodians" and their Roman overlords. So closely do the movements crystallizing about the two resemble each other that the only observably incontrovertible difference between them is that the Christianity born of Jesus' death developed a non-Jewish overseas wing because of the general oppression in the Roman Empire at the time. In addition, it is arguable that this latter gradually supplanted the native and indigenous one in perspective and via retrospective historical insight obscured it, so that its actual nature has become lost to us. The Scrolls have restored the balance in viewpoints by helping to rescue these native sectarian movements from the oblivion into which they were cast by both "Roman" Christianity and "Rabbinic" Judaism either intentionally or via benign neglect.

Apostles". *N.b.* tradition often confuses Simon Cephas with Simeon bar Cleophas. identified as "a Rechabite priest" in *E. H.* 2.23.17 (cf. *Haeres.* 78.14)—"cousin" and "uncle" often being euphemisms for brother and father.

[15]Judas' messiahship is reflected in the "Messianic" sword episode of 2 Macc 15:12-16 where Onias and Jeremiah (a kind of "Ancient of Days") play the role of priestly forerunners.

[16]Jesus' Temple-cleansing activities are well known, as are Judas', though they are rarely linked. In the wake of the latter *Hanukkah* is ratified by a vote of "the people"; 2 Macc 10:5ff. much as Judas' priesthood was; cf. Ezra's similar activities below, p. 26.

Chapter Two
THE ZADOKITE PRIESTHOOD

The Scrolls have delineated what a Zadokite priesthood has to have been from the second century BCE onwards. Though there might be a genealogical component to this conception, its main thrust is qualitative, namely, "those who keep the Covenant" or "follow the Law".[17] Primarily, the Zadokite priesthood must relate, as the Zadokite Document explicitly denotes, to the Book of Ezekiel where it was first introduced.[18] In Ezekiel "the Priests", who are "the *Bnei-Zadok* Levites, *kept charge of My sanctuary*", *i.e.*, "kept the Covenant", while "the sons of Israel *went astray* from Me" (translation and italics mine).[19] That there may be a genealogical connotation to this description is self-evident. However, it is also clear from

---

[17]Cf. "Keepers of the Covenant" for "Sons of Zadok" in 1QS, v, 2-9. In CD, ii-iv's exegesis of Ez 44:15 the definition turns more eschatological, *i.e.*, it is linked to the role of the *Zaddikim* ("First" and "Last"—*Rishonim* and *Aharonim*) in "the last days" and probably the Resurrection. Here, too, the stress is on "doing the exact sense of the Law" (4.8 and 6.15). "Doing" and its variations, *ma'asim* and *ma'aseihem*, are constant themes at Qumran linking up with the stress on "works" and "keeping the whole Law" in Ja 2:7ff. In the Letter of James, "keeping the Law" is repeatedly stressed as opposed to its ideological opposite "breaking the Law". "Doing" or "Doers of the *Torah*" is, also, important in 1QpHab, viii, 1-3, and xii, 4-5 regarding "the delay of *the Parousia*", the exegesis of "the Righteous shall live by faith" (also eschatological), and "the Last Judgment". This is also true in 4QTest, including both "True Prophet" and "Star" proof- texts ("the Star" is the *Doresh ha-Torah* in CD, vii, 18). The reference there to Deut 33:8ff.'s "teaching the Law" and "keeping (*yinzor*) your Covenant" is the clue to "Nazoraean" terminology; cf. *Nozrei-Brito* (paralleling *Shomrei-Brit*) in Ps 25 and Ps 119 addressing "the Perfect of the Way walking in *Torah*" and saturated with Qumran imagery. Cf. too the use of Ez 44:7's "Covenant-Breakers" in 1QpHab, ii, 6 for "the Liar" and his confederates "the Traitors" (*Bogdim*) and "Violent Ones" (*'Arizim*).

[18]See Ez 40:46, 43:19, 44:15, and 48:11. The best discussion of 'the Zadokite Statement' is by J. Bowman, "Ezekiel and the Zadokite Priesthood", *Transactions of the Glasgow University Oriental Society,* xvi, 1957, pp. 1-14. Albright, too, understands the problem noting that the Greek Septuagint conserves a reading of "sons of Saddouk", not Zadok; and he understands that "sons of Zadok" can just as easily be understood as "sons of the righteous one"; cf. the reading "sons of the Zadok" in 1QS, ix, 14 and W. F. Albright and C. S. Mann, "Qumran and the Essenes: Geography, Chronology, and Identification of the Sect", *BASOR,* Suppl. Studies, 10-12, 1951, pp. 17ff. Le Moyne in *Les Sadducians,* Paris, 1972 shows little insight into these problems. His preconceptions resemble Nlilik's: cf. his comments about the "righteousness" of the Sadducees, p. 160.

[19]In Ezekiers wording "priests" and "*Bnei-Zadok* levites" are appositives. "*Bnei-Zadok*" is used adjectively to describe which "levites" will serve as "priests"; not *vice versa*. Any genealogical sense this might have had is broken open in CD, iii. 21ff. by the deliberate addition of *waw*-constructs. There, "sons of Zadok" are defined as "the *Elect of Israel* called by *name* (n.b. the predetermination) who will *stand* in the *last days*" (italics mine—the usage is from Ez 37:10 and also carries with it the implication of "be resurrected"). The usage "wandered astray" is common at Qumran and is usually used in contradistinction

studying Ezekiel's account (whether authentic or pseudepigraphic is beside the point) that there are other priestly levites, members of families as respectable as Shaphan's (who was involved in "the reform of Josiah"). These, comprising the former reigning priestly aristocracy, doubtless could have made equally legitimate "Zadokite" claims (though it is not clear such claims counted for anything before the Restoration) and are now being disqualified on the basis of their idolatry, etc. from service in the Temple.[20]

The Dead Sea Scrolls further emphasize the ethical aspect of Ezekiel's usage. As they employ this terminology, it definitely has a component in "Righteousness", which is of course the root of the personal noun, "Zadok", or in observation of "the Law" (*i.e.*, what in other language might be characterized as *"zeal* for the Law"—phraseology current at

---

to "the sons of Righteousness" who "do the *Torah*", often in connection with allusion to the treacherous activities of "the Man of Lying", who "pours out the waters of Lying" and teaches "straying from the Law" and "stubbornness of heart": cf. CD, i, 15: ii, 13, 16f.: iii, 1. 4, 14; iv, 1; 1QS, iii, 21f.: iv, 11f.; 1QpHab, x. 9; 1QH, 23f.; ii, 14; iii, 21f. etc. The use of "sons of *Zedek*" twice in 1QS. iii, 20ff. in this context is deliberate; cf. also 4QpPs 37, iv, 15. The context here, important for all subsequent Second Temple problems from the "Zealot" opposition to the Herodian family to the Pauline Gentile Mission's problems with the Jerusalem Community, is keeping "the uncircumcised in heart and uncircumcised in flesh" out of the Temple (Ez 44:7-10). It belies Josephus' contention that the 66 CE rejection "by those in charge of Temple service" of gifts and sacrifices from *any* foreigner (including the Emperor and presumably "Herodians") was an "innovation". The "heart" and "flesh" imagery forms the backbone of the allusion to "Holy Spirit" baptism from 1QS, ii, 1-iv, 26 and is the basis of Josephus' description of John's baptism. The "idolatry", "fornication", and "riches" charges (all themes associated in extant data with James) comprise "the three nets of Belial" accusation against the priestly hierarchy in CD, iv, 18ff. For the confrontation between "Simon" and Agrippa I (probably the original behind Acts 10:1-11:18) and the related "Temple wall" incident directed against his son Agrippa H (which leads inexorably to James' death), see below pp. 19 and 43 and *Ant.* 19.7.4 and 20.9.11. In *War* 2.17.1 Agrippa II *is* ultimately barred from the Temple and all Jerusalem by "the innovators".

[20] See Ez 44.10: "those levites who abandoned me when Israel strayed from me ... They are to become servants in my sanctuary ..." ;these are contrasted to those levites who are *"Bnei-Zadok"* in 44:15. It becomes clear that "sons of Zadok" is being used as an antonym of "going astray" and "broke my Covenant". Cf. 4QFlor, i, 17, where "the sons of Zadok and the men of their community" are identified with those who "shall not defile themselves with idols" (the reading here is disputed, but the context is clear). For Ez 8:11 those levites who abandoned their duties "to follow idols" include the former priestly establishment including the family of Shaphan. Cross does not treat these matters in "Reconstruction of Judean Restoration", *JBL*, v, 1975, pp. 4-18.

Qumran).[21] It cannot be stressed too strongly that this moral component is the absolute determinant of a proper "Zadokite" priest at least as far as the Zadokite Document is concerned, and probably Ezekiel as well. The play-on-words implicit in this esoteric analysis of the term constitutes a favorite device at Qumran. The artful craftsmanship practiced there is missed on many Qumran scholars who do not adequately come to grips with literary devices in such an environment. This play-on-words is reinforced in the conjunction of the *Moreh ha-Zedek* with the "son of Zadok", or more precisely the "Zadok" *par excellence*. It is extended even further in *the pesharim*, where the identification is always consciously and explicitly drawn between "the *zaddik*" in the text and "the *Moreh ha-Zedek*" in the exegesis.[22]

What would be Jesus' relationship to the kind of ideology we are developing here? According to perhaps the oldest and probably most "Jewish" stratum of New Testament Christology, Jesus was the suffering "Just One"; *i.e.*, "the suffering *Zaddik*" and is specifically so designated in Acts. The origin of this phraseology is "the suffering servant" simile of Isaiah 53. Here, it should be noted, not only is "the

[21]See, for instance, the introduction of the Zadokite Document addressed to "all Knowers of Righteousness" amid the language of "the heart", "the Way", "works" (*ma'asei/ma'aseihem)*, and "Walkers in Perfection". 1QS, ii, 15 and iv, 4 refer to "zeal for his Judgements" and its variant "zeal for the Judgments of Righteousness" as opposed to "stubbornness of heart", "zeal for fornication", "slackness in the service of Righteousness", and "a tongue full of insults" (cf. "the tongue" imagery in Ja 3:5ff. itself generically parallel to "lying"/"spouting"/"scoffing" imagery at Qumran). See also 1QH, ii, 15 "a spirit of zeal" against "the Seekers after Smooth Things". In 1QS, ix, 23 the usage "zealous for the Law" actually occurs relating to two citations of the famous Is 40:3 "making a Way in the wilderness" and reference to the three central "priests" as a spiritualized "Holy of Holies" who *atone for the land* by "suffering the sorrows of affliction" and practicing Righteousness and "Perfection of the Way". They are "the offering": their Righteousness, "the fragrance", and through them "the Holy Spirit is established on Truth" (viii, 1-ix, 25): cf. also the "Cornerstone", "Wall", "Rock", and "Fortress" symbolism in this passage and in 1QH, vi, 25f., vii, 7f., etc.

[22]I have treated this correspondence in two SBL papers, "James as Righteous Teacher" (1977) and "The *Zaddik*-Idea and the Zadokite Priesthood" (1979). but its verification is readily made by even a cursory inspection of Habakkuk and Ps 37 *peshers*. 1QpHab, i, 12 actually draws it in the exegesis. The context of "the Wicked devouring" or "seeking to slay the Righteous" (4QpPs 37. iv, 7) also closely parallels Is 3:10. another *zaddik*-passage expressly applied to the death of James (about whom "the Prophets declared") in *E. H.* 2.23.15. Cf. also CD, i, 20 specifically referring to "the *Zaddik*" and alluding to the *nephesh-Zaddik* vocabulary of the Is 53:11f. *zaddik*-passage. If one catalogues all references to *zaddik* in Prophets and Psalms (the usual exegetical texts employed at Qumran), further collating them with words like Lebanon, *Ebionim*, *'Anavim* ("the Meek"—also *Dalim)*, *Bogdim* (Traitors), etc., one achieves an approximation of the method used for choosing exegetical texts at Qumran; cf. Is 2-5, 10f., 14, 25, 29-33 (Zech 10-11), Hab 2-3, Na 1, etc.

servant" identified with "the *Zaddik*", but his "justifying" action is to be accomplished by his "Knowledge" (probably through teaching; cf. that *Da^cat* widespread at Qumran) and his *^camal-nephesh, i.e.,* works with soteriological force. This *yazdik-zaddik* theology of Is 53 is not only recognizable in the Pauline corpus, it is also present in the Zadokite Document and the Qumran Hymns.[23] By extension, it is also present (working off the word *^camal*) in recognizably parallel fashion in the Habakkuk' *pesher* and the Letter of James; however, Paul parts company with these on whether this "justification" is to be achieved by "faith" or through works of Righteousness and "the Law".[24] According to the esoteric interpretation of "the Zadokite Priesthood", as we have expounded it, since Jesus was *"Zaddik"*, to his heirs belong the high priesthood. The word-play we have already signaled is further extended in the Letter to the Hebrews with the allusion to "the priesthood after the order of Melchizedek". The reference here is not only to the concept of "Righteousness" as being the primary basis of legitimacy in the

---

[23]See CD, iv, 6f. in the Ez 44:15 exegesis. Here "the sons of Zadok", now identified with "the *Kodesh Shonim*", *i.e.*, "the *Rishonim*" or "the *Anshei-Kodesh Tamim*" (usage widespread in CD and 1QS), "through whom God grants atonement", "justify the Righteous", *i.e. yazdiku zaddik*. Cf. the purposeful reversal "justify the Wicked" in CD, i, 19 in relation to "the Lying Boaster" who abolishes "the Ways of Righteousness" and his attack on "the soul of the Righteous One" and the parallel reversal of *yizadek* ("to be justified") in 1QS, iii, 2f.; cf. also Rec 1.70. *For yizadek* in Hymns see 1QH, vii, 28; ix, 14f.; xiii, 16f. etc. See also "you justified" used in relation to righteous "works" in 1QH, i, 7 and "to justify" in 1QM, xi, 14 in relation to eschatological reference to "the Poor", the "Star" prophecy, and Messianic "rain" imagery. That Is 53:11f. was very early applied (presumably in the Jerusalem Church) to Jesus' death is confirmed by Paul in 1 Co 15.3ff. in his preface to resurrection-appearance sequences. It is never remarked that the whole structure of Qumran organization of *Moreh-Zedek/Zaddik* and *Rabim* is based on Is 53, *i.e.*, "my servant the Righteous One will justify"/"bear the sins of the Many" (*Rabim*). Cf. as well Ja 5:6 below, pp. 19 and 43.

[24]The preservation of something resembling the "Jerusalem Church" or "Jamesian" interpretation of Hab 2:4 in 1QpHab, viii, 1ff. is often missed. Not only does the exegesis parallel Paul's, but in contradistinction to the more antinomian Gentilizing approach of the latter, its effect is twice restricted to "all *^cOsei ha-Torah* in the House of Judah", *i.e.*, only to *Jews*, and of these, only to those "who do the Law", with an accent on "doing". These "will be saved from the House of Judgments by their works (*^camalam*) and their faith in the Righteous Teacher". *N.b.* the telltale reversal of the sense of the underlying text as per Pauline exegesis. Its eschatological nature is confirmed in 12.3ff. where it is now "the Simple of Judah doing *Torah*" who will be "saved at the Last Judgment", "Lebanon" is referred to, and the usage *Ebionim* is deliberately introduced into the *pesher* (though rani does not appear till Hab 3:15). Cf. how in x, 9ff. "the *Matif ha-Chazav* leads Many astray ... with works of Lying so that their *^camal* will count for nothing".

succession, but also to the personality of the righteous priest/king Jesus, in whose name the new order is established.[25]

Here, it should not be forgotten that the title, "the *Zaddik*", was also accorded to Jesus' brother James, who was on this basis in addition to being Jesus' genealogical successor, his spiritual heir. Early Church literature, whether through over-enthusiasm or otherwise, depicted James as having worn the breastplate of the High Priest and actually entering the Holy of Holies.[26] Whether this priesthood of Jesus and James was also "the Zadokite" one is debatable. In terms of the analysis we have presented of Righteousness or "the Righteous One" being the basis for the esoteric understanding of Ezekiel's prognoses, it was. Through this analysis, also, sense can be made of the testimony, referred to above, of James actually functioning as high priest. Whether the Maccabean priesthood "of the Most High God" is, also, to be identified with the Melchizedek one of Christianity and the Letter to the Hebrews remains open to question. Whether this latter usage of the term can be extended to the Qumran (or Zadokite) use of the term as well has been debated. The writer would take a position in the affirmative, considering all such juxtapositions of the letters *Z-D-K* to be interrelated. In this regard, it should be remembered that the formula, "men of the lot of Melchizedek", of 11QMelchizedek corresponds almost precisely to the

---

[25]Heb 3:1ff., 4:14ff., and 7:1ff. *N.b.* Heb 7:26 already knows the doctrine that only "an absolutely pure and holy high priest beyond the influence of sinners" (in the peculiar code of this period "Herodians" and "foreigners"), *i.e.*, a priest-Zaddik, can provide an efficacious atonement for sin. Cf. too its evident Qumranisms: "the doctrine of Righteousness" (5:14), the doctrine of "Perfection" (2:10 and 7:28), adoptionist sonship (5:50, and in connection with "bearing the sins of the Many", *the end* of the last age" (9:27f.) actually echoing CD, iv, 10f., "the completion of *the end* of those years", and "*ha-kez ha-aharon*" of 1QS, iv, 16f. and 1QpHab, vii, 12 (italics mine).

[26]*E.H.* 2.23.6 and Epiphanius, *Hanes.* 29.3 and 78.13. Jerome. *Vir. ill. 2.* supports Epiphanius' claim that James went into the Holy of Holies, which suggests his atoning activities in his role as Righteous "Priest" and appears to relate to at least one *Yom Kippur.* These testimonies are contemptuously dismissed by most scholars. T. Zahn's reference to James as "the pope of Ebionite phantasy" (quoted in H.J. Schoeps, *Paul: The Theology of the Apostle in the Light of Jewish Religious History,* Philadelphia, 1961, p. 67) is representative. Since it has become possible within the framework of the opposition "Priest"/*Zaddik/Moreh-Zedek* at Qumran to make sense out of such testimonies, I submit they should be treated more seriously. *N.b.* Talmudic tradition preserves material that the sons of Rechab married the daughters of the high priests (Siphre Num 78 on 10:29 reverses this) and their sons did service in the Temple; Yalqut Shimᶜoni on Jer 35:12—"sons of Rechab" being in our view a euphemism for "Essenes"/"Zadokites", evoking (like "life-long Nazirite" allusions) the similarity in life-styles.

terminology "sons of Zadok" in the Zadokite Document; and therefore, by simple reduction, Zadok and Melchizedek are equivalent usages.[27]

Finally, if there is substance to any of these extensions and identifications, "the priesthood after the order of Melchizedek" must be related to what we have called "the Zealot", based on "the zeal of Phineas" and invoked on behalf of Simeon the Righteous, Mattathias, and Onias in the Hebrew version of Ecclesiasticus, 1 Macc, and 2 Macc respectively.[28] Correspondingly, J. Bowman has argued in a much overlooked article on this subject that the Zadokite one bases its claims for legitimacy on this selfsame "covenant of Phineas".[29] By now it should be clear that these are not all separate reckonings, but rather esoteric or poetic variations around the same theme, "Righteousness" and/or "zeal"; just as the various phraseologies the community at Qumran used to refer to itself,

---

[27] 11Q Melchizedek has been translated and commented upon variously by A. S. van der Woude, "Melchisedek als Himmlische Erlfisergestalt in den Neugefundenen Escatologischen Midraschim aus Qumran Höhole XI", *Oudtesamentische Studien,* iv, 1965, pp. 354-73; J. T. Milik. "Milkī-sedq et Milki-reŝa ^cdans les anciens écrits juifs et chrétiens", *JJS,* 23, 1972, pp. 95-144; J. Carmignac, "Le document de Qumran sur Melkisédeq", *Qumran,* vii, pp. 343-78; M. de Jonge and A. S. van der Woude, "11Q Melchizedek and the New Testament", *NTS,* xii, pp. 301-26; J. A. Fitzmyer, "Further Light on Melchizedek from Qumran Cave 11", *JBL,* 86, pp. 25-41, etc.; but it is incontrovertible that "Men of the Lot of Melchizedek" of line 8 is used synonymously with "the Sons of Light" in the line 7 and with the general way "sons of Zadok" is used throughout the Qumran corpus; cf. 1QS, iii, 18ff. equating "sons of *Zedek*" with "sons of Light". Once the basic parallelism of all these usages, *i.e.,* "sons of Zadok", "Truth", "Light", "Heaven", etc., is comprehended, and with it, adoptionist sonship-notions centering around the "Perfection" ideal, the question whether or not the Melchizedek priesthood is found at Qumran becomes academic.

[28] See Sira 50:24, 1 Macc 2:26f., and 2 Macc 3:1 and 4:2. *N.b.* Onias III plays the same literary role in 2 Macc as Mattathias does in 1 Macc.

[29] *Op. cit.,* pp. 4f.; J. Trinquet, "Les liens 'Sadocites' de l'écrit de Damas des Manuscrits de la Mer Morte et de l'Ecclésiastique", *V. T.,, i,* 1951, pp. 290ff., is also aware of the same point, but is able to develop it less. For confusion of "Zadokites" and "Sadducees", see Justin Martyr, *Dialogue with Trypho* 80, where "Sadducees" are listed with other Jewish heretical groups; Filaster in *Diversarum Haereseon Liber* 5; and Jerome in Migne, *Patrolog. Lat.,* xxvi, pp. 163ff. For problematic Talmudic reference (which abound), see b. Erub 68b-69a, Sanh 38a and 100b, Hullin 87a, Niddah 33b-34a, M. Yadaim, iv, 6-8, etc. In the Pseudoclementine Rec 1.53-54 it is specifically asserted that the Sadducees are a group considering themselves "more righteous" than the others who came into existence about the time of John the Baptist; cf. Josephus' characterization of them as "harsher in judgment", *Ant.* 20.9.1 and his play on John Hyrcanus' desire "to be righteous"; *Ant.* 13.11.5f. Cf. also Mt 11:12 and Lk 16:16 associating the beginning of "the men of violence" with John's coming and the material in *ARN* 5.2 associating sectarian strife with "Zadok and Boethus" (*i.e.,* "Saddouk" and Joezer b. Boethus). Strikingly, Josephus' discussion of Jewish sects in *War* and *Ant.* is also triggered by mention of Judas and/or "Saddouk"; see below pp. 42 and 82.

e.g., "sons of Light", "sons of Truth", "sons of Zadok", "sons of *Zedek*" , "the sons of *Hesed*" , "*Ebionim*", "the Elect of Righteousness", "the Meek", "*Ebionei-Hesed*" ("the Poor Ones of Piety"), "*Nimharei-Zedek*" ("the Zealous for Righteousness"), "*Tamimei-Derech*" ("the Perfect of the Way"), "*Anshei-Tamim ha-Kodesh*" ("the Men of the Perfection of Holiness"), etc., do not all designate different groups , but function as interchangeable metaphors.[30] In this view, the Covenant of Phineas operated over and above the general Aaronite one (Bowman considered the Covenant of Phineas to be the prior one), setting forth which among the various Aaronite heirs could be considered suitable candidates for the high priesthood, *i.e.*, the "zealous" or "righteous" ones. It is significant that one of the original demands at the time of the first uprising in 4 BCE, inspired according to Josephus by "the Zealots", was to appoint "according to the law" a high priest of "more perfect purity".[31] For their part it was the "messianically"-inspired zealous young priests who by stopping sacrifice on behalf of the Romans gave the signal for the start of the uprising in 66 CE.[32] Commentators who cannot make a determination as to whether the Dead Sea Scroll sect was anti-Herodian or pro-Herodian, pro-Hyrcanus or pro-Aristobulus, and consequently are unable, for instance, to make any sense out of the destruction of the community in the forties or thirties BCE by fire, are equally unable to understand any of the considerations delineated above; or rather simply do not wish to, preferring to take a position on the relatively safer and less controversial questions of palaeography and archaeology.[33]

---

[30]See 1QH, ii, 10, 12, 33f.; iii, 22; v, 8, 31-32; vi, 20, 29; ix, 35f.; 1QS, iv, 28; v, 13; viii, 17ff.; ix, 8; CD, viii, 24ff. etc. Unfortunately for the premises of most modern scholarship terms like: *Ebionim, Nazrim, Hassidim, Zaddikim* (*i.e.*, Ebionites, Palestinian Christians, Essenes, and Zadokites), turn out to be variations on the same theme. The in- ability to relate to changeable metaphor, particularly where subversive or esotericizing groups are concerned, has been a distinct failure in criticism ancient as well as modern.

[31]*Ant.* 17.9.1. One should follow the variations of this "Perfection" terminology. *i.e.*, *tom, tamim/tamimim hatem*, etc., at Qumran and in the New Testament. At Qumran it is often used in connection with "the Way" terminology. Since it is based on the description of the first *Zaddik*, Noah, as *"tamim"* in Gn 6:9, it should perhaps be called "Noahic".

[32]*War* 2.17.2. That these priests who halted the sacrifice on behalf of or paved for by foreigners in the Temple were moved by the "Messianic" prophecy is made clear in *War* 6.6.4. The application of it to Vespasian by Josephus and R. Yohanan b. Zacchai, not only testifies to its currency in 68 CE events, it is also in keeping with general "Pharisaic" policy. It further illustrates Josephus' description of the followers of "Judas and Saddouk" in *Ant.* 18.1.6 as being "in all matters like the Pharisees except they have an inviolable attachment to liberty and ... could not bear to call any man Lord".

[33]See below, pp. 34. and 86.

Chapter Three
ECCLESIASTICUS AND PRIESTLY LEGITIMACY

The all-important Hebrew text of Ecciesiasticus, found at three locations over the last century: the Cairo Geniza, Qumran, and Masada (each of which is important in itself), is crucial to the matter of Zadokite/Sadducean priestly claims and one of the keys to unraveling the Second Temple sectarian puzzle. The "Sadducean" or scribal character of the text has generally been recognized. What was not so plain was its sectarian character, nor how the all-important material in chapters 50-51, missing from the Septuagint/Vulgate version, was used to legitimatize priestly claims by all the sects heir to the legacy, spiritual or otherwise, of the saintly Simeon the *Zaddik*. These include, as we shall see, the Maccabees, Zealots, Zadokites, and probably even the Christians, *i.e.*, all the groups outside of the Pharisaic/Herodian establishment of 40 BCE onwards. The Pharisees also used Simeon, but not to establish priestly legitimacy; rather as a link in the transmission of right-guided tradition .[34]

I have left both Essenes and "Saducees" off the list. It is, strictly speaking, imprecise to refer to the "Zadokites" at Qumran as "Essenes", which the majority of scholars in the field tend to do for polemical reasons of their own. The sectaries at Qumran might be "Essenes", but the case is by no means proven. Nor is it clear how "the Essenes" saw the problem of priestly succession, nor how they would then differ from Hassidaeans, Zealots, partisans of Judas Maccabee, or even his enemies. One is on safer ground to use the sectaries own terminology, whether "sons of Zadok", *"Ebionim"*, *"Zaddikim"*, *"Hassidim"*, or some other, all terms found generously sprinkled throughout their literature and meaningful in the light of sectarian history in Palestine. For their part, the so-called "Saducees" are dominated by the Pharisees in their post-Herodian embodiment, as Josephus tells us in no uncertain terms.[35] They are in no way

---

[34]The association in both Pirke Abot 1.2 and *ARN 4.1* (the section delineating R. Yohanan's relations with the Romans and applying "Lebanon" symbolism to the 70 CE Temple fall) of "Torah", "Temple-service" (the basis of Ezekiel's 'Zadokite Statement'), and "Hesed" or "the practice of the *Hassidim*" with the person of Simeon the *Zaddik* needs no further elucidation. *N.b.*, this section of *ARN(4.4)* associates *rain-making* with proper *Temple-service;* drought with its cessation.

[35]*Ant.* 18.1.4. It is noteworthy that what Josephus describes as "Saducees" and "Pharisees" in *War* 2.8.14 sound very close to what Rabbinic literature is referring to as "*Beit-*Shammai*" and "*Beit-*Hillel". In this period one has to be careful with one's terminologies which tend to become unglued. Terms like "Zealots", "Essenes", even "Pharisees", which we take to be "parties", Josephus and his sources often use generically. Josephus himself confuses "Essenes" and "Pharisees" saying the same things about "Pollio" and "Sameas" as he does about "Essenes". "Menachem the Essene" repeats a prophecy earlier ascribed to Sameas, and Pollio and Sameas are even confused with each other; cf. *Ant.* 14.9.3f., 15.1.1, and 15.10.4f. Elsewhere, Josephus cuts a part from his description of the Essenes in *War* 2.8.10 and adds it to his description of "the fourth philosophy" of Judas and Saddouk in *Ant.* 18.1.6. See below, pp. 36 and 58.

"Zadokite" if Qumran is typical of what we mean by Zadokite. We have/already noted that their legal and spiritual legitimacy was called into question by those Josephus calls "desirous of innovation" as early as 4 BCE (*War* 2.1.2); quite properly, as it were, since these new-model "Sadducees" are thoroughly compromised by their Roman/Herodian connections.

Let us attempt a reconstruction following priestly lines of legitimacy, but without adhering to the interpretation of "Zadokite" as implying only or even primarily genealogical descent.[36] It is generally accepted that Simeon the *Zaddik* (whether the earlier one of Josephus and imprecise Rabbinic speculation or the later one of Ecclesiasticus) is a true son of Zadok, *i.e.*, a lineal descendant of the Davidic/Solomonic High Priest, but there is nowhere any proof of this.[37] This is one of the implicit assumptions of Qumran scholarship, and should it be found wanting, most of the edifice so artfully constructed upon it becomes extremely fragile. There is no proof that Ezra is "a Zadokite" priest, or Ezekiel who first employs the term in a significant way, or even Elijah for that matter. It is true that someone wants us to think that Ezra is a Zadokite priest, and he is supplied" with With a good "Zadokite" genealogy, but on closer inspection one finds he is given the exact same genealogy as Jesus ben Yehozedek a hundred years earlier, the first high priest after the return from captivity.[38] Even this genealogy has gaps in it and contradicts what is known about priestly succesion in other parts of the Bible.[39] For Bowman, all such genealogies are artificial since very little survived the Babylonian destruction. Biblical ploys (old or new) on matters of genealogy are, in any event, something to be handled with circumspection.

[36] See Albright, *loc cit.* The idea that "*Zaddik*" *is* as good a basis for the derivation of the term "Sadducee" as Zadok is also understood by P. Wernberg-Møller, "*Zedek, Zaddik, and Zadok in the Zadokite Fragments (CDC), the Manual of Discipline (DSD) and the Habakkuk Commentary (SSH)*", *V. T.*, iii, 1953, pp. 309-315, and R. North, "The Qumran 'Sadducees' ", *CBQ*, 17, 1955, pp. 164-188. Wernberg-Meller incisively states in his conclusion, p. 315, "Probably *Zadok* is not meant as a name at all, requiring the reading *Zaddik;* and we may translate: 'it was (not) revealed until a *righteous one* arose' (of CD, iii)". Le Moyne, p. 160, is unable to understand North's presentation, no less rebut it. See also A. Michel, *Le Maitre de Justice*, Avignon, 1954. That *waw* and *yod* are indistinguishable at least in 1QpHab was developed by Y. Ratzaby in *JQR*, 41, 1950, pp. 155ff. See also Rec 1.54 and John Hyrcanus' "Righteousness" associated with Sadducees above, p. 16.

[37] The problem of the dating of Simeon the *Zaddik* has been discussed in detail by G. F. Moore in "Simeon the Righteous", *Jewish Studies in Memory of Israel Abrahams*, New York. 1927, pp. 348-64, including all the relevant references from the Talmud, Josephus, and Ecclesiasticus.

[38] Cf. Ezra 7:11. with 1 Chron 5:34ff.

[39] For instance, Josephus tells us in his famous statement about the priesthood in *Ant.* 20.10.1 that there were eighteen in number "one in succession to the other from the days of King

More importantly, what has never been remarked is that the claim being put forward on behalf of Ezra is not the normal "Zadokite" one at all, but rather what we have been calling "the Zealot" (as Bowman has argued, this is prior to and functions as the Zadokite). Indeed, Ezra is the "zealous" priest *par excellence,* showing incontrovertible zeal for the Law even to the extent of demanding the divorce of alien, including Samaritan, wives—a typical Phineas-style procedure.[40] No doubt Ezra would have preferred a harsher penalty than excommunication had the Yehud of his day not simply been autonomous and had he had the powers to impose the death penalty. In any case, his powers seem to have reached right into the "Zadokite" high priestly household itself. Not only does he occupy its Temple chambers, but he banishes one of its heirs, Sanballat's son-in-law, which seems to be the birth-moment of Samaritan "Zadokite" claims.[41]

Solomon until Nebuchadnezzar ... took Josadek the High Priest captive", but this contradicts the numbers on the list of *Ant.* 10.9.6—only 15 names, which in turn contradicts the genealogy given Ezra and Yehozedek in 1 Chron 5:34ff.—only 6 names—or 1 Chron 5:5-14, which gives thirteen names. With so many repetitions, the last-named has the air of concoction about it; for instance, a second Azariah far down the list is said to have officiated in Solomon's Temple. Even a cursory examination of Josephus' list will reveal several significant omissions as well as conflicts with known facts he himself provides: for instance, the Amariah who served in Jehosephat's time and the Azariah of Hezekiah and Hilkiah's time. One garbled genealogy of 1 Chron 9:10 gives the ancestors of Yehozedek's grandfather, Azariah, but, lists only three generations between him and the Zadok of Solomon's time. In addition, it groups him in a genealogical milieu that seems to reflect a pre-Davidic time—*pace* genealogical knowledge at the time of the composition of Chronicles. In Neh 11:10, one Jedaiah (the name Chronicles gives to the second priestly course and evidently meant to be a high priest) is listed as the son of Joiarib (the first priestly course) and given the genealogy of Ezra and Jesus ben Yehozedek. Cf. too Eusebius' statement following Julius Africanus *in E.H.* 1.7.12 about Herod's purported destruction of all priestly genealogical records.

[40]For this grisly episode, see Num 25:6-15: "Phineas the priest ... has turned *my wrath* away from the sons of Israel ... In reward for his *zeal* for his God he shall have *the right to perform the ritual atonement* over the sons of Israel" (italics mine). It is precisely the problem of "Gentiles" in the Temple that forms the background to the Zadokite Statement in Ez 44:7 as we have seen, and later surfaces in the Herodian period with the posting of "Zealot" warning markers. Cf. too *Ant.* 19.7.4 on "Simon's" opposition to Agrippa I entering the Temple noted above, p. 7.

[41]Ezra 10:6ff. and Neh 13:4ff. Strictly speaking, the banishment recorded in Nehemiah is claimed by Nehemiah, which raises questions as to who is actually behaving in this zealous way, Ezra or Nehemiah. Ezra 10:18f. only mentions the members of the high priestly family whose marriages Ezra dissolved. Curiously enough, one of these last is named "Jarib", which must be identical with the first priestly course in Chronicles, the one the Maccabees later claim affiliation with. For Ezra with his Phineas-like behavior as a priestly gloss (possibly Maccabean), see below, p. 24.

If we are unable to prove the legitimate "Zadokite" descent of any priestly hero of the Bible after the Solomonic period, imagine the embarrassment of the priests of Judas' day, who certainly could not do so either. Of the twenty-four courses of the Temple, only sixteen could even be "Zadokite", and which ones these might be is impossible to determine. Though Chronicles attempts a retrospective portrait of these, the names it includes are identifiably Second Temple.[42] One of these is accused in Ezra's time of not even being of priestly descent.[43] In any event, the Maccabees put forth in the safest manner possible their "Zadokite" claim in 1 Macc by signaling their membership in the first and largest priestly course, that of Jehoiarib. It is as good a claim as any, especially when reinforced by the portrait of Mattathias' Phineas-like behavior. Where did the assumption come from that the Maccabees could not be considered "Zadokite", or even that they were not "priestly", appertaining rather to some lower "levitical" order?[44] This is nothing but a confused distortion of historical data to suit desired theoretical aims. We do not even know to what course Simeon's family belonged (unless it be that of Jedaiah), and it is not at all outside the realm of possibility that the Maccabees constituted a lesser branch of his family as the Tobiads had in a previous generation.[45]

To claim Zadokite descent in Jesus' time (not to mention Davidic) would be like being able to claim descent from Dante in our own. Ecclesiasticus, especially Chapter 51, was so important because it delineated an instrumentality for claiming priestly legitimacy the days

---

[42]The sixteen orders are given in 1 Chron 24:3ff. and dated to David's time. The genealogy of Azariah of 1 Chron 9:10 above presents three of the course names as brothers and dates them in Saul's time. The names figure prominently in the list of returnees in Ezra 8 (repeated in Neh 7-8). Many are repeated among the signatures of the agreement of Nehemiah 10, in the population list of Neh 11, and the list of returnees of Neh 12. One course, "the sons of Delaiah", Ezra 2:34ff. considers not even to be able to prove "that their families and ancestry *were of Israelite origin*" (italics mine).

[43]Ez 2:34ff.

[44]1 Macc 2:1, 24-28, 50, 54, 58, etc. *N. b.*, how in what can only be called Mattathias' *Zealot* farewell, Elijah is said to be consumed by "zeal for the Law." For good examples of this kind of assumption, see Milik, pp. 82-3, and Cross, pp. 129-41. Josephus in *Ant.* 20.10.1 never doubts the legitimacy of Maccabean family claims to the priesthood con trasting them to the meaner ones of the Herodian priesthood, and as *Vita* 1 confirms. never considered his own Hasmonaean priestly ancestry an embarrassment.

[45]For the relation of the Tobiads to the high priestly family, see *Ant.* 12.4.2. The garbled high priestly genealogy of Neh 11:10 also points to a relationship between the first and second courses, Joiarib and Jedaiah, one or the other of which presumably being the reigning high priestly line.

when all priestly genealogies had difficulty in going back to Ezra's time. First, Simeon is the high priest, but he is so on Zadokitelines; *i.e.*, he is a *Zaddik,* a pious man. *"Hassid"* and *"Zaddik"* are in some sense parallel usages probably going back to Isaiah and have continued as such in Scroll literature, Karaism, and Jewish mysticism up to the present day. In this manner, the crucial list of *"Anshei-Hesed"* (the familiar "famous men" of Greek translation) in the Hebrew Ecclesiasticus begins and ends with the *Zaddikim,* Noah and Simeon.[46] I think we must grant that Simeon the Just (Mattathias too) is "Aaronite" according to the normal usage of that term. In Second Temple period times the priests (or "sons of Aaron") seem more of a caste, as they were in Zoroastrianism or as "the Brahmins" in India, than a specific genealogy. But is he a "Zadokite" to whom in Ezekiel's language "the charge of God's Sanctuary" must go until the end of time? He is, says Ecclesiasticus, on the basis of his perfect Piety (*Hesed*) and Righteousness (*Zedek*). In this we have the stirrings of both the "Hassidaean" and "Zadokite" movements, which are related (cf. *War* 2.1.2 where the demand of "the innovators" is for greater priestly *"Piety"—Hesed*). The Hebrew version of Ecclesiasticus adds that as such he also accedes to "the Covenant of Phineas". This covenant is a bridge over any supposed genealogical deficiencies, since being based on "zeal for the Law", it is qualitative extending to all descendants of Aaron through Eleazar. It is also to a certain extent "Zadokite" in a genealogical sense, since theoretically it should not extend to the descendants of Ithamar. It is not clear, however, if it ever should be construed in this sense, though originally this might have been part of its thrust. It is also "Zadokite" in the esoteric sense explaining just how "a son of Zadok" or "a *Zaddik*" distinguished himself, *i.e.*, through "zeal for the Law".

---

[46] Is 57:1 is perhaps the best example of this coupling of *"ha-Zaddik"* with the *"Anshei-Hesed"*, the exact language of Ecclesiasticus. For "Noah the Righteous", see Hebrew Ecclesiasticus 44:17 (actually found intact at Masada and in the Geniza). For Enoch "the Righteous" see Enoch 1:1-2, beginning with the revealing words "he (Enoch the Righteous) blessed *the Elect* and *the Righteous* who will be living in the day of tribulation when all the wicked and godless are to be removed". In 12:4 Enoch is "the scribe of Righteousness", and both titles are coupled again in 15:1. Cf. T. Levi 10:5 and Nis 10:4 in the context of Genesis history told in *Zaddik* symbolism. The coupling of *Hesed* and *Zedek* also forms the backbone of Josephus' description of John the Baptist's baptism; *Ant.* 18.5.2. Justin Martyr in *Dial.* 23, 47, and 93 uses them to describe early Christianity and they form the basis of Josephus' description of Essene doctrine in *War* 2.8.2ff. and *Ant.* 15.10.5 on Menachem above. See also how Josephus applies these two categories to the person of Simeon the *Zaddik* himself in *Ant.* 12.2.5.

Ecclesiasticus is patently a "priestly" book as the amount of space spent praising Aaron and Phineas, to say nothing of Simeon—more than for Jacob, Moses, David, and others put together—attests. That it should have been prized at Qumran among the Zadokites, at Masada among the "*Sicarii*" (the terminology is Josephus'), and in a probable Karaite synagogue in Old Cairo is not surprising.[47] What is often overlooked by those considering Josephus' data is the link of what he ultimately chooses to label as "the Zealot" movement to the priestly class despite the fact of his own affiliations as a young priest with this movement.[48] The Talmud

---

[47] Josephus relates how 600 surviving *Sicarii* (*sic*) fled to Egypt. to escape Roman repression, as a consequence of which the Temple at Heliopolis was very likely suppressed. The terminology "*Sicarii*" is pejorative, since this group obviously did not refer to itself in this fashion. The first use of concealed weapons in this manner in Palestine was actually employed by a Roman Governor, Pontius Pilate; *War* 2.9.4.; *Ant.* 18.3.1. Seen in this light, the *Sicarii* were simply adopting already existing Roman stratagems. Their hostage tactics (*War* 2.13.2; *Ant.* 20.8.5) resemble those of modern Islamic revolutionaries. The connection with Shi'ism is not fanciful, the *Sicarii* being Apocalyptic Judaism's *Assassins*. The Imam-idea at the heart of Shi'ism closely parallels the preexistent *Zaddik*-idea at Qumran; cf. 1QH, i, 20ff.; ix, 28ff. (in the context of adoptionist sonship); xv, 5 (echoing Nazirite-from-womb themes in Ga 1:15 and *E. H.* 2.23.4); and CD, ii, 7ff. Rec 1.52 conserves a perfect facsimile of "the Hidden Imam" doctrine (cf. "hidden" themes below, p. 24): "Know then that Christ, who was *from the beginning and always*, was *ever present with the Pious, though secretly*, through all their generations" tying it to "the Righteousness doctrine" (italics mine; cf. also Paul in 1 Co 2:8 and Col 1:16. *N.b.* he hints here at the "hidden" ideology and in 1 Co 15:44f. at that of "the Primal Adam". For the *Zohar* on Noah the Righteous as the progenitor of the "hidden" notation, see below p. 31; on the Primal Adam, p. 96).

R. De Vaux's criticism of "the Zealot" hypothesis of Roth and Driver again displays the peculiar inability to come to grips with the true nature of such groups: "According to its literature the community of Qumran was pre-eminently a religious group and was opposed pre-eminently to the official Judaism. The party of Zealots, on the other hand, was, according to all that Josephus tells us of it, first and foremost a nationalist party and was opposed, first 'and foremost to the Romans"; R. De Vaux, *Archaeology and the Dead Sea Scrolls,* Oxford, 1973, p. 120. De Vaux misunderstands that Josephus describes events to the Roman public in terms that they can understand; cf. the language he uses in describing revolutionary events relating to the downfall of Caligula and the elevation of Claudius, *Ant.* 19.1.2. The rise of militant Islam, particularly Shi'ite Islam, in modern times should help place such movements in a more realistic light.

[48] S. G. F. Brandon, *Jesus and the Zealots,* New York, 1967, pp. 114-141, has dealt at length with this issue of priestly connections. Not only did Josephus as a young priest oc cupv an official position in Galilee under what should probably be termed the "Directorate" period of the Revolt, 66-68 CE, but his earlier trip to Rome (where he probably made the connections that he later used to betray the Zealot cause) is also interesting in this regard; cf. Vita 3. Technically, Josephus never actually calls "the fourth philosophy" or Judas' 'Galilean' movement "Zealot" until after the "election" of Phannias/Phineas in *War* 4.3.8f.; even here he applies it only to Eleazar's group in *the Temple* (5.1.1), but the usage has attained a wide currency.

in its own manner alludes to the priestly connections of the orientation.[49] Though Josephus describes it to his Roman readers in the primarily political terms they could understand (the same could be said for how they could understand "Christianity"—a deficiency the New Testament goes a long way towards making up); "the Zealot" movement is first of all a movement making certain claims about priestly legitimacy, and not the primarily revolutionary one Josephus and the New Testament have caused us to think of it as Chief among these claims is the requirement of zeal for the Law" as a prerequisite for service at the Temple altar in an age where the high priesthood was to a certain extent up for barter, that this should have political ramifications is not surprising. Jesus himself displays some of these attitudes in the Gospel portrayal of the Temple cleansing affair where "Zealot" language is explicitly attributed to him.[50] Similar "zeal" for the Temple is attributed to his brother James in the portraits of his "Piety" (*Hesed*) and Righteousness in early Church literature. Not only does Ja 2:10 stress his "zeal for the Law", but all accounts dwell on how the flesh on his knees resembled "camel's hide" from all the importuning of God he did in the context of what appears to have been a *Yom Kippur* atonement.[51] Similar "zeal" (as well as "Rock", "Fortress",

---

[49]The famous passage in M. Sanh. ix. 6 implies at least some connection of the *Kanna'im* with priestly matters. B. Salomonsen in "Some Remarks on the Zealots with Special Regird to the term '*Qannaim*' in Rabbinic Literature", *NTS*, 12, 1966, pp. 164-76, has supplied a list of others; but his general orientation reflects the same general preconceptions as Milik, De Vaux, Le Moyne, *et al.*

[50]Noted above, p. 6. The whole problem of Jesus and the Zealots has been debated at length in well-known works by Brandon, Cullmann, Hengel, etc. The lack of issue relates very much to the inability to grasp that Zealotism as such was an orientation and not a religio-political movement with a distinct ideology as, for instance, Messianism was.

[51]Epiphanius and Jerome, *loc.* cit., mention entering the Holy of Holies, and in general all accounts agree that James' praying involved "atonement" on behalf of "the people"; cf. sectarian difficulties over the issue of *Yom Kippur* in 1QpHab, xi, 4ff. between the Righteous Teacher and the Wicked Priest. *N.b.* James' nemesis Ananus was "called by the name of truth" (*War* 4.5.2; cf. the parallel *E.H.* 2.23.20 about James), twice "ruled over Israel", and "his corpse" was violated (in 1QpHab, ix, 2 the word *is* "corpse"). That James' surpassing "Righteousness", revealingly testified to by his sobriquet, and "Piety" would have entitled him in Zadokite circles to make such atonement should be clear. In connection with these priestly claims, *Haeres.* 78.14 evokes his *rainmaking*, performed too by his Zaddik-precursor, Honi (whose death anticipates James'), which Rabbinic tradition also ascribes to Phineas/Elijah and *Habakkuk*; cf. *Ant.* 14.2.1f., b. Ta⁽an 22b-23b, and *ARN 4.4.* M. Sanh. 9:6 specifically notes: "If a priest served in a state of uncleanness ... the young men among the priests took him outside the Temple and split open his brain with clubs", which appears to have been absorbed into accounts of James' death in *E.H.* 2.23.17 and *Haeres.* 78.14, as opposed to *Ant.* 20.9.1. Whatever James' ritual purity, he

"Shield", and "Protection" imagery) is also referred to in the Qumran Hymns usually attributed to the personal composition of the Righteous Teacher himself.[52]

Here, it is significant to remark that Ecclesiasticus has also been conserved by what perhaps should be called "non-Palestinian Christianity", *i.e.*, Roman, Greek Orthodox, Ethiopic, etc., albeit in a somewhat sanitized form, though not by Rabbinic Judaism true as always to its Pharisaic/Herodian roots. Many readers will be shocked at my linking of the latter two and yet the Talmud proudly proclaims the link of Pharisaic Judaism with the Herodian family,[53] as it does Rabbi Yohanan ben Zacchai's Romanizing self-humiliation before Vespasian by way of disassociating himself from the Zealot (and in this case "Messianic") movement.[54] Josephus, another self-professed "Pharisee", not uncharacteristically flaunts his own similar behavior.[55] If the extant literature is any yardstick, Vespasian must have become very impatient at all these Jewish turncoats vying with each other to proclaim him Messiah. The anti-nationalist, Romanizing policy of the Pharisees

---

was subjected to "Sanhedrin" trial by the Herodian priestly establishment. In this regard, one should take seriously the violent attitude towards "the Rich"- in Ja 2:6 and 5:1-10, following which Elijah's rain-making miracle is evoked (5:17). *N.b.* the first political act when "the Zealots" took over the uprising in 68 CE in its "Jacobin" phase, apart from the wholesale slaughter of the high priests (including Ananus), was to destroy the debt records "to enable *the Poor* to rise against *the Rich*" (italics mine); *War* 2.17.8. Cf. in this context Ja 5:6 blaming "the Rich" for the death of "the Righteous One" (and Paul in 1 Thess 2:15 blaming *the Jews*).

[52]1QH, i, 11; ii, 15; iii, 37; iv, 3; vi, 17ff.; vii, 8ff.; viii, 22ff., ix, 28f., etc.; cf. James as "*Oblias*" ,"Protection of the People", and "Bulwark" in *E.H.* 2.23.7, 3.7.8, and *Haeres.* 29.4 and *n.b.* the Cleophas/Alphaeus/*Oblias*/Lebbaeus tangle.

[53]See particularly M. Sota 7:8 and the cry there, when Agrippa (whom "the sages praised") reads the Law on *Succot* and comes to the passage, "You may not put a foreigner over you which is not your brother"; cf. also Bikk 3:4 and Siphre Deut 157 on 17:15. The mirror image of this episode for Zadokite history must once again be that Simon with "a very accurate knowledge of the Law" who convenes "an assembly" in Jerusalem in *Ant.* 19.7.4 and wants to exclude Agrippa from the Temple *as a foreigner* ("since it belongs only to native Jews"); see above, p. 7.

[54]For this clear misuse and cruel mockery of the Messianic prophecy in the episode usually taken as being the birth moment of Rabbinic Judaism, see *ARN* 4.5. Those who doubt that the fall of the Temple discussed in the Qumran Habakkuk and Isaiah *peshers* applies to the one in Vespasian's time should note that the same passage, Is 10:33-4 applied to the 70 CE fall in *ARN* above, is also to be found subjected to exegesis. Since there is no evidence of exegesis of this kind relating to an earlier fall, the burden of proof in the face of such decisive evidence must rest on its detractors.

[55]*War* 3.8.8f. For his discussion of the "Messianic" prophecy see 6.5.4.

will be dealt with at length below. It can be traced back to the earliest stages of the party in 2 Macc and the time of Alexander Jannaeus and his son Hyrcanus II. At this point it is sufficient to assert, that if the patriarch Hillel was ever head of the Sanhedrin, as Pharisaic tradition proclaims, then the Sanhedrin in which he exercised such influence was the Herodian one.[56] Of all the parties so far mentioned, the Pharisees alone make no perceivable insistence on the high-priestly qualification of "Righteousness", being satisfied to accept appointment from foreign or non-Jewish rulers. In this orientation probably is to be found the original basis for their "split" with the "Zadokites".[57]

---

[56]For the relationship of the Hassidaeans in I Macc to the Pharisees, see below, pp. 28. For Alexander's crucifixion of the 800 Pharisees, see *War* 1.4.6 and *Ant.* 13.14.2. That these are Pharisees is clear from the revenge they take against Alexander's associates when they come to power after his death, under his wife Alexandra, as it is from their support of the priestly claims of her eldest son Hyrcanus II against the Sadducee/Zealot supporters of his younger brother Aristobulus. We have already noted Herod's affection for "Pollio the Pharisee"; equally illuminating is the famous *Prozbul* associated with Hillel, which is at the root of the problem of debt records above. For its relationship to James' attitude towards "the Rich", see below, p. 44.

[57]This "split" is vividly illustrated in 1 Macc 7:9-18, where the "Hassidaeans" are said to be "the first among the Israelites to ask them for peace terms". This is in line with their policy under Alexander and Hyrcanus. It accords vividly with the words of "Polio the Pharisee and Sameas, a *disciple of his*" (italics mine), who, "when Jerusalem was besieged ... advised the citizens to open their gates to Herod, for which advice they were well requited"; *Ant.* 15.1.1 (*Ant.* 14.9.3 attributes this advice to Sameas alone). The same policy is followed by Yohanan ben Zacchai, who before having himself smuggled out of Jerusalem in a coffin, had his friends shoot an arrow "over the wall saying that Rabban Yohanan ben Zacchai was one of the Emperor's friends". It also epitomizes the foreign policy of two other self-professed Pharisees. Josephus and Paul (cf. Ro 13:1ff. for Paul's views). Our use of the term "Pharisees" here parallels what Qumran calls "Seekers after Smooth Things" and their fellow-travelers, the "Liar", "Traitors", and "Men of Violence"; cf. CD, i, 12ff.; 1QpHab, ii, 1ff.; 4QpNah, ii, 1ff, etc.

Chapter Four
THE MACCABEES AS ZEALOTS AND ZADOKITES

The "Zealot" and "Zadokite" claims of the Maccabees are put forward in the "official" history of these claims, 1 Macc. Made in the name of the eponymous family head the Hasmonaean, Mattathias, these are meant to be blanket claims covering not just Judas and his descendants,[58] but all of Mattathias' descendants, including most notably Jonathan, Simon, and the latter's progeny. 2 Macc puts forth the same "Zealot" claim for the person of the saintly Onias III, presumably the son of Simeon the Just.[59] In this account Judas is the "Messianic" savior/priest and Onias plays the role of Mattathias. For it, there is no interruption between the family of Simeon the Righteous and Judas. Judas and the nine others who go out into the wilderness to live in caves and subsist on vegetarian fare are nothing but Noahic *Zaddikim*.[60] Here, of course, is the archetypical episode for the founding of a community such as Qumran,

---

[58]Here one might wish to quote from Mattathias' testament to his sons (itself a paraphrase of Ecclesiasticus' famous "Praise of the *Anshei-Hesed*"). *1* Macc 2:49-64: "This is the time my children ... to have a burning zeal for the Law and to give your lives for the covenant of your ancestors. Remember the deeds performed by our ancestors, each in his generation and you shall win great honor and everlasting renown. Was not Abraham tested and found faithful, was that not counted as making him just? ... Phineas, our father, in return for his burning zeal received a covenant of everlasting priesthood ... Elijah for his consuming zeal for the Law was caught up to heaven itself. ... My children, play the man and be courageous for the Law, for it will bring you glory." *N.b.*, the reference to the zeal of Phineas/Elijah, combined with the favorite Pauline allusion, "justification by faith". The question of Judas' descendants we cover elsewhere. Unlike Ezra, who confines himself to excommunication, Mattathias' zeal is expressed in killing the backsliding Jew about to offer illegal sacrifice on the altar at Modein. His cry in 1 Macc 2:21-28 to his followers, "Let everyone who has *zeal for the Law* and takes his stand *on the Covenant* follow me" (italics mine) resembles nothing so much as the behavior of *Levites* in Ex 32:25-30, who slaughter their backsliding countrymen, and to whom Moses says, "You have won yourself investiture as priests of Yahweh today".

[59]2 Macc 4:2 calls him "this Zealot for the laws" and "Protector of his fellow countrymen" after already applying the Hesed/"Perfection" imagery in 3:1f. *N.b.* the "Protection" (in Hebrew probably *Maᶜoz*) imagery once again, prefiguring its later application to James. See below, p. 26.

[60]2 Macc 5:27. The significance of this concept of "the ten *Zaddikim*" for the events surrounding the birth of the Hassidaean movement should not be underestimated. Judas' behavior, including his vegetarianism, is the prototype of John the Baptist's. The problem relates to Noah's vegetarianism before the institution of sacrifice (Gen 9:1ff: *n.b.* the additional theme of abstention from *blood*) and has to do, as 1 Macc 1:62-7 suggests with "standing firm and having the courage to refuse unclean food". Cf. the second escape and salvation episode involving *Zaddikim* in Gen 18, also including the theme of "cave-dwelling" (in a Qumran locale).

but so thick is the obscurity surrounding Maccabean claims in Qumran research, it is never remarked. Judas is a *Zaddik* in the sense that Noah the Righteous was considered a *Zaddik* (so surnamed in various Second Temple books). In some sense the continued existence of mankind is predicated on his righteous behavior,[61] and his "Nazirite" (Or "Rechabite") style vegetarianism is tied to this.

This episode regarding Judas also relates to the second episode in Genesis regarding Righteous Men, the Lot episode, and takes place in a locality very near that of the events recorded in Lot. Lot, too, is a "*Zaddik*". The Lot story goes further even than the Noah and specifies the minimum number of *Zaddikim* required for the world to continue in existence—ten.[62] It is important to note that Abraham, too, is usually referred to in these sources as "Righteous", an appellation which has clung to him in Islam and by which he is referred to several times in the Koran, *i.e.*, Ibrahīm *as-Sadiq*[63] Here, one should be aware that the Koran, preserving as it does lost traditions from sectarian and Apocalyptic Judaism, provides us with the reference to Ezra as "the

---

[61]In the words of Pros' 10:25, "the *Zaddik* is the foundation of the world". This passage is subjected to exegesis in *Zohar* 59b with the conclusion that the existence of the world is predicated on the Righteous (*n.b.* the *Zohar* 218a-b on *Phineas* knows the doctrine of "the suffering *Zaddik*", whose death is expiatory and who "suffers to protect the people"). 59b and 222a use the "Pillar" imagery, which relates to its application to "James, Cephas, and John" (the central triad) in Ga. 2:9. *Zohar* 59b on Noah explains the mysterious saying about James in the Gospel of Thomas, *i.e.* "In the place where you are to go, go to James the Just for whose sake Heaven and Earth came into existence." The "Heaven and Earth" theme is reiterated in relation to Jesus' words in Mt 24:34ff. (somewhat condensed in Mk 13:30f. and Lk 21:32f.) amid eschatological allusion to "the days of Noah". Of course, according to this ideology, when James, "the Protection of the People" and "Just One", is killed, Jerusalem could no longer remain in existence. This is reflected in the attribution in Origen's Josephus of the fall of Jerusalem to his death and in the appearance directly thereafter of a man Jesus ben Ananias. whom Josephus describes as having suddenly appeared on the streets at that time crying "Jerusalem is doomed", *War* 6.5.3. Josephus relates this episode in the context of discussing the relationship of "the Star" prophecy to the events culminating in the fall of Jerusalem. It is perhaps helpful to point out that the treatment of Jesus ben Ananias by the Jewish and Roman authorities is exactly parallel to that described in the N.T. for Jesus, except Jesus ben Ananias is freed; in the Slavonic Josephus so is Jesus.

[62]Noah and Lot are specifically so designated in Gen 6:9ff., 7:1, and 18:22ff. Later Rabbinic tradition is fond of augmenting this to 36.

[63]See for instance Koran 2:35 and 3:67; the second reflects the justification material in Gen 15:6, which in turn is reflected in the 1 Macc 2:52 and of course Paul. *N.b.* the Koran in 3:39-59 and 6:86 knows that both John and Jesus were *Zaddikim*, and Jesus as "Primal Adam".

son of God", in what is perhaps a more interesting testimony to his Zadokite heredity than the genealogy provided him in the book by his name.[64] John the Baptist is portrayed as another of these *Zaddiks,* who goes out in the wilderness in imitation of Judas Maccabee and his nine *Zaddikim;* and whose followers will be saved in good Noahic fashion from the universal flood of fire and water soon to descend on mankind.[65] He is distinctly referred to as *"zaddik"* in the New Testament and possibly in Josephus as well. The latter reference is followed by a capsule description of John 's philosophy of "Righteousness" more perfect as a reflection of its time and place than anything comparable in the New Testament and containing within it the explicit mention of the two key words, *"Hesed"* ("Piety") and *Zedek* ("Righteousness") so characteristic of these tendencies as we have described them.[66]

[64]Koran 9:30. Ezra's sonship is here grouped beside Jesus'. Such a peculiar notion can be understood if one consults Ecclesiasticus 5:11 on almsgiving, *zedakah* (*zakat* in Islam): "you will be like a son to the Most High" and the parallel passage in Wis 2:16: "the Righteous Man (*Zaddik*) is God's son". Cf. *Zohar* 222a above and 1QH, ix, 28-36: "You have known me before ever my father was and from the womb of my mother, you have dealt kindly with me ... for my father knew me not and my mother abandoned me to you, for you are a father to all the sons of your Truth. ..." and xv, 14f.: "You alone created the *Zaddik* and established him from the womb". These allusions to "the preexistent *Zaddik*" and adoptionist sonship at Qumran are often presented in association with baptismal imagery and the language of the descent of the Holy Spirit and "being joined to the Community of the Sons of Heaven": cf. 1QS, iii-iv; xi, 2ff.: 1QH. iii. 20ff.. etc.; cf. also adoptionist sonship and baptism in Justin. *Dial.* 88 and 103: also Heb 1:15 and 5:6. In particular, the pre-existent *Zaddik* links up with the *Logos* doctrine in the Gospel of John and the notion of the *Imam* in Shi'ism ("the Hidden *Imam*"—like the Hidden Messiah—to return at the end of time in the person of "the *Mandi*"). That all the *Zeddikim are* the sons of God and as such will be resurrected at the end of time (an event of which Jesus is but the special case) is widespread in the literature: cf. Mt 5:9ff., 45ff.: Lk 20:36 etc. A parallel idea is expressed in CD. iv, 5 on Ez 44:15 above, p. 6.

[65]For the coming fire and "burning" (which the Righteous will of course escape) see Mt 3:10f. and Lk 3:16f. At Qumran its counterpart is to be found in 1QM, xi, 10 where the "fire in the chaff"-allusion is actually employed following allusion to "the Star"/ "Messiah" and Judgment executed by "the Poor" leading up to the eschatological "rain" imagery. Mt 24:37, cited above, also compares the saving activity of the Messiah with that of Noah at the time of the Flood, *viz.;* "as were the days of Noah, so shall be the coming of the Son of Man." We consider all these escape and salvation episodes involving *Zaddikim* to be "Noahic".

[66]Mk 6:20. Curiously enough, but in line with the New Testament's working method, it is always foreigners or their satraps who first recognize and/or identify *Zaddiks* like Jesus and John. John, according to the ideology of 1 Macc, even in his role of Elijah/ Phineas *redivivus,* would be a priest/*Zaddik* as well as being a "Zealot". The last he confirms by hounding Herod over a minor legal point. The New Testament also refers to Joseph the Righteous (in this case Jesus' father, but classically, too, the Biblical Joshuah was "ben

We are now in a position to reconstruct some of the history of the so- called "Sadducean" or Zadokite movement. I propose this to stand as an alternative to some of the "History of the Essenes" we see so often in Qumran research and which have stood so unchallenged for the last twenty years.[67] Perhaps the first truly "Zadokite" priest, leaving aside the originator of the terminology Ezekiel himself, was Ezra. Here, too, we leave aside possible plays on the name of the last high priest before the Captivity, Yehozedek, and the possibility that the author of the Zadokite Statement was preparing the way for the return of Yehozedek's family in the person of his son Jesus. A century later Ezra, with the same genealogy as Jesus, is superficially at least more substantial, though much overlapping exists between his actions and those of Nehemiah's. For this reason, the possibility that the character of Ezra himself might simply be a priestly fiction superimposed on more secular material should not be ruled out, but this does not affect the "Zealot/Zadokite" character of the presentation. Given the portrait we have however, Ezra certainly can lay claim to the priestly "zeal" of the Covenant of Phineas, for no more zealous priest is on record unless it be the Lawgiver himself. Whether he actually did service at the altar is impossible to determine since our

---

Joseph") and Abel the Righteous, Mt 1:19 and 23:5, characterizations perhaps derived from the Zaddik-style history in Wis 10. In *Ant.* 18:5.2 Josephus characterizes John as "a good man who commanded the Jews to exercise virtue, both as concerning Righteousness (*Zedek*) towards one another and Piety (*Hesed*) towards God and so to come to baptism ... for purification of the body, supposing still that the soul was thoroughly cleansed beforehand by Righteousness." The Slavonic adds, "God sent me to show you the Way of the Law". Cf. 1QS, viii-ix, where the words attributed to John in the N.T. are expounded in terms of "the Way" terminology and "studying the Law", and 1QS, iii-iv's description of Qumran baptismal procedures against a background of "heart/"body" imagery evocative of Ez 44:9 (see above, p. 7) and varying Josephus' "soul"/"body" notation above. This *Zedek* and *Hesed* dichotomy constitutes the surest basis for confirming the identity of these various Second Temple groups. Justin Martyr, as noted (*Dial.* 93), pinpoints it as the basis of Jesus' teaching (cf. Mt 22:34-40): "He summed up all Righteousness and Piety in two commandments, *viz.*, 'You shall love the Lord Your God with all your heart' (*i.e.,*"Piety towards God") and 'your neighbor as yourself' " (*i.e.*, "Righteousness towards one another"); and we have already shown it.to constitute the totality of Josephus' description of "the Essenes", whom he calls "despisers of Riches" (an extension of "the Righteousness towards men" theme into the sphere of economic equality; cf. "the Poor") who "exercise Piety towards God and Righteousness towards all men"; *War* 2.8.2-7.

[67]See, for instance, Milik, Chapter 3, pp. 44-98; J. Murphy O'Connor, "The Essenes and their History", *RB*, 81, 1974, pp. 215-44; A. Dupont-Sommer, *The Essene Writings from Qumran*, Oxford, 1961; and Cross, Chapter 2, "The Essenes, the People of the Scrolls", and Chapter 3, "The Righteous Teacher and Essene Origins".

sources are so imperfect. He presides over festivities in the Temple like some powerful vicegerent.[68] The rededication of the Temple implicit in his reading of the Law is echoed in Judas Maccabee's presiding over a similar rededication 250 years later accompanied by the institution of a similar festival.[69] Whether Ezra's piety and zeal are sufficient to entitle him to the sobriquet "the *Zaddik*" as the Koran would imply, is open to question. If the Zadokite priesthood does not go back to pre-Exilic times (and there is little evidence that it does), then our renascent "Zadokite" or "Righteous" priesthood must date from this period.

From Ezra's time to the time of Simeon the Just in the 3rd to 2nd centuries BCE we go into something of a 'tunnel', and very little is clear until we emerge with what appears to be a "Zadokite" priesthood in the person of Simeon the *Zaddik* himself. Whatever else this priesthood adhering to Simeon's family might have been, it was obviously considered a "Righteous" one with the title of "the *Zaddik*" prominent among its accoutrements. The confusion of dates for this first definitive "*Zaddik*" *may* simply be the confusion of two Simeon the *Zaddiks,* since the family names seem to alternate back and forth between use of the names Onias and Simeon. Onias III (possibly also surnamed "the Just"), martyred at the time of the Maccabean uprising and probably the son of the Simeon in Ecclesiasticus, is very definitely presented as a *Zaddik* and probably "a suffering servant" as well. In an extremely important

---

[68]See above, p. 15. That Ezra might be a priestly fiction was proposed some time ago in a book by C. C. Torrey, *Ezra Studies,* Chicago, 1910. When viewed from a Maccabean/Zealot point-of-view, the suggestion has considerable merit. Whether true or not, the fundamentally Zadokite/Zealot/*Zaddikite* character of the presentation of Ezra remains unaffected.

[69]That Judas' Temple rededication was also accompanied by an Ezra-like reading of the Law is implied by the institution of *a Succot-like* festival commemorating another wilderness sojourn, *Hanukkah.* This in turn is actually ratified by popular vote (a democratic feature of the new "Zealot" mentality that has escaped most modern criticism anxious as it is to distance Christianity from movements like the Zealots, Maccabees, and Zadokites); 1 Macc 4:59 and 2 Macc 10:1-8. 2 Macc actually recommends that the "feast of Tabernacles now be kept in the month of Chislev" (1:9), and the more one reads it the more one sees it as a kind of *Hanukkah Haggadah.* The implication of moving the feast of booths to *Hanukkah is* of course that just as Moses went into the wilderness for the first Law, so Judas and his nine *Zaddikim went into* the wilderness for its reconsecration—the second. 2 Macc 2:13-15 even compares the collecting activities of Nehemiah concerning Kings, Prophets, and Psalms with how "Judas made a complete collection of the books dispersed in the late war, and these we still have. If you need any of them, send someone to fetch copies for you." It is striking too that this correspondence knows no Ezra (1:18-36); neither does Ecclesiasticus (49:13f.). Both refer only to Nehemiah.

section of 2 Macc (the book which presents Judas' claims to be a *Zaddik* and as "Messianic" battle-priest, the leader of the "Hassidaean" movement) Onias is not only called a "*Hassid*" ("Pious One") and "this zealot for the laws", but also "Protector" or "Shield of his fellow countrymen".[70] Despite its equal importance to the notice about Judas and his nine *Zaddikim*, this passage has also been totally ignored by modern scholarship, though it is quite possibly the basis for similar statements about the person of James the Just the brother of Jesus, another *Zaddik* and putative priestly heir according to early Church testimony.[71]

It is perhaps because of this extremely pious presentation of Onias (who cures/resurrects an enemy of God through his righteous sacrifice and is resurrected himself along with the prophet Jeremiah as a kind of "Ancient of Days" to offer Judas the Messianic battle sword in the concluding episode) and the miraculous appearances of heavenly horsemen, that 2 Macc is held in such low esteem.[72] Yet, aside from these lapses of pious

---

[70] 2 Macc 3:1, 4:2, and 15:12. We have already mentioned the titles "*Zaddik*" and "*Oblias*" ("Protection" or "Strength of the People") above, p. 19, as being repeatedly (or intrinsically as it were) applied to James in *E. H* . 2.1.2ff., 2.23.4ff., 3.7.8 and *Haeres.* 29.4-7 and 78.7-14; cf. too Josephus in Origen, *Contra Celsum* 1.47, 2.13, and *Comm. in Matt.* 10.17.

[71] Recently J. Brashler has suggested re-interpreting the difficult "*Oblias*" to read "*Obdias*", or what he would translate as "Servant of Yahweh". It is at least as plausible to consider "*Mize* a garbled version of Onias. That Onias is distinctly surnamed "Protection of his fellow countrymen" in the passage above seems the clear prototype of the statement about James. The implication, of course, in both instances was when this Shield, Strength, Pillar, or *Zaddik* was removed from the city, the city could no longer remain in existence. *E.H.* 3.7.8 puts this proposition as follows: "By their dwelling in Jerusalem (*i.e.* James and his companions), they afforded, as it were, a strong Protection to the place". Origen, *loc. cit.* (echoed in *E.H.*), insists that Josephus affirmed that "so great was James' reputation for *Righteousness* among the *People*" (*italics mine*), *that* the more discerning attributed the siege of Jerusalem and its subsequent destruction to his death. Origen's own impatience with this notice is probably not a little connected with its disappearance in extant texts. In *War* 4.5.2, Josephus makes a precisely parallel statement about James' nemesis, Ananus. He calls Ananus "venerable and very Righteous", "egalitarian", "concerned for the proletariat", etc.; even though later in *Ant.* 20.9.1, he calls him "overbearing", "insolent", and in *Vita* 39 "corrupted by bribes". That there is some confusion of Onias III with Honi *the Circle-Drawer* (circle-drawing is the mechanism for rain-making—in Josephus, "Onias the Just"), the events of whose life are mirrored in James', further strengthens the Onias/James connection and raises the additional possibility of an Onias *redivivus* tradition alongside the Phineas/Elijah one, if all three are not in fact variations on the same theme; cf. also Goosens, *op. cit.*

[72] For it, there is no break between the priesthood of Onias and the activities of Judas. The Zadokite (or the equivalent *Zaddikite*) and the Hassidaean movements are the same. Its stress is on resurrection of the dead and "making a pious end", providing the *sitz-im-leben* out of which Christianity was to emerge. Following its terminology, Jesus very definitely "makes a pious end" and in so doing must be resurrected. That 2 Macc has not been found at Qumran requires explanation, because of its patently similar orientation to Qumran literature. However, that Josephus does not seem to know it argues very

enthusiasm, it describes itself as being based on an earlier and much longer work by Jason of Cyrene. It contains much that is authentic, including official correspondence, a portrait of Onias patently more reliable than the confusion of 1 Macc, and first-rate material on Judas' relation to the Hassidaeans. As should be obvious by now to the reader, unlike majority scholarly opinion, I consider it more reliable on the whole than 1 Macc. The latter suffers from certain apologetic aims regarding the whole of the Maccabean family—in particular the progeny of Simon through John Hyrcanus, the real hero of its narrative.[73] Pro-Hassidaean in a manner that 1 Macc is not, 2 Macc exhibits many of the characteristics of what must be called "Hassidaean-type" literature (to cite two: "thorough-going" apocalyptic and a stress on resurrection of the dead). Besides having something of the appearance of a *Hanukkah Haggadah,* it seems to have been written to correct the inaccurate portrayal of Judas Maccabee and the slanderous presentation of the Hassidaean movement he headed in 1 Macc. That Judas and Onias are found so closely linked in its account argues very forcibly that its author(s) felt no break from the "Zadokite" priesthood of the one to the "Zadokite" priesthood of the other. That both were also "Zealots" needs no further elucidation.

The testimony of books like Daniel, Enoch, the Testament of Levi, etc., can be employed at this point to clinch the case for the similarity in aims between the Maccabees (perfectly good Zadokites in the several senses of that word as I have argued), the previous priesthood of Simeon and Onias, and the Hassidaeans.[74] One must, to be sure, concede the

---

strongly either that it was not written yet or was not known in Palestine. Indeed, it has the form simply of a letter to the Jews of Egypt (cf. Hebrews). 1 Macc would have been rejected out of hand by the Qumran sectaries (as Esther probably was) because of its slanderous portrayal of the Hassidaean movement.

[73]It may even have been written to combat certain slanderous material regarding John Hyrcanus' origins, perhaps originally set forth in Jason of Cyrene's earlier work championing the cause of Judas Maccabee; see *Ant.* 13.10.6. Here a mysterious Eleazar (an Essene-type) castigates him with the words, "if you would really be *Righteous,* lay down the priesthood and content yourself with the civil government of the people" (italics mine). *N.b.,* the play on the *Zaddikite* aspect of the Zadokite priesthood. The thrust of the episode concerns priestly purity or a priesthood without blemish, not genealogy. It does not dispute John's right to serve, nor his family's. It only complains that his mother was a captive and carries with it the imputation of bastard birth. Here, too, the text first introduces Pharisees and Sadducees and we hear of John's being priest, prophet, and king, as well as his desire "to be Righteous". The attempt by 1 Macc to acquit Simon, John's father, of the treachery of handing over his brother Jonathan's two sons to be slaughtered is patent and also bears on the problem of John's dubious origins; cf. 1 Macc 13:17-20.

[74]See Dan 9:26 and 11:22 and the subsequent rising of the *Kedoshim,* "the learned" and "the elect" who will be "made white", implied thereafter in 11:33 and described in 7:15-23.

point that the saintly *"Kedoshim"* of Daniel are equivalent to what is called "Hassidaeans" in the Maccabee books and Josephus, a correspondence not difficult to acknowledge.[75] I take Daniel in any event, if not Enoch as well, to be products of this "Hassidaean-type" literature. Here, among other things it will be objected that 1 Macc portrays the Hassidaeans as having deserted Judas Maccabee for a Quisling high priest loyal to the Seleucids.[76] For 2 Macc, Judas is the leader *par excellence* "of those Jews called Hassidaeans ... who are warmongers and revolutionaries".[77] As at Qumran and in Ecclesiasticus no distinction is made between *"Zaddik"* and *"Hassid"*, and Judas' *Zaddikim* double as Hassidaeans. In one account the Hassidaeans are the loyalist partisans of Judas Maccabee; in the other they are treacherous backsliders who go over to his Seleucid-backed opponents.

How can the two be reconciled? Actually it is not so difficult if one remarks that the behavior of the so-called "Hassidaeans" in 1 Macc resembles very much the behavior of the Pharisees during the reign of Alexander Jannaeus at the time of the incursion by Demetrius.[78] The way out of the impasse is to assume both accounts are true and that there are *two groups* of Hassidaeans: one loyalist or purist who must be identical with those whom we have been calling "the Zadokites"; the other a break-away which has rightly been termed "Pharisees". It even might be assumed that both saw themselves as authentic "Hassidaeans" until gradually the new terminology supplanted the old. What was "the

---

As most scholars have realized there can be little doubt of the provenance of these events. The reference to Jeremiah and "the Ancient of Days" is picked up in the Messianic sword scene with Judas Maccabee at the climax of 2 Macc. Enoch 90:8 refers to the martyrdom of Onias in portions extant at Qumran, followed immediately in 90:9 with the description of Judas, probably "the Great Horn", and his activities which follow in 13-19; cf. the "Horn" imagery applied to the teacher in 1QH, vii, 22f.

[75] I think there can be little doubt that those who are called "Saints" in Daniel must relate to those who are called "Hassidaeans" in the Maccabee books. In any event, the terminology is used interchangeably at Qumran with a host of other epithets including *Zaddikim, Ebionim*, sons of Light, etc.

[76] 1 Macc 7:8-18. *N.b.*, the interesting use of Qumran-style exegesis in applying *Hassideieha* in Ps 79 to this break-away party who sue for peace and are prepared to recognize foreign appointment of high priests. It is not yet a case of confusion of terminologies since the terminologies are fluid and still developing. It is this Josephus fails to appreciate when taking his sources too literally and later speaking about "Pharisees" and "Essenes".

[77] 2 Macc 14:6.

[78] That these men are Pharisees is clear from the vengeance they take in retribution later under Alexandra; cf. *War* 1.4-5.

split" about? When viewed in this light it is about instrumentalities—in particular, who should appoint the high priest: whether it should be by a native and purist procedure, *i.e.*, "an election" or "by lot", or whether appointment by foreign rulers or their agents was to be considered legitimate. Josephus mentions the "high priesthood of Judas" three times and that it was "bestowed on him by the people".[79] He also tells us that the Zealots not only demanded selection by lot in 4 BCE, but actually proceeded to carry it out in the extremist phase of the uprising against Rome in 68 CE For their part, the Pharisees consistently supported and upheld the legitimacy of priests appointed by foreigners.[80]

How can the presentation of 1 Macc be explained according to this picture? What it has preserved is probably the birth moment of the Pharisee Party, but according to Josephus the later Simon and the early John supported the Pharisee Party.[81] Later John went over to the Sadducees and was followed in this by his son, Alexander Jannaeus. The latter together with his son, Aristobulus, are the epitome of what we must mean by "Sadducees" in this period. Aristobulus very definitely exhibits the "nationalist" tendencies of this movement. as we have described it, and the telltale inability to fawn on foreign potentates (in Josephus' words, "he turned sick of servility and could not bear to abase himself in order to secure his aims at the expense of his dignity"). In this he is supported by a "zealous" lower priesthood in the Temple who go about their chores and sacrifices even while the Romans are slaughtering

---

[79] *Ant.* 12.10.6 and 11.2. That he did not mention this in *The Jewish War* is perhaps best understood in terms of his fuller and freer elucidation of events in the *Antiquities* when his position in Rome had become more secure. *N.b.* the parallel "election" of James as "Bishop of Jerusalem" in early Church tradition and its likely reflection in the story of "the election" of the twelfth Apostle "Mathias" who defeats "Barsabbas *Justus*" in Acts 1:23f. Note, also, the *bloody* "Jamesian"-like *fall* "Judas Iscariot" purportedly takes in 1:18.

[80] Cf. *Ant.* 17.9.1, where the main demand of the followers of the two rabbis slain in the Temple Eagle incident was that "the people" should choose the high priest. For the election of Phannias (*i.e.* Phineas) ben Samuel, see *War* 4.3.8 and Tos. Yoma i, 6.180. Josephus' words of indignation over his elevation are worth quoting: "He was a man not only unworthy of the high priesthood, but that did not even know what the high priesthood was: such a mere commoner was he! Yet did they haul this man without his own consent from the countryside. ... put upon him the sacred garments, and upon every occasion instructed him what he was to do". It is hard to imagine a 'poorer' priesthood than this. That he was a "stone-cutter" as well is not without its symbolism; cf. "Rock" and "Cornerstone" symbolism in the early Church and at Qumran. *N.b. War* 6.8.3 mentions a Temple Treasurer named "Phineas", who gives over to Titus what is left of the Temple treasure.

[81] *Ant.* 13.10.5.

them.[82] As against this, his brother Hyrcanus II returns, following his mother's lead and her connections with Simeon ben Shetach, to the Pharisee fold. Hyrcanus is definitely Pharisaic, which his connections

[82]*War* 1.7.1: "Pompey was amazed at the unshakable endurance of the Jews ... Not even when the Temple was being captured and they were being butchered around the altar did they abandon the ceremonies ordained for the day ... the priests quietly went on with the sacred rites and were cut down as they poured libations and offered incense putting the *service to God before* their own preservation" (italics mine). Josephus adds the important political note: "Most of those who fell were killed by their own countrymen of the rival faction" (*i.e.*, the Pharisees and proto-Herodians). Nothing could be more "Zealot" (and "Zadokite") than the dedication to "Temple service" exhibited by Aristobulus' priestly supporters.

Even the typically Zealot resort to suicide finds expression here. Cf. the "Zealot" suicide of the old man (whom Josephus identifies with cave-dwelling "robbers" of *Galilean* origin) and his seven sons in a Jordan valley location 100 years before Masada, below p. 56 and *Ant.* 14.15.4f. Not only is this event reflected in "the Seven Brothers" episode in 2 and 4 Macc, which definitively link the doctrine of resurrection to the martyrdom ideal; it coincides with the period of the end of phase 1B of Qumran habitation, *i.e.*, 37 BCE when Herod is on his way like Pompey before him and Vespasian after him to assault Jerusalem. *N.b.* the purposeful trivialization of this "Seven Brothers" episode in the Mt 22:23, Mk 12:18, and Lk 20:27 responses to "Sadducee" beliefs on *resurrection*. These parodies, following references to Jesus' "right-teaching" on the question of "paying taxes to Caesar", conclude with citation of Justin Martyr's "all Righteousness" dichotomy of *Hesed* and *Zedek*, *i.e.*, the *Piety* commandment of "loving God" and the *Righteousness* commandment of "loving one's neighbor as oneself". Jesus quotes these in order "to silence the Sadducees". *N.b.*, the general context of the allusion to "the Way of Righteousness", and "God in Truth", "the Prophet", "Stone" and "Cornerstone" imagery, plural son- ship, and spiritualized sacrifice; cf. Ja 2:8ff. on the "all Righteousness" commandment.

For Honi ("Onias the Righteous")'s attitude towards these Pharisee and Romanizing supporters of Hyrcanus, see *Ant.* 14.2.1. Honi's refusal to condemn Aristobulus is the direct cause of his murder. Here, Josephus alludes to the "hidden" tradition, which appears to have attached itself to Honi's family, seems to involve cave-dwelling, and comes all the way down through Simeon bar Yohai, the *Zohar's* eponymous source (see below, pp. 63f. *N.b.* the *Zohar*, 63a and 67b on "Noah", knows the "hidden" tradition. For it, Noah, who "sought *Righteousness*", "*withdrew*", "*hid himself in the* ark" or "*was hidden* in the ark on *the Day of the Lord's Anger*, and was placed beyond the reach of *the Adversary*"—italics mine. Note also the connection of these notions with "rain" and eschatological "flood"). Josephus tells us that Honi "hid himself" because of the war; but his grandson "Hanan", possibly identifiable with John the Baptist, is also called "Hidden" in the Talmud, and the thrust probably relates more to what goes by the name of "the Hidden *Imam*" ideology in Shi'ite Islam than it does Josephus' rather charming misunderstanding of it. The Talmud, too, misunderstands the true implications of the ideology when it recounts a "Rip van Winkle" story about Honi and tells of another, otherwise unidentifiable, grandson Abba Hilkiah, who repeats his grandfather's rain-making feat; b. Ta'an 23a-b. Not only must "Abba Hilkiah" have been a contemporary of James; but if the Lucan account of a kinship between Elizabeth and Mary has any substance, then James, too, was very likely a descendant of Honi. Epiphanius' (*loc. cit.*) ascription to James of a parallel rain-making miracle increases the points of contact (*n.b.* the common elements of "working in the fields" and antagonism to the Pharisaic Herodian establishment in both traditions').

with Herod's family and cooperation with the Romans to secure his priesthood conspicuously confirm.[83] But Jonathan and Simon Maccabee have already at an earlier time betrayed the purist program of their brother Judas and in effect assimilated themselves to the policies of "the Pharisees" who 'split' with Judas and supported the Seleucid appointee Alcimus on the grounds of his supposed greater purity.[84] This break can explain the negative portrayal of the Hassidaean movement in the official family history of 1 Macc, an attitude of antagonism, which by the time of its composition, had permeated the Hasmonaean family. But 1 Macc, while conserving the anti-"Hassidaean" spirit of Jonathan and Simon, 'forgets' that the original Hassidaeans were Zadokites and followers of Judas conserving only their current embodiment in the Pharisee movement. John Hyrcanus very soon attains the status of an independent monarch (Josephus tells us that he alone embodied in his person the three attributes of prophet, priest, and ruler, and his son, Aristobulus, actually assumed the crown) and, therefore, has no further need of the temporizing policies of the Pharisees.[85] He returns to the policies of the Zadokite wing, which he assimilates to his own, no longer treating it as an independent entity, nor remembering its original differences with his two ancestors. For him, the Hassidaeans are the group who

---

[83]See *War* 1.6.2; *Ant.* 13.16.1. For Hyrcanus' general connections with the Herodian family, see his relations with Antipater, *Ant.* 13.16-14.6. That Aristobulus is ant-Pharisaic is confirmed in *Ant.* 14.5.4. For Hyrcanus' behavior towards Pompey, see *Ant.* 14.4.2. *i.e.*, "Hyrcanus zealously assisted him (Pompey) in everything." As we have suggested, such behavior also epitomizes Pollio and Sameas', Josephus' "Essenes" Yohanan ben Zacchai's, and Josephus' own attitudes towards Emperors or their agents, as it does Paul's. It has also been retrospectively assimilated into the portrait of Jesus in the N.T. Here the charge in Acts 15:5 (echoed in modern scholarship) that Christianity was infiltrated by "Pharisees" at an early stage is true; but its import is rather the opposite of what the N.T. implies. The "Pharisee the son of a Pharisee" is Paul and his approach in Ro 13:1-7 typifies "Pharisaic" policy, as no Pharisee rabbi other than Akiba is on record as having been crucified or beheaded. Akiba, in any event, is ridiculed by his colleagues for his behavior; see below, p. 52.

[84]Which is why 2 Macc chooses to end on the triumphal note of Judas' Messianic appointment. For it, Jonathan and Simon have already betrayed the "Zadokite" Hassidaean ideal of their brother. Given the almost obligatory martyrdom of those who espoused it, their defection is not surprising.

[85]*Ant.* 13.10.6 and 11.1. His father, Simon, had assumed the high priesthood "until a trustworthy prophet should arise"; 1 Macc 14:41 (prefiguring the later "True Prophet" ideology); Simon no doubt must have considered this to mean permanently. We have already seen above, p. 28, how the Pharisees, who contest John's right to the high priesthood, do so on the grounds of his questionable purity and prod him on the basis of his own presumable interpretation of the Zadokite Covenant, *i.e.*, on the basis of *Righteousness*.

betrayed his uncle Judas and follow a temporizing foreign policy inimical to the new interests of his "Kingdom". On this basis 1 Macc, though Phariseeizing of necessity in its portrait of Jonathan and Simon, .is a product of the later part of John Hyrcanus' reign (or even early Alexander Jannaeus). It purposely obscures the connections of the original "Zadokite" Hassidaeans led by Judas with the priesthood of Onias and Simeon, and at the same time uses the terminology "Hassidaean" to heap abuse upon the breakaway temporizing Pharisee movement.[86]

---

[86] 1 Macc's rather clumsy handling of the priestly infighting in which Onias is replaced by Mattathias gives further evidence of its unreliability. By comparison, 2 Macc clarifies the political ramifications of the squabbles over priestly succession.

Chapter Five
ARCHAEOLOGICAL RECONSTRUCTION

Here, some archaeological evidence based on the coins so dear to Qumran archaeologists should perhaps be employed.[87] If one observes in a general way the distribution of coins found at Qumran, it will be remarked that it increases and decreases in a consistent pattern. The first rise in distribution begins at the time of John Hyrcanus (the later period) and reaches a peak under Alexander Jannaeus. It then falls away almost to zero in Herod's reign. It starts increasing again around the time of Herod's death and the revolts of 4 BCE-7 CE, rising steadily until it hits a peak during the crucial years 50-60 CE before the war against Rome. To judge by the numerical distribution of coins, the monastery is destroyed at the height of its power.[88] Numerous scholars have been particularly puzzled over the clear destruction of the settlement

---

[87]See R. De Vaux, "Fouille au Khirbet Qumrân", *Revue Biblique,* 60, 61, and 63, 1953, 1954, and 1956, pp. 93, 229-231, and 565-569, and *Archaeology and the Dead Sea Scrolls,* pp. 18-23, 33-41, 44-45, 64-67, 70-71. De Vaux, and almost all specialists who base their work on his, employ this coin data to arrive at a final determination for the abandonment of the site by the sectaries. De Vaux himself, however, states, p. 138, "It is quite certain that in the study of the Qumran documents archaeology plays only a secondary role." Elsewhere, though, he states in response to Driver's contention, *The Judaean Scrolls,* Oxford, 1965, p. 394, that "internal evidence afforded by a document must take precedence over external evidence": "No—other things being equal, there is no precedence between the two kinds of evidence: a correct solution must make use of both, must prove the worth of both", *NTS,* 13, 1966-7, p. 97.

[88]De Vaux, *loc. cit.* There are some 94 coins which are all from the second and third years, 67-8 and 68-9 of the Revolt (6 too oxidized to read). By contrast there are only about 11 coins from the period of Archelaus, 1 for Herod (though there are 78 coins from the period of Agippa I, another period of high revolutionary activity ending with the execution of Judas' two sons). By contrast there are 143 coins from Alexander Jannaeus. 5 coins from Hyrcanus II and four for Antigonus b. Aristobulus. One cannot resist remarking here that if one coin had been found from 69-70. De Vaux's theory of abandonment, and that of those basing their theories on his, would be in grave jeopardy. See, also E. NI. Laperrousaz, *Qoumrán L 'Établissernent Essénien des bords de La :Vier Morte,* Paris, 1976, p. 30. No coins have been found for instance from the first year of the revolt. Should we therefore conclude the sectaries only arrived during the second? No coins have so far been found from the second year of the Revolt in Jerusalem. Should we likewise conclude the Temple fell before then? Y. Meshorer confided in a personal comment to me that he has not even seen De Vaux's coins, which are safely locked up in the École Biblique, and doubt must persist as long as 6 are too oxidized to read. Very few coins would have escaped from the city when it was under siege from CE 68 onwards in any event: and at least in the Jericho area, under Roman occupation as it was, they would have been of no use even if they had. De Vaux points to one hoard of coins found near Jericho from the fourth year, but this is just that, a hoard.

N.b. the precipitous rise in coin distribution during the periods of Alexander Jannaeus and Agrippa I. These correspond chronologically to two known flights in these periods: Alexander's flight with "6000 of his followers" to a mountainous area outside Jerusalem (*War* 1.4.7 and

somewhere on or before 31 BCE.[89] The usual conclusion drawn is that the monastery was destroyed by fire during the earthquake of 31 BCE. De Vaux, whose hypothesis this was, admitted its weakness when criticized, but this admission never made the same impression as his original proposal.[90] Or, for those who realize the absurdity of thinking that the sectaries could not have rebuilt the monastery in 30 or 29 BCE if they did so in 4 BCE, comments such as, "perhaps the Persians destroyed the monastery in the war between Antigonus and Herod/Hyrcanus", are common.[91] To these I should like to add a third.

Cross was very close to the mark when he observed that control of the Jericho road was all-important, and the sectaries could not maintain themselves at Qumran in the face of Roman control over it. But he missed the self-evident corollary of this, of which the settlement's several destructions give unmistakable proof. Only some twenty-odd walking miles from Jerusalem, the monastery could not maintain itself in the

---

Ant. 13.14.2) and James' flight with "5000" of his followers to an unspecified location "outside Jericho" after the attack by Paul on the Temple Mount; Rec 1.70ff. Significantly, this last actually places James and his community in the region of Qumran, from where he sends out Peter on his first missionary journey to Caesarea. It also contains the highly original notice that James broke his leg in a fall down the Temple steps and was still "limping" some weeks later when Peter arrived in Caesarea. For an additional numerical parallel to this flight of the "5000", see Philo's remarks in *Quod Omnis* 12, numbering "those people called Essenes ("who derive their name from their Piety") at something more than 4000".

[89]See Milik, pp. 51ff., Bruce, pp. 49-52, Cross, p. 60, etc.

[90]Though originally extremely dogmatic on the question of the earthquake, in his final work De Vaux took a much more conciliatory stance: "The question remains open, therefore, and my real reason for believing that the fire coincided with the earthquake of 31 BCE is that this solution is the simplest and that there are no positive arguments to contradict it." The criticism came from De Vaux's own colleague, Milik, pp. 51ff., and a despised enemy, S. Steckholl, "Marginal Notes on the Qumran Excavations", *Revue de Qumran*, 7, 1968, pp. 34ff. But *there are positive* arguments to contradict it, namely, besides the question of evidence of some habitation in the Herodian period, why a group that returned in 4 BCE could not return in 30 BCE, or even left in the first place instead of quite simply repairing the damage? To think an earthquake could have caused, in addition to masonry damage, the kind of total conflagration the evidence suggests, is farfetched. (Those who contend that superstition could have kept the sectaries away—Morton Smith in a personal comment to me—still must explain why they subsequently returned and the evidence for a less than total abandonment.) But De Vaux's methods were already being criticized by R. North as early as 1954 in "Qumran and its Archaeology", *CBQ*, 16, pp. 426-37. and more recently by Laperrousaz.

[91]See Milik, p. 94, Laperrousaz, pp. 41-45, and B. Mazar, T. Dothan, and I. Dunayevsky, *En-Gedi, The First and Second Seasons of Excavations: 1961-62*, Jerusalem, 1966, p. 5.

face of a strong determined central authority in Jerusalem.[92] Alexander Jannaeus was .one such ruler; Herod the Great another. The Romans under Vespisian and subsequently under Titus plainly constitute a third such determined force, as they do under Hadrian and Severus when Bar Kochba's guerillas first occupied the site and then abandoned it and made a more determined stand further into the Wadi Murabbacat or Nahal Hever.[93] I do not consider the period of the tetrarchies and procurators by definition to at anytime have exhibited this characteristic of 'strong central government'. The power of the procurators probably

---

[92]Cross, pp. 75ff. His sharp critique of Driver, Rabin, and Roth in these pages is in-, temperate. It is true that the theories of Driver and Roth could not account for the whole expanse of Qumran literature, but they at least had the virtue of pointing out the expansive "Zealot" nature (*i.e.*, non-pacifist and apocalyptic) of the sectaries. Even De Vaux finds himself in difficulty on this account, stating in *NTS,* p. 93, that "the Essenes, who were pacifists, offered resistance to attack ..." and in *Archaeology,* p. 122, "We were already aware that the Essenes took part in the Revolt". Milik was forced by the theories of Roth and Driver to admit that in the last phase, "Essenism had taken on something of the character of the Zealots ... ", *NTS,* p. 93. Oblivious to the contradiction he has involved himself in, De Vaux held to his pacifist preconceptions, while at the same time terming the Essenes, "eschatological".

Here, it is worth quoting Cross, "Military control of Qumran from Masada in the face of Roman power immediately north (*i.e.*, Jericho) is quite incredible." Additionally, Cross assumes the Masada group participated in the final stages of the war, although like the Christians before them they had already withdrawn from Jerusalem in 68 after the assassination of Menachem. As long as they refrained from harassing commerce on the Jericho road, which most evidence suggests they did, the Romans would have had no interest in bothering any final holdouts, who might have remained in or slipped back to the caves and ruins. Control of the Jericho road by a hostile and determined authority would make life difficult at the monastery, but *in wartime conditions* not impossible, and the site was a good forward observation post for Masada. It is just as likely the Romans did not immediately garrison it (coin data notwithstanding—otherwise why burn it?), but rather moved on to the siege of Jerusalem (actual garrisoning would have come later in the course of operations against Masada). Life could certainly have continued at Qumran, its isolated location and natural caves being the *raison d'être* for its settlement in the first place.

[93]For description of Nahal Hever finds, see Y. Aharoni, "Expedition B—The Cave of Horror", Y. Yadin, "Expedition D", and "Expedition D—The Cave of Letters", *IEJ,* 12, 1962, pp. 186-99; 11, 1961, pp. 36-52, and 12, 1962, pp. 227-257. Here, too, the evidence shows that Bar Kochba's followers returned to site at Qumran at a time of weakened central authority and abandoned it in the face of superior, more determined, forces. Actually, as Driver has noted, the presence of Bar Kochba's forces at the site must be explained, particularly in relation to Cave IV, which they could not have remained unaware of. 68 CE, far from being a *terminus ad quern* for the deposit of the scrolls, is only a *terminus a quo, i.e.*, not the last, but rather *only the first possible moment* for their deposit.

rarely extended very far outside Jerusalem except in occasional bursts of energy as under Tiberius Alexander and Felix.[94]

That the monastery seems to have flourished under Alexander while it lay buried in ashes under Herod (the same monarch who built a winter palace nearby and had the last of the Maccabean claimants to the high priesthood strangled while frolicking in its swimming pool) *must say something*. Yet majority opinion tends to identify Alexander Jannaeus as "the Wicked Priest"; while at the same time identifying the sect with "the Essenes", about whom both Herod and Josephus speak with such evident cordiality.[95] Very few specialists doubt that the sect was vociferously (even vindictively as John the Baptist was) anti-Pharisaic;

---

[94]The robbery of the crown messenger, Stephen, not far outside the walls of Jerusalem (see below, p. 66, for the relationship of this Stephen to the "Stephen" in Acts) shows the impunity with which guerrilla forces operated in these years. The bandit chief, Eleazar bar Dinaeus, operated for almost a generation until Felix was able to curtail his activities. The inability of procurators to protect Galilean pilgrims on their way through Samaria, and even the activities of John the Baptist and Jesus, give further proof of this proposition; Cf. *Ant.* 20.5.4; *War* 2.12.2; *Ant.* 20.6.1 and 8.5; *War* 2.13.1-3.

As for Felix' activities in the years 52-60, Josephus states "as to the number of the robbers whom he caused to be crucified and of whom were caught among them, and those he brought to punishment, they were a multitude not to be enumerated". Still the next procurator, Festus, was forced to tackle "the chief curse of the country" killing "a considerable number of the bandits" and capturing "many more"; *Ant.* 2.14.1. Elsewhere, Josephus calls the "cheats and deceivers claiming inspiration" and scheming to bring about revolutionary changes by leading the people "*out into the wilderness* on the pretenses that there God would show them *signs of approaching freedom*" an even greater scourge (italics mine); *Ant.* 2.13.4., and claims "the religious frauds and bandit chiefs joined forces and drove numbers to revolt, *inciting them to strike a blow for freedom*" (language reminiscent at once of the two rabbis in the 4 BCE Temple Eagle incident and the Slavonic descriptions of John the Baptist and Jesus); *Ant.* 2.13.6.

[95]Milik understands this proposition very well, pp. 93-5. citing the relevant data from Josephus (*Ant.* 15.10.4-5: "He always treated all the Essenes with honor and thought higher of them than their mortal nature required"); yet resists its self-evident corollary, preferring to hold out for token habitation of the monastery in the Herodias period. For Josephus' own pro-Essene sentiments, one has only to cite his description of the sects in *War* 2.8.2ff. This is not really a description of the sects at all, but a description of the Essenes, the customs of whom he labors over in loving detail: sec above, p. 13, for Josephus' incorporation of elements from this description in his expanded treatment of the movement of Judas and Saddouk in *Ant.* 18.1.1ff. He first mentions "Essenes" in the period between John Hyrcanus and Alexander Jannaeus: cf. *War* 1.3.4 and *Ant.* 13.11.2 on "Judas the Essene" portrayed as a Temple fortune-teller on the fringes of the establishment (see similarly "Simon the Essene" in *Ant.* 17 .13.3). We have already called attention to the overlap in the portraits of "Menachem the Essene" and the Pharisees, Pollio and Sameas. The obsequious behavior of all three resembles nothing so much as Yohanan ben Zacchai's (and Josephus' own) treatment of Vespasian. The technique is always the same, predicting

yet the scholarly consensus insists that Alexander Jannaeus, who in his person exhibited the same characteristic, persecuted the sect: while Herod, whose open alliance with the Pharisee-sponsored Hyrcanus and special treatment of Pollio and Sameas (who advised the Jerusalem polity to open its gates to him) patently show to have been pro-Pharisaic (as his descendants, Agrippa I and Agrippa II, indisputably were confirming the Gospel picture of the "Herodian"-Pharisaic alliance), treated it with solicitude.[96] One text at Qumran actually deals with these events—the Nahum *pesher*. While it does not condone crucifixion *per se* for reasons that in the first century CE should be obvious (and even palaeographers agree that this is what they call a "Herodian" text, *i.e.*, first century CE), it does not condemn the "furious Young Lion's" action in taking vengeance on the members of the party who invited "Demetrius" into the country. The stance, rather is very similar to that of Honi the Circle- Drawing *Zaddik,* who when called upon to condemn the priestly supporters of Aristobulus in the next generation who had opened the

---

for the patron either his imminent coming to power or long life on the throne. Once again. I feel our explanation of the origins of the "Hassidacan" split goes a long way towards resolving these discrepancies. Whoever these early "Essenes" are they are not our Qumran sectaries, who are never obsequious and whose eschatology never panders to anyone; on the contrary, it is violently apocalyptic. Nor are they the "Essenes" whose martyrdoms Josephus describes in such detail in the *War*, a description probably embodying elements of his own eye-witness account of the fall of Qumran. Milik's description of a change in the character of the Essenes is not sufficient to explain these discrepancies.

[96]See n. 95 and above, p. 32. The grouping of "the Pharisees and the Herodians" together on the questions of loyalty to Caesar and paying taxes in the section of the N.T. preceding the discussion of "the Sadducees" and "the Seven Brothers" is for once very incisive; Mt 22:15ff., Mk 12:13ff., and Lk 20:20 (parodying the "Righteousness" notation; cf. also Mk 3:6). Once the two groups of Hassidaeans/Essenes are understood, as we have described them, *i.e.*, as "Pharisee" Essenes and "Zadokite" Essenes, then most of these problems that so bedevil Josephus' narratives, evaporate. When "Essene" is used, we must often substitute "Pharisee", as for instance, in all the examples of Herod's regard for "Essene" teachers. When "Pharisee" is employed, we must *sometimes* substitute "Essene" (or better yet, "Zadokite"), as for instance, in Josephus' reference to "Saddouk a Pharisee". In the Slavonic (in what is perhaps as good a proof as any of its authenticity), we hear how Simon, a toadying "scribe of Essene origin", runs at "the wild Man" and attacks him, which is patently preposterous since John is the "Essene"-type (cf. "Simon the Essene" in *Ant.* 17.13.7, possibly identifiable with the legendary "Shammai"). If we read here "Pharisee", the situation is clarified considerably; for more on the relationship of Saddouk and John, see below, pp. 95f.

Temple gates to him and given him refuge, refuses in good "Zadokite" style. In return, these Herodian-aligned and Romanizing Pharisees stone him.[97]

---

[97]This event has been rightly signaled in the work of Goosens and Dupont-Sommer as very important. We have noted it above, pp. 2f. In it, we must see the basis for the charge, repeated so often in the N.T. and early Church history (and then echoed in the Koran), that Israel stoned all the Prophets and Righteous Ones; Mt 23:29ff. and Lk 13:34ff., 11:47 etc. There can be little question that Honi is one of "the Righteous Ones" referred to, the "tombs" of whom are also mentioned in Mt 23:29 (cf. "the whitened sepulchers" in the Rec 1.71 reference to James' flight to Jericho probably related to the "making white until the time of the End"—allusion in Dan 11:35. See, also, how this imagery is picked up in the Koran 73:13 in the description of "the Day on which the hair of the children will be turned white"). Other than Zechariah, and excluding the apocryphal Martyrdom of Isaiah, no other prophets are on record as having been killed by Jews unless we include Honi's namesake Onias and John the Baptist. the latter linked in N.T. tradition with Zechariah. The connection of both Onias' to James has already been signalled. In addition to the rain-making; the bringing of James (again by "Sadducees and Pharisees") into the Temple at Passover to quiet the Jewish masses, the "Messianic" proclamation he makes, and his subsequent stoning are extremely close to the circumstances of this Honi episode; cf. Eusebius. Epiphanius, and Jerome. *loc. cit.* The reference to James' fall from "the pinnacle of the Temple" in these accounts is a garbled version of his earlier "fall" from the steps in Rec 1.70 which has been assimilated by Church tradition into a single attack.

Chapter Six
A "ZADOKITE" RECONSTRUCTION

Our hypothesis is that the "Zadokite" monastery at Qumran is "Sadducean", but not Sadducean according to the portraits in Josephus and the New Testament, which relate to a later period.[98] In like manner the so-called "Karaites" of the Middle Ages refer to themselves and are referred to by others as "Sadducees" (strikingly enough they also seem to have used this terminology interchangeably with "*Zaddikim*"), but have more in common with the Qumran sectaries than they do with what I shall call "Herodian" or normative Sadduceeism.[99] Far from being at odds with the Jerusalem authorities during the Maccabean period, Qumran Sadduceeism was in large measure sponsored by them. Therefore, its highpoint according to coin data comes in the Hyrcanus/Jannaeus period, also the highpoint of the Maccabean family priesthood. Its rise is coincident with the split in the later part of Hyrcanus' reign between the Maccabean family and the Pharisee

---

[98]The hypothesis is not new; see for instance the articles of North, Goosens, Wernberg-Møller, Trinquet, and the remarks of Albright above, p. 14. However, none of these ever developed the proposition in any detail; neither did they couple it with "Christian" and "Zealot" hypotheses as we are doing. Up until now it has been something of a three-corner hat—the partisans of the "Zealot" theory and the Sadducees knowing nothing about Jewish-Christianity; the partisans of Jewish-Christianity (Teicher is its only well known representative, but actually Margoliouth preceded him) knowing little or nothing about Sadduceeism and Zealotism.

[99]See Maimonides on *Abot* 1.3 and Abraham ibn Ezra on Dan 11:31 in Gallé, *Daniel avec Commentaires*, p. 141 for the view from outside. From inside, see Embden and Filipowski, *Liber Juchassin ... R. Abraham Zacuti*, 13a; Trigland, *Diatribe de Seta Karaeorum*, pp. 16f., and Hassan b. Massiah, quoted in Poznanski, *REJ*, xliv, pp. 76ff. That the Karaites actually referred to themselves as *Zaddikim* is confirmed in S. Luzki, *Orah Zaddikim*, Vienna, 1830, pp. 19ff. Indeed, no one has yet satisfactorily explained the double "d" in the Greek transliteration of Sadducee, nor the fact that the Zadok in the Zadokite statement in the Septuagint Ezekiel is rather transliterated, *Saddouk*, just as the teacher who arose with Judas the Galilean as the shift to "Messianism" occurred is called "Saddouk" in the *Antiquities*.

Here it would be worth quoting from the Karaite author al-Kirkisani, who not only knows (as Rabbanites did not., or had forgotten) that Jesus was "*a Zaddik*", but "that his Way was the same as that of Zadok and Anan ... Jesus forbade divorce just as the Sadducees did (but the Sadducees did not forbid divorce; rather the sectaries at Qumran and the early Christians did). As for the religion of the Christians which they profess today, it was Paul who introduced and established it. He was the one who invested Jesus with divinity and he claimed to be a prophet ordained by his Lord Jesus ... As for the religion of the Christians which they profess today, it is outright heresy"; *al-Qirqisani's Account of the Jewish Sects of Christianity*, tr. by L. Nemoy, *Hebrew Union College Annual, v. 7*, 1930, pp. 364-5. A more "Ebionite" account of "Christian" history could not be imagined. Even today one has to be amazed by al-Kirkisani's perspicuity in an age of otherwise utter confusion.

Al-Kirkisani also preserves the tradition from *ARN* 5.2 that there were *two* groups of Sadducees (*i.e.*, "the Sadducees and the Boethusians") taking their origins from the "split"

Party which is carried to an extreme of brutality in the conflict of the Jannaeus period.[100] How then could John Hyrcanus have 'returned' to the Sadducee Party? He did so because this was the original party of Judas Maccabee, deserted by his family during the somewhat dubious machinations of his uncle Jonathan and father Simon to curry Seleucid favor for their claims to the high priesthood.

The monastery at Qumran was probably the extreme expression of Sadduceeism. In the manner of both Daniel and Maccabees II, this extreme and pietistic expression of Sadduceeism, embraced by the Hassidaean partisans of Judas Maccabee, differed from normative Sadduceeism of the Herodian period (which seemed to have more in common with Samaritanism or the Shammai wing of the Pharisee Party) in its radical espousal of the relatively "new" doctrine of resurrection of the dead, or rather resurrection of "the Pious Ones" or "the Righteous Ones", for these were the only ones to whom the privilege applied, all others in the language of the time going straight to *Sheol*."[101] That

---

between two leaders, "Zadok and Boethus"; pp. 326 and 364. Though Kirkisani's generation count places this in the second generation after Simeon the *Zaddik* (*i.e.,* the time of our Zadokite "Hassidaean"/Pharisee "Hassidaean" split); dose attention to generation counts in *ARN* 5.2 ("they taught them to their disciples and their "disciples to their disciples") places it *three* generations beyond that or in the period of the confrontation (the *second split*) between "Saddouk" and the Herodian "Sadducee", Joezer b. Boethus, over the issues of *taxation,* priestly *Hesed,* etc. (n. *b.* for *ARN,* Zadok's "Sadducees" *espouse* the doctrine of resurrection, not reject it and heap abuse on the "Pharisees" on this basis). Not only is this the *sitz-im-leben* of Josephus' discussions of sectarian strife, it links up with traditions in the N.T. and Pseudoclementines dating "Messianic" and sectarian strife to the time of the coming of John the Baptist; see above, p. 11. Note also that for the *Ant.* and the Slavonic, "Saddouk" and "the Wild Man" play parallel roles; see also below, p. 95. For Kirkisani, Zadok broke with the "Rabbanites" (and presumably their "Boethusian" confederates) on *the issue of marriage with a niece.* The practice was widespread in the first century establishment, particularly among "Herodians" themselves, and constitutes the basis of the "fornication" charge at Qumran, a matter that also exercises James; cf. CD, iv. 15-v, 11 specifically delineating these matters in connection with "the standing up of Zadok", and Acts 15:20ff., 21:25, and 1 Co 5-7 on James' directives to overseas communities, in particular, "fornication".

[100]Both Laperrousaz, p. 31 and Cross, p. 122, realize that the evidence of coin data invariably points to an origin about the time of John Hyrcanus. We should add the corollary that its establishment was not inimical either to the aims of John or his children (it is in relationship to the demise of the first two of these that John derives his reputation as a "prophet" in *Ant.* 13.10.7; cf. the parallel "prophesying" of "Judas the Essene").

[101]This idea is so widespread in Second Temple literature, including the Scrolls and the Gospels, that one hardly knows where to begin; cf. Wis 1:1, 1:15, 2:16ff., 3:1, 4:7ff.; Enoch, Chs. 38-62, where the doctrine is developed in its entirety and "the Righteous" and "Elect" are identified, 92:3, 93:10, 94:1, repeating the 'love Righteousness' admonition of

the Sadducees of the Herodian period did not embrace the doctrine is difficult to understand, except that Herod after destroying the Maccabean family (those who doubt the popularity of the Maccabean family should note the reaction of the crowd to Herod's murder of Miriamne and her brother, Aristobulus, and its support of Antigonus in opposition to the advice of Pollio and Sameas) brought in a priest from Egypt, Simon ben Boethus, whose daughter he married as he had the Nlaccabean heiress previously.[102] For this, the "new" priesthood he instituted should more properly be called "the Boethusian", as it is often referred to in Talmudic literature.[103]

Wis 102:4-5, the basis of a similar Koranic expectation, and 103:1-4; Test. L. 5:7 and 13:5; A. Bar 14.12 and 15.7f.; A. Ezra 7.17-8, 35ff., 99 (encouraging martyrdom), 102 (adding the additional notion of intercession on the Day of Judgment), 8:33, 55, and 9:13ff.; cf. CD, i-iv; 1QS, xi; 1QH, vi, 29 and xi, 10-14. That the doctrine, announced first in 2 Macc 12:38-45, was meant (as implied in A. Ezra 7.99) to encourage martyrdom is dear from the 'Seven Brothers' episode, the martyrdom of Eleazar, and the words, "If he had in view the splendid recompense reserved for those who make a pious end, the thought was holy and devout"; cf. 6:28, 7, and 14:46. What better inducement could there be for sacrifice in Holy War? This is the thrust which is picked up in Islam. Paul, while stressing the doctrine, rather emphasized its Greek mystery parallels, *i.e.*, "entering the tomb with Jesus", in the interests of appealing to a wider (less "Zealot"-minded) clientele.

[102]For the crowd's reaction to Aristobulus/Jonathan, see *War* 1.22.2: "When he put on the sacred vestments ... the whole crowd burst into tears." Josephus is even more effusive in *Ant.* 15.3.3f.: "... a warm zeal and affection towards him appeared among the people, and the memory of the actions of his grandfather Aristobulus evidently came to their minds ... The city ... was in very great grief, every family looking on this calamity (his death) ... as if one of themselves had died". That Miriamne's memory was also cherished by the progenitors of Christianity is clear from the proliferation of Marys in the Gospels. In Antigonus' case, it is because of his equally wide *popularity* that Herod bribes Mark Anthony to *behead* him—the first recording of such in Palestine. Like stonings, these beheadings are worth cataloguing; they are all applied to *popular* leaders for the same reason. Josephus (*Ant.* 15.1.2) quotes Strabo of Cappadocia to explain: "Anthony supposed he could in no other way bend the minds of the Jews to receive Herod ... for by no torments could they be forced to call him king (cf. Josephus on "the Essenes" in *War* 2.8.10: "though they were tortured and tormented ... they could not be forced to flatter their tormentors"), so he thought that this dishonorable death would diminish the value they had for Antigonus' memory'—this directly following his description of how Herod paid such honor to "Pollio the Pharisee and Sameas" *n.b.* the progression: Antigonus. John the Baptist, and *Theudas* (a contemporary of the N.T's "James the son of Zebedee"; see also below, pp. 67f.).

[103]*Ant.* 15.9.3. This Simon ben Boethus is a citizen of Jerusalem but comes from an Alexandrian priestly family "of great note". In typical fashion Josephus seems to confuse him with Simon Kanthera "the son of Boethus" under Agrippa I more than fifty years later (*Ant.* 19.6.2), while at the same time comparing the Boethusian family with that of Simeon the *Zaddik* in the number of sons doing the high priestly service and in the process providing the interesting aside that the latter had three sons. J. Jeremias, *Jerusalem in the Time of Jesus,* Fortress Press, 1975, pp. 194f.

Herod also "leased" out the priesthood to a variety of other pro-Pharisaic claimants as the procurators did after him. This importation of foreign claimants is a typical totalitarian or colonial device for controlling local party unrest, and probably is very much evidenced by the pliant Hillel's arrival from Babylon at about this time coincident with Herod's destruction of the previous "classically" Sadducean Sanhedrin that had opposed him.[104] Anyone who doubts the "flexibility" (even

and 229f., gives credence to this suggestion. For Talmudic references, see Tos Sukk iii.1.193; Tos Yoma i.8.81; Yal R. Sh. L15.210; b. Sukk 43b; b. Shabb 108a; b. Men 65a; b. Yoma 18a, etc. The ancestral tomb of the Boethusian family is probably to be found in the Kedron Valley beneath the "Pinnacle of the Temple" at the foot of the Mt. of Olives. There the memorial plaque identifies a family of the course of "Hezir" and contains the names of some four of the Boethusians who actually served as high priests. Curiously enough, this is the tomb which is usually ascribed in Christian tradition to St. James, i.e., James the Just. Allegro romantically queries, though perhaps not without substance, whether this could be the "tomb of Zadok" mentioned in the Copper Scroll, line 52, *The Treasure of the Copper Scroll*, New York, pp. 103-112.

The Christian tradition linking this tomb with James is extremely old and one should be chary of lightly setting such folk memories aside. If indeed James was buried here—and most Church fathers make pointed mention of the location of James' burial place just outside the Temple wall—the question of an actual link with the Boethusian family is not completely far-fetched. Indeed, this is precisely what is implied in the Rabbinic nickname for Jesus, "ben Panthera", i.e., probably a slight distortion of "ben Kanthera". If there is any truth to this suggestion, then the takeover of the Boethusian tomb (whose in-laws the sons of Kanthera were) by Christian tradition becomes more comprehensible; cf. Epiphanius' constant assertion that "Joseph the brother of Cleophas" (sic) was called "Panther"; *Haeres* 78.7. Since Joseph Cabi (and possibly Joseph Kami, as well, if the two can be separated), the high priest preceding the execution of James, was one of the sons of Simon ben Kanthera, i.e., a Boethusian called "Joseph"; we have the additional possibility of material relating to the burial of James being assimilated into the "Joseph of Arimathaea" legend in Jesus burial traditions; cf. *Ant.* 20.8.11f. In fact, it is Agrippa II's removal of Joseph Cabi that sets the stage for the judicial murder of James. One should remember, that Agrippa II, like his father before him in the confrontation with "Simon", was already smarting from his defeat by the Temple "Zealots" in the Temple wall incident. It was shortly after these events that Josephus undertook his mission to Rome to see Poppea on behalf of certain "Essene"-type priests who, because of their "Piety towards God", ate only "figs and nuts"; *Vita* 3.

[104]Josephus records in *Ant.* 15.2.4 that he had first set up "an obscure priest from Babylon", named Ananel, though the Talmud, M. Para, iii, 5 considers him to have been an Egyptian; see Jeremias, pp. 66-69. Herod seems to have elevated four principal families, the Boethusians, that of Ananus, Phiabi, and Kamith; see Jeremias, pp. 193ff. Their popularity may be judged by the well-known lament preserved in Tos Men xiii.21.533 and b. Pes 57a: "Woe to me for the Boethusians; woe'unto me for their curses. Woe to me from the sons of Ananus; woe unto me for their slanders. Woe to me for the sons of Kantheras; woe unto me because of their reed pens. Woe to me for the house of Ishmael ben Phiabi: woe unto me because of their fists. For they are the high priests, their sons are treasurers, their sons-in-law are Temple Captains, and their servants smite the people with sticks." Josephus' opinion of these families, even

the "exploitability") of the Pharisaic *Nasi* and Davidic descendant from Babylon should examine his celebrated innovation of the *Prozbul* and compare the attitude it evinces towards the rich or upper middle classes (by this time all with Roman, Herodian, and "Pharisaic" connections) with the attitude in the Letter of James (a true *Zaddik* in the parlance of this period) towards these same classes.[105] That this

though severely compromised by his relationship with them, is as follows: "And Herod, who was made king by the Romans, did no longer appoint high priests out of the descendants of the Hasmonaean's house, but appointed to that office men of no note and barely priests, with the single exception of Aristobulus" (Miriamne's brother); *Ant.* 20.10. The key to this process. of course, was possession of the high priestly garments, which Herod took over immediately on coming to power and which the Roman governors inherited in succession to him. The machinations concerning this are well described in *Ant.* 20.10. Of course. what had in effect been instituted from 37 BCE onwards was the Greek custom of selling the priesthood to principal families of wealth on a temporary basis: *cf. Ant.* 15.11.4.

[105]"Isn't it always the Rich who are against you? Isn't it always their doing when you are dragged before the court (cf. Paul's "only criminals have anything to fear from magistrates")? Aren't they the ones who insult the honorable name to which you have been dedicated? ... Now an answer to the Rich. Start crying, weep for the miseries that are coming to you. It was a burning fire that you stored up as treasure for the last days (cf. John's attack on "the Pharisees and Sadducees" in Mt 3:7ff. and CD, vi-viii—also referring to "vipers"—on "riches" and "fornication"). Laborers mowed your fields and you cheated them ... realize that the cries of the reapers have reached the ears of the Lord of Hosts. In the time of slaughter you went on eating to your heart's content. It was you who condemned the Righteous One and killed him; he offered you no resistance. Now be patient brothers until the Lord's coming" (Ja 2:6f. and 5:1ff.). Echoing this passage's climax in the allusion to "Messianic" rain, James actually proclaims "the Lord's coming" or the Messianic return in the Temple on Passover in terms of "coming on the clouds of Heaven" (*E. H.* 2.23.13; cf. CD, vi, 10), thereby linking, as already suggested above, the Dan 7:13 "clouds" allusion with this "rain" imagery as per "the Star Prophecy" and "rising up of the Poor" material in 1QM, xi, 5-xii, 7. Though early Church accounts have conflated two separate attacks on James (one in the forties by "the enemy" Paul in the Temple with one in the sixties by the High Priest Ananus; cf. the two adversaries of "the Righteous Teacher"/ "Priest" whose presence dominate the Habakkuk and Ps 37 *peshers*—"the Pourer out of Lies"/"Scoffer" with "a tongue full of insults" within the community and "the Wicked Priest" outside it); such a proclamation in these circumstances was incendiary. James' attitude, of course, cannot be separated from that of the priestly "Zealots", who having regard for "the Messianic Prophecy" start the final uprising by stopping sacrifice "on behalf of foreigners". We have already signaled their concern "to persuade the Poor to join the insurrection" by burning all the debtors' records (a demand initially voiced *70 years* before in the 4 BCE events) and their election of the lowly stone-cutter Phannias as high priest; see above, p. 30 and *War* 2.1.2 and 2.18.6.

We have also already noted above, p. 6, the common theme of "admission of Gentiles" whether into Church or Temple. Hostility towards "Herodians" is but a variation of this theme, as is the Pharisaic/Pauline involvement with them. *N.b.* among the founders

Boethusian priesthood abjured the doctrine of resurrection of the dead probably is attributable to its overseas and earlier roots. These are discernible in both Ecclesiasticus (despite its preservation in all the localities so far described) and the Samaritan "Zadokites" going back to a time before its introduction by the Maccabean/Hassidaean practitioners of "Holy War".[106] The Pharisees true also to their "Hassidaean" roots embraced the new doctrine.

As we have discussed, Simon probably broke with this original Hassidaean movement. 2 Macc is anxious to counter the charge that

of the Church at Antioch, where "the disciples were first called 'Christians' " (Acts 13:1f.), were "Herodians"; and Paul's "Gentile Mission", overriding the demands of the Law and addressed equally "to Jews and Gentiles alike" (cf. Ro 3:22, 1 Co 12:13, etc.), is perfectly in line with the exigencies of Herodian family policy. Timothy, for instance, "whose mother was a Jewess" and who carried Roman citizenship, is typical of this "Herodian" mix, as is Paul himself; cf. Ro 16:11, where Paul hints at his own Herodian ties, and Acts 10:15ff., 11:20ff., 16:1ff., and Ga 2:4ff. See, also, that "Saulus", a "kinsman of Agrippa who used violence with the people", in *Ant.* 20.9.4, who is the go-between between "the Men of Power" (the Herodians), "the high priests". and "the principal Pharisees" and Agrippa II in *War* 2.17.3f. and 2.20.1. The constant linking of Saulus in these episodes with the Idumaean convert "Costobarus" and a namesake of Herodias' husband "Antipas" probably reflects his genealogy back through Bernice Ito Agrippa I's maternal grandfather Costobarus (*n. b.* the repetition of the telltale themes of *marriage with nieces* and blatant *fornication* here). "Saulus" is also closely associated in these descriptions with "Philip b. Jacimus", the intimate of Agrippa II *in Caesarea* and commander of his guard. For Josephus' pointed reference to "Philip's" *two daughters,* see *War* 4.1.10 and *Vita* 36.

Among other Herodians at Antioch are very likely "Niger" and "Silas", namesakes of whom desert from Agrippa II's army and are grouped along with *Queen Helen's son* and "John the Essene" as some of *the bravest commanders of the Revolt;* cf. *War* 2.19.2. 2.20.4, 3.2.1ff., and 4.6.1. These Herodian *Men-of-War* present valuable parallels to "the Men of War"/"Men of Violence" allusions at Qumran themselves linked to the mysterious "Idumaeans" of Josephus' allusion (responsible for the death of Ananus and participants, as well, to a certain extent in the War). Brandon, *op. cit.,* pp. 124ff., has already discussed in detail James' relationship with the Messianic/Zealot lower priesthood, and Josephus describes how the, high priests "ventured to send their slaves to the threshing floors to take the tithes ... so that the *Poor* among the priests died for want" (italics mine); *Ant.* 20.8.8—developed with greater emphasis on "the Riches" of the high priests in the context of *the stoning of James* and the notice about Saulus' violent rioting in Jerusalem in *Ant.* 20.9.1ff.; cf. the parallel sequencing in Acts 6-8, including problems in collection distribution and the reference to the conversion of "a large number of priests"—also our further remarks below, p. 66.

[106]Ecclesiasticus is still following the Stoic/Cynic/Epicurean philosophy of Ecclesiastes, though in "the Zadokite Statement" at the end, there is a distinct shift: cf. 10:11f, and 15:20 with 49:12, 50:24f., 51:1-22 (extant as a separate psalm at Qumran), and 51:30. The doctrine was probably abjured as much at Leontopolis (the probable venue of "the Boethusians") as at Samaria both because of its revolutionary tendencies and the innate conservatism of each.

Judas was not a Hassidaean and pointedly ignores the subsequent priesthoods of Jonathan and Simon (with their "Pharisaic" tendencies) as being unworthy of note. Associated with this pietistic Sadduceeism that believed in resurrection of the dead and was more zealous for the Law even than the Pharisees (*n.b.* Jesus' stance in this regard in the Sermon on the Mount: "Unless your *Righteousness exceed* that of the Scribes and Pharisees..."[107]) was the production of apocalyptic literature which in turn gave rise to both the "Messianic" and "Zealot" movements of the first century CE.[108] This pietistic Sadducee movement did not follow Pharisee *Halachah,* nor its style of expressing this in "traditions" culled from the practice and teachings of "the fathers" (much like Sunni Islam). Rather, in the style of the Temple Scroll and much other similar literature at Qumran, including Jubilees, it expressed itself in pseudepigraphic pronouncements of an exoteric kind whether *halachic* or apocalyptic.

---

[107]Mt 5:20. For other statements in Matthew on "Righteousness" and "Righteous Man", see 3:15 on the commands of "all Righteousness" (cf. Justin's use of the "all Righteousness" phraseology in *Dial.* 93 in summing up the *Hesed* and *Zedek* commandments and the reference to the "all Righteousness" commandment in CD, vi, 20 above); 5:6, "blessed are those thirsting for Righteousness"; 5:10, "those persecuted for Righteousness"; 10:41, "He that receives a Righteous Man in the name of a Righteous Man shall receive a Righteous Man's reward (cf. Wisdom); 21:32, "John came in *the Way of Righteousness*" (italics mine—terminology current at Qumran and reminiscent of statements in Josephus and al-Kirkisani); 25:37, Jesus' followers as "the Righteous"; 25:46, "the Righteous (shall go) into eternal life"; 13:43, "then shall the Righteous shine forth as the sun in the Kingdom of their Father" (*n.b.* the sonship motif); and 13:49f., "so shall it be at the end of the world; the angels shall come forward and sever the Wicked from among the Righteous". The reference to Abel as "a Righteous One" in 23:35 comes in the context of comparing his fate with that of Zechariah ben Barachiah, obviously another *Zaddik* (*n.b.* the traditional ascription of the Kedron Valley tomb next to James' to his name). See also Paul in an unguarded moment in 2 Co 11:5ff. amid "light" imagery referring to the *Hebrew* "Archapostles" as "dishonest workmen disguised as *Servants of Righteousness*" (*italics* mine). For other Qumranisms, see "sons of Light" and light imagery in 1 Thess 5:4ff., Eph 5:9, Col 1:12, and 2 Co 6:11ff. (including reference to "*Beliar*"); the reference to Noah as "preacher of Righteousness" in 2 Pe 2:5; "the service of Righteousness" in Ro 6:17ff.; "weapons of Righteousness" in 2 Co 6:7. adoptionist sonship in Ga 3:24ff.. Ro 8:14. Eph 1:5, 1 Jn 3:1ff.; and 3 Jn 11's "he that does what is right is a son of God"; the "heart" imagery in Ro 10:10; the "fragrance and offering" metaphor of 1QS, viii.9 and ix, 4, in 2 Co 2:14ff. (including reference to Qumran-stvie *Dacat*), Eph 5:2f., and Phil 4:18, and the allusion to "Perfection of Holiness" in 2 Co 7: 1 . For a combination of "Perfection", "sons of Light", and "Truth" motifs, see Ja 1:17f.; for "Truth" motifs in Paul, see 2 Thess 2:11, Eph 5:9, Ro 2:20. 9: 1 , etc.

[108]See below, pp. 93ff., for our contention that the "Zealot" movement was not new in 4 BCE to 7 CE, only what we are delineating as its "Messianic variation.

This is the literature found at Qumran. It is massive as it is widely disseminated through the Oriental world via Jewish Christianity, other "Zealot"/"Messianic" movements (in fact, all groups outside the orbit of Phariseeism and official Judaism), and apocryphal literature. As the disappointment of its Messianic hopes became permanent, its covert tendencies increased, and its ideas grew ever more esoteric. These, in turn, were transmitted to various groups outside the orbit of official Judaism and Christianity in the East, e.g., Elkasaites, Ebionites, Manichaeans, Gnosticizing groups like Sabaeans, Mandaeans, and at Nag Hammadi, and even Syriac Christians, Nestorians and Jacobites (*n.b.* the telltale nomenclature). Many of its fundamental ideas, while distorted by subsequent overlays, were preserved in *Kabbalah:* and traces of them are clearly discernible in Karaite and Islamic literature, most notably in its Shiᶜite variation. Indeed, the latter is the Islamic counterpart to the Zadokite movement as we have described it (as Sunnism is to Rabbinism).[109] Judas, following in the footsteps of Simeon and Onias before him, is the quintessential "*Zaddik*" or Righteous Teacher-type, who in Rechabite/"Essene"-style "withdrew into the wilderness" (usage current at Qumran) and lived "like a wild animal" (presumably in caves), eating "nothing but wild plants to avoid contracting defilement". He is the type of the warrior high priest presented in the War Scroll.[110] This is not to say that any Qumran identifications should be attached to

---

[109]For the pre-existent Zaddik-notion at Qumran and its connections with the *Logos-* doctrine of John's Gospel and the incarnate Imam-doctrine of Shiᶜism. as well as its relation to Proverbs' "The-Zaddik-the-foundation-of-the-world", the Gospel of Thomas. and the *Zohar,* see above p. 23. The constant reiteration of the notion of *Daᶜat (Knowledge),* itself tied up with the justification processes of Is 53:11, in all Qumran sectarian texts easily translates itself into what goes by the name of *Gnosis* in other milieus. For the comparison of "the coming of the Son of Man" to "the days of Noah" amid imagery regarding the passing away of "Heaven and Earth", see Mt 24:34ff., already cited above. For Noah as the "Perfection" ideal or "the Perfect Man" who was, therefore, like *Shem* and *Melchizedek* "born circumcised", see *ARN* 2.5 and *Zohar* 59b. For the relationship of "the Poor" and "the Pious" to Phineas and David, see the section on "Balak and Balam" preceding "Phineas" in *the Zohar* 193a-197a. Not surprisingly, this section knows "Yunus and Yamburus" (cf. the material in CD, vi-ix, including Ms. B). Though the *Zohar* may be the thirteenth century forgery it is often considered to be, the whole "Phineas" section, which includes reference to the Book of Enoch and "the supernal Priest" (as well as "the future Jerusalem", "the celestial Temple", "the supernal Israel" and "the Primal Adam"), should be studied very carefully.

[110]For the role of this warrior high priest and the priests generally (in their white "battle dress" in the War Scroll which De Vaux refers to as "apocalyptic"), see 1QM, vii, 10-ix, 9. The war in question is not metaphorical, though it is idealized. Here, the same preconceptions which inhibit coming to grips with the metaphor in "Zadok" now dictate an allegorical approach to the war. Attention to literary genre and care over literary devices would help.

Judas, either in the *peshers,* which are late, or the Zadokite Document, whose date for the moment must remain indeterminate).[111]

That these priests do not follow the Pharisaic policy of compromise with foreigners is plain: "they are not to defile the oil of their priestly anointment with the blood of vain heathen". One battle priest is separate and goes up and down the line encouraging the ranks. This is undoubtedly the same priest who "is chosen by the vote of his brothers" to officiate on "the Day of Vengeance" (xv, 4-7). This "Vengeance" is to be accomplished by "the Saints of his People", as well as "the Poor" and "those downtrodden in the dust", with the help of the heavenly warrior angels. Cf. the employment of these angels for just such a purpose in 2 Macc and the general discussion of the angel Michael in Milik's "Milkī-sedq et Milkī-reša[c] ..." , pp. 106ff. and 141ff., van der Woude, pp. 304ff., and Fitzmyer's "Further Light on Melchizedek", *JBL,* 86, 1967, pp. 32ff.

Compare, too, this priest's "election" with both "Phannius" in the last phases of the uprising and that of Judas Maccabee discussed above. We have, also, noted the parallel theme of the election of James as successor and head of "the Jerusalem Church" in early Church literature and its counterpart the election of "the twelfth apostle" in the Book of Acts. Though some accounts speak of a direct appointment of James by Jesus (Gos Th 12 and Rec 1.43), others generally agree that an "election" of some kind occurred (*E.H.* 2.1.2-4, 2.23.4, 7.19.1 and Jerome, *loc. cit.;* cf. *E.H.* 4.22.3f. on Simeon bar Cleophas' succession after James' martyrdom, because "being a cousin of the Lord, *i.e., the son of his uncle,* it was *the universal demand* that he should be *the second"*—italics mine. If Acts had at this point discussed *the succession to Jesus* and not *the succession to Judas Iscariot,* then. of course, the puzzling appearance of James in 12:17 would need no further explanation).

Whether this avenging battle priest is identical with the "High Priest" who rises to recite the War Prayer from the Rule and also all their Hymns, and generally "arranges all of the order of formation according to what is written in the War Scroll" (xv, 4f.) is difficult to determine from the context. Cf. Eisler, pp. 262ff., interpreting Lk 3:14ff. in terms of "John's field sermon"; also Jesus' arranging of those who follow him "into the wilderness" in military formation (Mk 6:40). We have already called attention to such battle order, "warrior angels", and "the horsemen who come like clouds" over the earth to rain "Judgment on all that grows on it", which is mentioned in the context of reference to the "Messiah" who "justifies the true Judgment of God in the midst of mankind"—"the Mighty One" whose foot will be on the necks of his enemies, who will smite the nations, and whose "sword will devour the flesh of the sinners filling the land with glory"; 1QM, xi-xii. For Enoch 90:9ff., Judas was considered "a Great Horn" and probably even "a Great Sword" (cf. 2 Macc 16:16), an appellation which is probably echoed in Ps 148:14: "He lifted up the horn for his people; the praise for all his Pious Ones" (*i.e., Hassidim*) quoted in the Hebrew version of Ecclesiasticus (51:15). *N.b.* Philo, *Quod Omnis* 12.75 and 13.91 knows very well that the name "Essenes" derives from the word "Piety", *i.e.,* "Hassidaeans".

[111]Cf. below, pp. 81ff. The dating of the Zadokite Document is complex because of one exemplar considered "early" on palaeographic grounds. Many point to the doctrinal shift that appears to occur between it and the Community Rule on the issue of "the Messiah of (from) Aaron and Israel" in the former (viii, 24; xii, 23f.; and xiv, 18) and "the Messiahs of Aaron and Israel" in the latter (ix, 11) as a dating aid. R. H. Charles, *APOT,* ii, Oxford, 1913, pp. 795ff., argued that the former related to an Israelite father and an Aaronite mother. G. Margoliouth, "The Sadducean Christians of Damascus", *The Expositor,* vols. 37-38, 1911-12, pp. 499-517 and 213-235, made the initial identification of this with Jesus. Curiously enough, and unremarked in subsequent commentary, the plural usage in 1QS may imply a series of "Messiahs of Aaron

Judas, too, is probably observing the extreme purity regulations associated with 'life-long Naziritism', reflected in both Philo's and Josephus' description of "Essene" practices—including sexual continency. As such, he is probably the model for John the Baptist, Jesus, and James (one could, also add Simeon bar Cleophas, Jesus' probable second brother, called "a Rechabite priest"—read "Essene"—in Eusebius). Where sexual continency is at issue, though argument from silence is not a proof, in each of the above-mentioned cases it offers a strong presumption. Where James is concerned, all early Church accounts make a point of calling him "a Nazirite from his mother's womb" (parodied to a certain extent by Paul's rival claims in Ga 1:15f.; cf. the stress on Nazirite oath procedures in Paul's confrontations with James). In Judas' case, any children would have changed the political picture for succeeding generations considerably, however none are mentioned.[112] Contrariwise, Judas' uncle Simon took care to dispose

---

and Israel", as much as it does *two separate* messiahs. When it is appreciated that the usages ^c*amod/*^c*omdim,* used in the exegesis of Ez 44:15, carry something of the sense of "be resurrected" with thtm (cf. "the Standing One" in Rec 2.7ff. and the phrase, "stand up", used with just such a connotation in *Zohar* 63a on "Noah") and that the *Messianic* "Shoot out of Israel and Aaron", after whom the teacher comes, of CD.i.7 has already died; then it will be realized that these usages, accompanying all references to "the Messiah of Aaron and Israel" and also coupled with references to "Zadok" and "the *Yoreh ha-Zedek*" in CD, v, 4f. and vi, 10f., are eschatological. *N.b.* that if, as per the suggestion of Milik, *op. cit.,* pp. 151f., pp. xv-xvi are inserted before p. ix; then, in fact, ms. A ends on p. xiv with fragments from 1QS, vii, 4ff. Since CD quite properly ends with the pious hope for the return (or "resurrection") of the Messiah of Aaron and Israel who "*will pardon their sins*" (xiv, 18—italics mine); the conclusion is that, whoever the Cairo redactors of the Zadokite Document might have been, they also knew materials from the Community Rule and they, anyhow, did not see the two documents as particularly separate.

[112]We have discussed why the note in 2 Macc 14:25 about Judas' "marrying and settling down" should not be taken too seriously; above, p. 4. For the Essenes, see *War* 2.8.2ff. The notice, after the one indicating their contempt "for Riches", about their view of oil as a defilement precisely accords with James' habits. Together with the notice about "bathing in cold water", it points the way towards the harmonization of James' and *Banus'* bathing habits noted above, p. 2. James only abjured *Roman*-style *hot* baths, where *oil was used, not ritual immersion:* (cf. how the Essenes in *War* 2.8.3 prefer "being unwashed"). The original model for such an extension of the rules of priestly purity, ultimately going back, as Ecclesiasticus well knew, to "the zeal of Phineas", was Elijah, but the ideology underwent a formidable development in the person of Judas.

Of course 1QM. vii, 1-7 provides the best explanation for Judas' family condition. as it also does John's, Jesus', James' and the people of Qumran generally: "No toddling child or woman is to enter their camps *from the moment they leave Jerusalem* to go to war until they return ... They shall all be freely enlisted (*i.e.* "volunteers") for war, *perfect in spirit and body* and prepared for and ready for 'the Day of Vengeance'. Moreover, any man who is not cleansed from a bodily discharge on the day of battle is not to go down with them: for *holy*

of the children of his brother Jonathan, who were killed under very questionable circumstances, thereby insuring the succession of his own heirs.[113]

At this point one is probably witnessing the break between the Hassidaeans supporting Judas and holding his memory sacred and the faction increasingly influencing the actions of Simon (by this time already beginning to be called "Pharisees") in his machinations to gain endorsement for his priesthood from the several Syrian Kings and pretenders. Judas is simply from the original and more pietistic wing of the Zadokite movement and proves it by the manner of his life (imitated to a certain extent by John the Baptist and Jesus) and in the "Zealot" manner of his death—*i.e.*, he makes "a pious end" as do John, Jesus, and James among numerous others after him. So "zealous for the Law", in fact, is John that he continually harangues the Herodian monarch, Herod Antipas, over a minor point of law (incomprehensible to anyone but the specialist) until the latter is forced to put him to death.[114] It is

---

angels march with their hosts" (italics mine). The echo of this in the use of the word "camp" in the Zadokite Document and "volunteer" in the Community Rule and 1 Macc 2:43 (used to describe "Hassidaeans") should not be overlooked. We have noted Eisler's presentation, above, p. 41, of John the Baptist as opposition High Priest of the last times calling his followers to the pursuit of Holy War or, as CD, xii, 22-3 puts it, "This is the rule for camp-settlements and those who live accordingly at the end of the Era of Wickedness until the rising ("standing up") of the Messiah of Aaron and Israel"; cf. CD, xiv, 18 above. So strict was the sect in the pursuit of ritual cleanliness that some have taken the Temple Scroll as implying copulation was forbidden in Jerusalem; cf., Uriah the Hittite's query to David when advised to enjoy his wife: "Are not the ark and the men of Israel and Judah lodged in tents?" (2 Sam 11:11).

[113] 1 Macc 13:17f.

[114] Cf. Mt 14:1-12 and Mk 6:14-29 with *Ant.* 18.5.2 and Slavonic Josephus. *N.b.* Slavonic Josephus knows the precise point, violation of the levirite law of marriage. Where al-Kirkisani's "Zadok" and Qumran are concerned, there is the additional issue of *marriage with a niece*, Herodias being Agrippa I's sister (as *Ant.* 18.5.1 is quick to point out while missing the connection with John's execution; cf. the tangle regarding Costobarus, Antipas, and Philip in relation to "Saulus' " genealogy above, p. 45). This, in turn, links this confrontation to the general hostility to Agrippa I's family and the recurrent theme of "fornication" at Qumran and in the Jerusalem Church. *Antiquities* knows that John was put to death as a public agitator (*i.e.*, the "Jewish" punishment of beheading), because Herod "feared the great influence John had over the people might lead to some rebellion": *n.b.* its prototype and only recorded precedent in the Second Temple period, the beheading of the last Maccabean priest/king Antigonus; above, pp. 42f. The N.T. portrait of Salome dancing at Herod's birthday party is childish fantasy; though in this instance consistent with its religio-political aims of acquitting the Romans or their appointees of complicity in the deaths of or malice towards "Christian" leaders.

interesting to note that aside from the relatively late example of Rabbi Akiba, who in any event is ridiculed by his Rabbinic contemporaries, this is not the Pharisaic way;[115] nor is it Josephus' or Paul's, both of whom identify themselves as Pharisees and prefer the obsequious self-abasement before Romans and their Palestinian appointees of Rabbi Yohanan ben Zacchai to martyrdom.[116] Nor was it the way of Simon Maccabee. It was, however, the way of the extreme wing of the Zealot party conserving Ecclesiasticus and Qumran material on Masada, *i.e.*, "making a pious end" in the manner recommended by 2 Macc. That they expected the imminent return of their bodies is implicit in the *purposeful* burial of the "standing-up-of-the-bones" passage from Ezekiel under the synagogue floor.[117] These "saints", who Josephus maligns, derogatorily referring to them as "*Sicarii*" (terminology which has stuck), were Hassidaean *Zaddikim par excellence.*[118]

Indeed, according to its polemic, non Jews never have any difficulty in recognizing Jesus' messiahship, where his closest disciples like Peter sink into the Sea of Galilee for *lack of faith* or deny him three times on his death-night. Caesarean legionnaires, whom Josephus identifies as the most brutal in Palestine (*Ant.* 19.9.2), are complimented for their "devoutness" and "generosity to Jewish causes" (Acts 10:1ff. means, of course, Agrippa I; see below p. 67. The provenance of this episode becomes clear from the reference to "Italica", the birthplace of both Trajan and Hadrian). That Herod, Pilate's wife, Pilate, and a centurion recognize John or Jesus as *Zaddikim* in Mk 6:20, Mt 27:19, 24, and Lk 23:47 is 'consistent with the working method we are describing. One particularly appropriate example of this kind, in the context of "receiving and keeping table fellowship with sinners" (read "Gentiles"; cf. Paul in Ga 2:15), is the statement that "there is more joy in Heaven over the repentance of one Sinner than ninety-nine Righteous Ones" ("in the wilderness"); Lk 15:1ff. Often the motifs of "prostitutes" (read "fornicators"), "publicans" (*i.e.* people who do not abstain from table fellowship), and "tax-collectors" are added for emphasis. The "wine-bibbing" assertion (Mt 11:19: Lk 7:34) serves to distinguish Jesus from James (and other "Rechabite"/ Nazirite-types). who, of course, shunned wine.

[115]P. Ta'an 68d. Yohanan b. Torta's retort to R. Akiba over the messiahship of Bar Kochba, "Grass will grow on your grave before the Messiah comes", is proverbial: cf. b. Sanh 97b. Akiba in the "Zealot"/"Messianic" tradition is operating within the framework of "the Star" prophecy and not subjecting it to mockery as Yohanan b. Zacchai, Josephus, and others did.

[116]For Paul's claims to be a Pharisee, see Acts 23:5, 26:5 and Phil 3:5: for Josephus'. *Vita* 2.

[117]See Y. Yadin, *Masada,* London, 1966. pp. 187ff. In his usual manner, Yadin is impressed with finding Chapter 37 buried underneath the synagogue floor, but at first sees no *special* significance in it. Finding also the last two chapters of Deuteronomy dealing with the *blessing and death of Moses,* he finally decides he has come upon a *genizah!* In like manner, finding a fragment of the Songs of the Sabbath Sacrifice from Qumran Cave IV at Masada, he sees this as proving only that "some Essenes" joined the refugees and took refuge on Masada with "the Zealots"; pp. 173-4 and "The Excavation of Masada', *IEJ,* 15, 1965, pp. 81-2, 105-8.

The behavior of Aristobulus' supporters on the Temple Mount during the siege of Jerusalem and its fall in 63 BCE is illustrative of the mentality of the whole Zadokite/Zealot movement. As we have noted, Hyrcanus, following the policy of Alexandra and her presumed relative Simeon ben Shetach (a Pharisee "father" is certainly the Pharisaic priestly contender and cleaves to a Pharisaic political line as we have expounded it. Who are Aristobulus' supporters? They are a combination of nationalists and Sadducees. That they are also "the popular party" is indisputable belying the oft-quoted testimony of Josephus in this regard, just as the popularity of his son Antigonus puts the lie to any claim that Pollio's (Hillel's?) typically Pharisaic recommendation to open the gates to Herod could in any way be considered "popular". But what kind of "Sadducees"? [119] Their behavior refutes, as nothing else can, the idea that they could have anything in common with

[118]The name, "*Sicarii*", was derived from the Roman *sicae*—a type of curved dagger they carried under their cloaks: *Ant.* 20.8.10; *War* 2.13.3 and 2.17.6. *N.b.* , however, that Pilate was the first to use such enlightened methods of crowd control in Palestine. Driver, pp. 183ff., thinks he has found a reference to this weapon in 1QM, v, 12: and Brandon, pp. 39f. and 203f., thinks he sees it in the episode of Lk 22:38, when the disciples appear to be armed with two concealed weapons in the *Sicarii* manner. Note, also, the reference in *Apost. Const.* 8.25 (v. mss.), identifying "Thaddaeus" with "Judas the Zealot" and the further variation of the latter name in "Judas Iscariot". Jn 6:71 speaks of "Judas the son of Simon Iscariot" (read "brother or) and Lk 6:16 speaks of "Judas the son of James" (read "brother of"). "Simon Iscariot" is, of course, equivalent to "Simon the Zealot" (cf. also "Cananaean") and his place in Gospel apostle lists approximates that of Jesus' *second brother* "Simeon bar Cleophas", e.g., "James the son of Alphaeus (read Cleophas), Simon which was called the Zealot, and Judas the son of James" (Acts 21:20, of course, testifies to the overwhelming number of "Zealots for the Law" the movement actually consisted of). For a complete discussion of these confusing matters, see below, pp. 67f.

[119]The most extensive testimony of the popularity of the Pharisees (as opposed to "the Sadducees") comes in relation to John Hyrcanus, *Ant.* 13.10.5-6; however this cannot represent the state of affairs two hundred years later at the time of the uprising against Rome. In addition, it contradicts what the *Antiquities* says about the followers of the *fourth* philosophy. Discussing the *innovations* of Judas and Saddouk and the calamities their movement brought upon the nation, Josephus states, *Ant.* 18.1.1: "So great did the alteration and change from the customs of our fathers tend to bring all to destruction who thus banded together, for Judas and Saddouk who introduced a fourth philosophic sect among us and had a great many followers therein, filled our state with tumults at that time and laid the foundations of future miseries by their system of philosophy which we were before unacquainted with ... and that the rather, because the infection which spread thence among our younger men, who were zealous for it brought our nation to destruction." The word "infection" was, also, used to describe the itinerant messengers the Emperor Claudius cautioned the Jews against receiving in his famous letter to the Alexandrians; cf. H. Idris Bell, ferns *and Christians in Egypt,* London, 1934, pp. 25ff. Paul, too, is described in similar terms in Acts 17:7, a passage that makes it clear that the problem concerned "Messianic" messengers like the apostles: "These are the people who have been turning the whole world upside down ... They have broken every one of Caesar's edicts by claiming

the corrupt Sadducee priesthood introduced under Herod and the procurators. They are of a different stripe altogether, of which the "Herodian" Sadducees are barely a caricature. They are zealous priests doing service for God on the Temple Mount even as the carnage going on around them ultimately overwhelms them eliciting even the grudging admiration of their Roman conquerors. They are what we have identified as "Zadokites", *i.e.*, the zealous lower priesthood, and very probably received part of their training at Qumran, as Josephus himself relates he received part of his training in a later period living three years among rock caves with a person he chooses to identify in his usual cryptic style only as *"Banus"* (*i.e.*, *"Bather"*).[120] Josephus is canny, always careful to cover his footsteps and not reveal the overt role of the priesthood—the lower at first (which would have inevitably implicated

there is another emperor Jesus"; and in 24:16: "The plain truth is that we find this man a perfect pest; he stirs up trouble among the Jews the world over and is a ringleader of the Nazarene sect"; cf, 16:20-22. For a recital of these "calamities" with inverted polemical intent, see all versions of "the Little Apocalypse": Mt 24:1ff.; Mk 13:1ff.; and Lk 21:5ff.

But the Pharisees are not even the popular party in Alexander Jannaeus' time, since in spite of his cruelties the people rally to him; nor in Aristobulus' or Antigonus' time; cf. *Ant.* 15.3.3. Josephus in *Ant.* 17.2.4 puts their number at "6000", the same figure he gave in 13.14.2 for the number of Alexander's supporters; cf. 2 Macc 8:2 putting Judas' supporters at "6000" and Jeremias' comments, p. 252. We must remember, too, that Josephus himself was working, usually in an uncritical manner, from sources—in this instance, probably Nicolaus of Damascus, a Herodian collaborator. Since we are dealing with a 200-year period, a party having a degree of popularity at one point might not even be the same one hundred years later—and Josephus doesn't take the trouble to inform us to which period his sources relate. From 4 BCE to 70 CE, and perhaps beyond, it is clearly the "Zealot" Party which is the popular one, as "nationalist" parties predictably are—not the Pharisees with their restrictive religious practices and contempt for the *'Am ha-Ares* (the "Zealot"/"Zadokite"/"Christian" sectaries?).

[120]*Vita* 2; cf. Ga 1:17-18, where Paul reports he went off immediately after his vision "to Arabia", possibly for "three years." Luke's knowledge of Paul's activities is probably defective; he states in Acts 9:22 for the same period that "Saul's power steadily increased and he was able to throw the Jewish *settlement at Damascus* into complete confusion" (italics mine; cf. below, p. 55).

For the resemblance of *Banus* to James see above, p. 2. That the bathing practices of both are highlighted by tradition is important in itself. We have already seen how Josephus' description of the Essenes points the way towards resolving discrepancies between how both are pictured. Both Eusebius and Jerome, *loc. cit.*, also link the question of James' bathing habits with anointing with oil, and *Haeres.* 78.14 confirms: "he never bathed in the (*public*) *baths*"; but, of course, if he went on the Temple Mount in the manner described, he underwent *ritual purification.* Josephus' charming transposition into Greek of "clothing that grew on trees" links up with the stress in all early Church sources of James' wearing only "linen", as it does the right won by the lower priesthood to wear linen shortly before him), but eventually the higher—in the so-called "Zealot" movement (and/or "the Messianic") in the revolution against Rome.[121]

Qumran can almost be considered a training center for the Jerusalem priesthood. As the "monastery" is probably very near the site where

the uprising (directly following the account of James' death, the high priests robbing "the poor", and "Saulus" 'violent behavior; *Ant.* 20.9.6).

[121]The *Autobiography* itself seems to have been written to combat damaging charges made in this regard against Josephus by Justus of Tiberius and others; *Vita* 65 and 74. For instance, it completely contradicts the claims made by Josephus in the *War* inflating his role in Galilee, though the business activities he describes in the *Vita* are no less shameful. He, also, as we have seen above, p. 27, completely contradicts himself on his personal assessment of his erstwhile associate, the high priest Ananus. Now and then he lets down his guard enough to reveal "the Star" prophecy as the moving force behind the uprising against Rome and the cessation of sacrifices in the Temple on behalf of all foreigners including the Emperor by the lower priesthood as the signal for its commencement. We have noted his mission to Rome to obtain the release of "certain priests" of his acquaintance above, p. 2. He describes them in *Vita* 3 as "very excellent persons" ("Righteous"?), who "on a small and trifling charge were put into bonds and sent to Rome to plead their cause before Caesar" (n.*b.* the Pauline-like appeal to Caesar, but the non-Pauline-like note of vegetarianism—Paul's pretensions in 1 Co 8:13f. notwithstanding—and abstention from "table fellowship"). He also reports the ritual shipwreck: cf. Acts 27:1ff. In Rome he makes the acquaintance of Nero's wife Poppea, whom in *Ant.* 20.8.11 he describes as "a religious woman", as well as the contacts he later employs so effectively to save himself and launch himself into Imperial favor. Poppea's obvious interest in "Jewish" causes (or "Christian"—in Claudian Rome there was no distinction: n.*b.* she takes the side of the Temple wall "zealots" against Agrippa II) parallels Helen of Adiabene's; *Ant.* 20:2. The "Christian" character of the latter's conversion emerges from the person of the Pauline-like "Ananias" and Helen's own intractable opposition to circumcision. In contrast, her more "zealot"-minded son, who later distinguishes himself in the uprising against Rome (cf. above, p. 45), embraces it. The "Christian" character of her conversion is echoed in Syriac sources, the antiquity of which is given additional support in *E.H.* 1.13.1ff. and 2.1.6ff. That the matter of famine-relief, whether involving Helen or Paul, the *Agbarus* legend, and the issue of Thaddaeus/Theudas/Judas Thomas lie behind the distortion of these same in Acts 5:34, 11:19, etc., is hinted at in *E.H.* 2.12.1ff.'s remarks on Helen; cf. below, pp. 67f.

Who the priestly beneficiaries of Josephus' rescue mission were and what the "trifling" charge was are interesting questions. In addition to Helcias and Ishmael retained at the pleasure of Poppea in the wake of the Temple wall affair, Josephus reports that the high priest Ananias and Ananus "the Temple Captain" were earlier sent to Rome in bonds "to give an account of what they had done to Caesar"; *Ant.* 20.6.2. This latter controversy apparently, also, involved both Jewish and Samaritan "innovators" persuading "the multitude to revolt from the Romans" and a crucifixion at Lydda (also reflected in Jewish "Messianic" tradition). It would appear, as well, to be the occasion of the consolidation of relations between Agrippa II and Ananus. It may be protested that Josephus was too young at this point for such a mission, which is true; however his youth may have been just the reason for sending him to Poppea in the first place, as Roman sources make no secret of her apparent preference for young men; cf. Tacitus, *Annales* 13.44ff. She evidently found him quite pleasing as he returned, as he himself attests, a success bearing "many presents" from

Judas Maccabee and his nine "*Zaddikim*" hid in "caves" (accepting the testimony of 2 Macc), one cannot resist the admittedly speculative suggestion that it might have been "founded" by John Hyrcanus to commemorate his return to the "Sadducee" Party of his uncle, much as his father had embellished the family's ancestral tombs at Modein before him. It is not sectarian until it is rendered sectarian after the assumption of power by Herod in alliance with the Roman-inclined Pharisees. Josephus and priests like him (John the Baptist for instance) probably went out to it for a two or three-year novitiate period as young men, where they were indoctrinated with "Zadokite" ideas.[122] As coin distribution testifies, it flourishes under the Maccabees; it is not inimical to them, though it is somewhat opposed to Phariseeism and any Pharisaic tendencies among them. It only begins to decline with the coming of the Romans under Pompey and the assumption of power by Herod the Great.

The Nahum *pesher,* already referred to, though condemning crucifixion (as any good "Messianic" text would in this period) is not otherwise antagonistic to Alexander Jannaeus, but rather to the presumable Pharisees he crucifies. The sectaries at Qumran knew their history as well as

her. Josephus tells us he was 26 at the time, which places the episode in 63-64, the year after the execution of James. Nero, who married Poppea in 62, proceeded to kick her to death not long before the uprising. However these things may be, we might be dealing with more "Essene"-like priests, as Josephus' account implies. Given the fairly positive attitude evinced in Josephus' writing towards both *Banu.s* and James, the possibility cannot be ruled out of a connection between these priests and events centering about the death of the latter described above.

[122]See 1QS, vi, 13-23. Cf. *Vita* 2 and *War* 2.8.7, where Josephus shows extensive knowledge of "Essene" customs; also Cross, p. 86, n. 61. It would have been impossible for anyone going "into the wilderness" in this region to have remained unaware of, or for that matter, unaffected by a settlement the size of Qumran.

Acts 9:3ff., after delineating Paul's commission to arrest "those of the Way" at "the synagogues in Damascus" and his vision on "the road to Damascus", speaks of how he "threw the Jewish settlement at Damascus into total confusion". Ga 1:17ff., following Paul's claims to being "specially chosen from his mother's womb", knows no Damascus-road vision. Rather it recounts how he went *directly* to "Arabia" (which is usually taken to refer to the area around Petra) and spent "three years" there and later in Damascus. CD, vi, 5; vii, 21, 35's references to "the land of Damascus" and "the New Covenant" associated with it (from which the followers of "the Lying" Scoffer who "departed from the Way" by abandoning the Law, and "the Men of War" who deserted to them, are to be excluded) are well known. Of particular interest, is the exegesis in vii, 18ff. identifying "the Star" as "the Interpreter of the Law who came to Damascus". We have already noted above, p. 4, the relationship of Paul's Damascus-road encounter to the Emmaus- road encounter associated with members of Jesus' family. Ga 1:15f., in parodying James' Nazirite claims, also makes a claim for "the Son in" Paul. Seen in this light, the possible parody of both

anyone else, in any event as well as Josephus, who may even have received some of his training with them, and this is just the point. The example of Alexander Jannaeus is cited for polemical purposes only, to condemn those who are guilty of having invited the Romans into the country in the first place (*i.e.*, the Pharisees, as they had previously the Seleucids under Demetrius and probably at the time of Judas Maccabee) and to condemn the effects of this presence, *i.e.* the crucifixion of the Just, which the Romans indulged in so promiscuously. At this point it is helpful to observe that the Zadokite Document actually prescribes death as the punishment for those "whose sworn testimony has condemned another to be executed according to the laws of the Gentiles".[123] It is also striking to see that the sectaries do not hesitate to call by name foreign opponents whose regimes are now regarded as past history, *i.e.*, "Demetrius King of the Greeks." It is another thing with regard to the present when their peculiar and by now familiar code comes into play. As anyone familiar with the technique of literary criticism will immediately grasp, the thrust of this commentary actually relates to the first century CE, "the period when the Seekers after Smooth Things hold sway", as do most of the other *pesharim* at Qumran, its examples being provided by way of historical confirmation of the points it wishes to make.[124] "The *Kittim*" in the Nahum *pesher* (as in Dan 11:30), regardless of how the terminology might be used in any other literary work, specifically denotes "the Romans"; since these are portrayed, not only as being

---

the Emmaus-road encounter and Qumran "Star" exegesis implicit in Acts' Damascus-road episode should not be discounted.

[123]CD, ix, 1-2; Garter's translation of sworn as "a private vow" and Vermes' vows another to destruction" make the extremely important thrust (clear from its placement at the head of what one should designate the civil law section) incomprehensible.

[124]Since the *pesharim* are found in single copies only, there is general agreement on palaeographic grounds on their fairly "late" character. The subject of the Nahum *pesher* is "the Seekers after Smooth Things", the period in which they hold sway (*i.e.*, according to our interpretation, the Herodian period), its effects, and the coming dispersal of "their community" (*n.b.* the stress on "leading Many astray"—the inversion of our interpretation of Is 53:11 "lying" and "the lying tongue"—cf. Ja 3:1ff.; and the grouping of "those who ____lying and evil during the last days" with "the Seekers after Smooth Things"). Driver, p. 94, attributes the suggestion that "the Seekers after *Halakot*" *is* a parody of that favorite Pharisaic legal activity "seeking *Halachot*" (equivalent in its thrust to the play on *Zaddik* and Zadok we have identified) to Brownlee. But there is, also, its wider, more generic, sense, applying to all those who sought accommodation with the Romans, *i.e.*, Pharisees, Herodians, Pauline Christians, "the Congregation of Traitors", and "the Men of War".

distinct from the Greeks under Demetrius, but as having succeeded them.[125]

There is no doubt as to how and why the monastery was destroyed after the events depicted in the Nahum *pesher*. It was destroyed in the struggle between Aristobulus/Antigonus and Hyrcanus/Herod, very probably by Herod himself. As governor of Galilee he hunted down insurgent leaders like Hezekiah, who had the support of the "Sadducee"-dominated Sanhedrin. When he was able, he then turned on this Sanhedrin killing all its members, except for the two Pharisees, Pollio and Sameas, the latter having already recognized Herod's "leadership potential" after the Hezekiah affair.[126] On his

---

[125] The same conclusion is unavoidable in relation to 1QpHab's use of the expression; cf. Driver's detailed discussion, pp. 197-216, which for command of difficult materials and its scope is unrivaled. Where the Habakkuk *pesher* is concerned, this is also true because of the presence in it of at least three exegetical interpretations identifiably current in 70 CE, *viz.,* the material on "the delay of the *Parousia*" (vii, 10ff, applied only to ⁽Osei-Torah —"Doers of the Law"), the "Jamesian" exegesis of Hab 2:4 (viii, 1ff., applied only to "Doers of the Law in the House of Judah", *i.e., only Jews walking in the Way of Torah*), and the use of "Lebanon" imagery (xii, 2ff., which *ARN* 4.5 definitively ties to the fall of the Temple in 70 CE) amid eschatological allusion again to "the Simple of Judah doing *Torah*", "the Wicked Priest robbing the Poor", and "the Day of Judgement". We have also provided the provenance for the alliance of "the Lying Scoffer", "the Men of War", and "the Congregation of Traitors" (cf. CD, i, 14ff. and viii. 38) with "the Seekers after Smooth Things". Our explanation of the generic use of expressions like "Seekers after Smooth Things", in this instance, applying to those who sought accommodation with the Romans, and our identification of "the Violent Ones" as Herodian "Men of War" (including Josephus' "Idumaeans"), who first support the uprising and later desert it (cf. *War* 6.8.2), goes a long way towards clarifying many of these seemingly complex relationships.

[126] A more obsequious speech is hard to imagine. The identification of Pollio and Sameas awaits final clarification. G. F. Moore, *Judaism,* i, 1927, Cambridge, p. 313 and n. 89a, puts the case for an identification with Abtalion. There is little disagreement that Sameas is Shammai (though some would prefer Shemaiah, if the two can in fact really be distinguished). I would submit that Josephus thinks he is talking about Hillel and Shammai, as his whole presentation implies they are *well-known*. In any event, the Talmud notes proudly that both Shemaiah and Abtalion were descendants of "Sennacherib" (*i.e.,* foreign converts or is the allusion metaphoric?); b. Sanh 96b and Gittin 57b. Cf. above, p. 13, for Josephus' confusion of Pollio and Sameas with each other, as well as his additional confusions of Pharisees and Essenes generally. Most scholars will agree that Hillel was patriarch at some point during Herod's reign, *i.e.,* c. 30 BCE; J. Neusner, *First Century Judaism in Crisis,* Abingdon, 1975. gives a *terminus ad gum* of about 20 CE, pp. 49-55, but rightly refers to these years as "obscure". Since there seem to be two sets of events referred to in Josephus, one dealing with the Sanhedrin that attempted to put Herod on trial say between 55 and 50 BCE; the other with his destruction of the followers of Antigonus after 37 BCE; a way out of the impasse is to assume *both* presentations contain some truth and that Josephus was referring to both sets of pairs, the earlier around 60-55 BCE and the later around 35-30 BCE

way towards his final assault on Jerusalem, he even stoped to brutally and mercilessly dispose of the "Galileans" of "Sepphoris" who had fled to "caves" with all their families.[127] In effect, this is the end of the first stage of our Zadokite movement. Its pious priests have been slaughtered on the Temple Mount by the Romans and their Pharisaic collaborators. Others fall victim to Herod's destruction of the Sanhedrin and though the struggle is protracted, their fate is sealed with Herod's final assumption of power around 37 BCE In the course of these events, the monastery is burned (giving way to the construction of Herod's pleasure palace nearby) and remains more or less uninhabited until the death of Herod when his sons were too weak to prevent its rehabilitation.[128] De Vaux and

---

[127]*Ant.* 14.15.4f. Josephus labors over this episode in loving detail. It includes the "Zealot" suicide of the old man, his wife, and "seven sons" while Herod begs them to desist, which we have already treated, including its parody in Mk 12:20ff., Lk 20:29ff., and Mt 22:25ff. The episode, together with the martyrdom of Eleazar, has received its literary transformation in 2 and 4 Macc; and the Eleazar material has received an additional transformation via *Gematria* (including the allusion to cave-dwelling) in the "*Taxo*" material in As Mos 9:1ff. In 4 Macc "Eleazar" has seven sons. The cave-like terrain is an important element in all traditions. The emphasis on "cave-dwelling" and martyrdom carries right through Bar Kochba times via Akiba's student Simeon bar Yohai, who functions as the keystone of *Zohar* tradition; cf. b. Shabb 33b. For Josephus the locale is south or east of Galilee, because Herod chases the refugees "as far as the River Jordan". That "the bandits" described are not bandits is made clear in the old man's impugning Herod's right to kingship (compare this with how the mass of Jews responded to Herod in connection with Antigonus' beheading; below, n. 130, *i.e.*, "by no torments could they be forced to call him king", which further translates into the more general, "nor could any such fear make them call any man Lord", so characteristic of Josephus' descriptions of the followers of Judas and Saddouk). As with Josephus' descriptions of the martyrdom of "the Essenes" coinciding with the end of period 2A of Qumran habitation, one can suppose that in this description one has a facsimile of the fall of Qumran ending period 1B.

[128]It was De Vaux who first proposed as a reason for the abandonment of the monastery the earthquake of 31 BCE; cf. "Fouilles de Khirbet Qumran," 1956, pp. 544f. and *Archaeology ...,* pp. 21-3, where he softens his stand under criticism. However, the conflagration that seems to have occurred on the site is not evidence of an earthquake; nor is an abandonment, as something else must explain the 30-40 year interruption in habitation. Laperrousaz in *Numen*, vii, 1960, pp. 26-76 would push the abandonment back to 67-63 BCE Milik, pp. 52-5, on the basis of some five Herodian coins questions the evidence for an abandonment at all, though he admits the evidence does suggest "a very violent conflagration ... the traces of an *intentional* destruction of Qumran" (italics mine) and a "substantial interval before rebuilding". He also questions his colleague De Vaux's archaeology on the question of the broken dishes which the latter associates with the earthquake, but which he rather equates with the destruction in 68 CE C. Roth, *The Dead Sea Scrolls: A New Historical Approach*, Oxford, 1958, pp. 22ff., took the interruption in habitation as demonstrating that a new group, "the Zealots", reinhabited the settlement after 4 BCE (and Milik agrees that the "Essenes" do appear to have changed character between 4 BCE and 70 CE)

Albright notwithstanding, the earthquake of 31 BCE was hardly of any consequence except as a possible archaeological aid in helping to date the period of the monastery's destruction and relative dormancy.[129]

Herod, as would any clever monarch interested in undermining his opposition, brings in leaders from outside, most notably Hillel from Babylonia and Simon ben Boethus from Egypt. The establishment which he sponsors and creates (partially by confiscating the wealth of the previous one, which had been destroyed much as its central figures, the members of the Maccabean family themselves, had been destroyed) is the Pharisaic/Sadducean one so familiar to us from portraits in the New Testament and Josephus.[130] With the appearance of "the Zealot movement" in 4 BCE, coincident with Herod's own demise, habitation

---

Roth's theory, while original, was poorly argued and hastily put together and he displays little or no knowledge of Jewish Christianity or the link of the "Zealot" movement to what we have been galling "Messianism". As it is, to him belongs the distinction of having pointed out the "Zealot" nature of the sect, even if he could not explain or account for it, and even if his identifications sometimes bordered on the absurd. Where identifications were concerned, Driver publishing seven years later, while giving a more solid presentation, was little better.

[129]Steckoll, pp. 33-4, argues that no earthquake damage ever occurred at Qumran. The kind of acidity that can be generated by these disputes can be measured by De Vaux's caustic aside on his critic: "The authorities of the Israel occupation have forbidden this Sherlock Holmes of archaeology to continue his researches at Qumran"; *op. cit.,* p. 48. This kind of comment compares with his final reaction to Driver. Having admitted on p. 133 that "The solution to the question (of the Essene character of the sect) is to be sought from the study of texts. and not from that of archaeology"; De Vaux then goes on to state on p. 138 "that in all probability none of the manuscripts deposited in the caves is later than this date" (*i.e.,* 68 CE) Finally, he puts it more unequivocally in his review in *NTS* of Driver's book: "No manuscript of the caves can be later than June CE 68", ending with the intemperate: "Driver's theory is not 'as nearly valid as possible', as he says on the last page of his book, it is impossible"; p. 104. Albright, who uncritically accepted De Vaux's archaeological explanation that Stratum 1B came "to an end with an earthquake and a fire, which can scarcely be separated from one another", dismissed Driver's work with the following words: "... the latest proposal for a different solution by a scholar of standing ... has failed completely. This failure is not caused by any lack of philological learning or of combinatory talent, but to an obvious skepticism with regard to the methodology of archaeologist, numismatists, and palaeographer. Of course he had the bad luck to run into head-on collision with one of the most brilliant scholars of our day—Roland De Vaux ..."; "Qumran and the Essenes", pp. 14f.

[130]The change is vividly evinced by Josephus' laconic comment after Pompey's troops stormed the Temple Mount: "So the Jews were now freed from kingly rule, and were governed by an aristocracy"; *Ant.* 14.5.4. The character of this aristocracy we have dealt with variously above, but it is perhaps best summed up in the following description: "Since Herod had now the government of all Judaea put into his hands, he promoted such of the private men in the city as had been of his party, but never left off punishing and revenging himself every day on those that had chosen the party of his enemies. But Pollio the Pharisee, and Sameas a disciple

at Qumran revives as the coin distribution verifies. But this movement is more than just "Zealot", as Josephus so pejoratively designates it to conceal its other tendencies after the election of "Phannius" and the killing of Ananus and the other high priests in the last stages of the uprising. The terminology is also picked up and applied in the New Testament, not to others, but to the followers of Jesus (cf. James in Acts 21:20 on the members of "the Jerusalem Church"). A better description of it would be "Messianic", as it is marked by a series of "Messianic" pretenders from the Shepherd Athronges and Judas in 4 BCE to "the Egyptian", for whom Paul is mistaken, Menachem ben Judas (who, if he was really the latter's son, must have been about 70 years old), and Bar Kochba.[131] It is "Messianic" because it believes the time of the end or "the last days" is at hand and that the Messiah of Israel (or of Aaron and Israel) must arise.

It is often overlooked how "Messianic" the Qumran sect actually was, and one is not just speaking here about the well-known notion of "the two Messiahs", which has been widely commented on presumably because it is so perplexing. Rather, what is even more striking is the reference to and quotation of the all-important "Star" prophecy from Numbers 24:17 upwards of three times in the extant corpus: once in the Zadokite Document, once in the War Scroll, and at least once in what

---

of Pollio, were honored by him above all the rest, because when Jerusalem was besieged, they had advised the citizens to receive Herod, for which advice they were well requited"; *Ant.* 15.1.1.

[131]The phrase, "I have called my son out of Egypt", of Mt 2:15 is perhaps better applied to this Egyptian, who also attempts the pro *forma* wilderness exodus. As it is, Matthew goes to considerable effort to get the infant Jesus to Egypt (an effort Luke and the other Gospel writers spare themselves). The movement, as we have stressed, is on the whole priestly, and is combined in interesting ways with the Messianic with the demise of the Maccabean priest/kings. A good place to begin the study of the early Christian concept of Jesus as High Priest is Justin Martyr's *Dial.*, where it is laboriously laid out, as are the associated doctrines of Jesus as *Zaddik;* Enoch, Noah, Abel, etc. as the *Zaddikim* of old; adoptionist baptism and adoptionist sonship; "Stone" and "*Ma^c oz*" imagery; and the Righteousness ideology (cf. Heb 7:26ff. on Jesus as the *perfect* "son" and supernal high priest and *n.b.* Justin never mentions Paul). Justin also provides the basis for Epiphanius' Essenes as "Jessaeans", *i.e.*, "Jesus" being a Greek pseudonym for Jesus' real name, "Oshea" or Hosea; cf. also *E.H.* 1.2.2ff. The priests, therefore, that should be coupled to this list of Israelite messiahs in this period are "*Saddouk*", *i.e.*, "a Pharisee teacher" (read "Essene") *who was* "the *Zaddik*" , John, Jesus, and James, just as the priest "Eleazar" is added to Bar Kochba's coins in a later embodiment of this duality. Only in Jesus' case, and James' (and Simeon bar Cleophas' following him) are we justified in thinking that a change in the ideology has occurred as per the Zadokite Document (and perhaps the series of "Messiahs of Aaron and Israel" in the Rule), becoming permanent in Christianity as it has been passed down to us.

should be called the sect's "Messianic" proof texts.[132] Josephus in a rare moment of candor describes this prophecy as the moving force behind the whole of the uprising against Rome, the signal for the actual start of which was the halting of sacrifice in the Temple by the zealous lower priests.[133] Examples and reflections of the currency of this prophecy in the first century CE and beyond can be seen in Josephus' and R. Yohanan ben Zacchai's derisive misuse of it (*i.e.*, in improperly applying

[132]CD, vii, 18-21; 1 QM, xi, 5ff.: and 4QTest 9-13, the last coming amid a flurry of references to "*ish-Hassideicha*" , "*yinzor*" , and "Yeshua" (not the Biblical "Yehoshua" one would expect), as well as "the True Prophet" citation of Deut 18:18f. so dear to the Ebionites.

[133]The young priests officiating at the Temple were persuaded "to receive no gift or sacrifice for any foreigner"; cf. the charge of "fornication, riches, and profanation of the Temple" leveled in CD, iv, 12ff. against the Jerusalem establishment. The first is explained, not only in the Document itself, but also in al-Kirkisani's account of the similarity of Jesus' and Zadok's teaching on the subject. Like Mt 19:4 and Mk 10:6, CD, iv, 21f. cites Gn 1:27, "male and female he created them", to explain the ban on taking more than one wife (cf. al-Kirkisani, pp. 363ff., who insists "Jesus forbade divorce just as the Sadducees did")—something we know, of course, that Herod *did* to excess. Yet Josephus' report of cordial relations between Herod and "the Essenes" is still taken seriously in many quarters.

The second aspect to this "fornication" charge, "marriage with a niece", we have treated in detail. It also relates to "Herodians". The charge of "Riches" is self-explanatory; n.b. James' antagonism to Riches is developed out of his citation of Justin's "all Righteousness" commandment (which James calls "the supreme law of scripture"), "love your neighbor as yourself"; cf. Ja 2:8f. (including his "keep the whole Law" directive) with CD, vi, 21f. The "large group of *priests* who made their submission" in Acts 6:7 (cf. Rec 1.44) certainly must be included among those "thousands" of believing Jewish "Zealots for the Law" James mentions to Paul in 21:20f. To quote Josephus: "And this was the true beginning of our war with the Romans ... And when many of the high priests and principal men (*i.e.*, the Herodian Pharisaic/Sadducean establishment) besought them not to omit the sacrifice which it was customary for them to offer for their *princes,* they would not be prevailed upon, relying much upon their *multitude*"; *War* 2.17.2f. When this is combined with the words: "But their chief inducement to go to war was an ambiguous oracle found in their sacred writings announcing that at that time a man from their county would become ruler of the world" (6.6.4), and this, in turn, with the quotation from *Ant.* 18.1.1: "the *infection* which spread thence (*i.e.*, the alteration in customs preached by Judas and Saddouk) among our younger men *who were zealous for* it, brought our nation to destruction" (italics mine); then I believe the true historical current of this period becomes clear. (This charge is only slightly deformed in the "Herodian" reformulation of it in the N.T.).

[134]For the most detailed account of this see *ARN* 4.3; also b. Gittin 56a-b. Cf. Mid. R. Lam i.5.31 and b. Yoma 39b. That the interpretation of Is 10:34, the classical allusion to the fall of the Temple in 70 CE in Talmudic literature, is to be found at Qumran (4QpIs^a) interpreted in exactly the same way points as nothing else can to the chronological *sitz-im-leben* of this interpretation; and, indeed, much of this exegetical literature generally, especially in the absence of any indication whatsoever that this passage was ever applied in like manner to any earlier fall of the Temple. This is also the case with Zech 11:1 (the fragmentary commentary of a related passage, Zech 11:11, also being found at Qumran spliced into 4QpIs^c). The "keys",

it to the Roman conqueror Vespasian,[134] behavior akin to the supposed jeering by the Jewish crowd at the Messiah Jesus crowned by thorns) and further afield in the peculiar twists given it in the infancy narrative of "the Star over Bethlehem" in Matthew's gospel and in the name accorded Bar Kosiba by tradition, i.e., "Son of the Star."[135] One might add to this, the obvious game being played by Tiberius Alexander, Philo's nephew (presumably with Josephus' connivance), to convince Vespasian that he was indeed the Messiah called from Palestine to rule the world.[136] This is to say nothing of Agrippa I's seeming possession by it and his posturing in silver garments in all probability to evoke "the Star's" glitter before a theater crowd in Caesarea prior to his suspiciously sudden death.[137]

---

which are flung into the heavens at the fall of the Temple in the Talmudic exegesis of Zech 11:1, and which for the Talmud are in the possession of the Sadducees or priests, are also a favorite topic in the New Testament. Cf. War 6.6.3 in the same section as that containing Josephus' explanation of the "Star" prophecy, the portents of the fall of the Temple, including heavenly hosts riding to and fro, the Temple gate opening of its own accord, and an overwhelming voice emanating from the Inner Sanctum crying, "Let us remove hence". The reference to "Lebanon", in some sense most often related to the priesthood and the fall of the Temple, is discussed in detail in Driver, pp. 458-9, G. Vermes. "The Symbolic Interpretation of Lebanon in the Targums", JTS. 1958, pp. 1-12, and Neusner, p. 75: cf. also Tacitus, Historiae 5.13.

[135]This star is also alluded to in Josephus' portents for the fall of the Temple, but here it resembles a sword that stood over the city for a whole year. That the early Christian community knew that "the star over Bethlehem" was connected to "the Star that would arise from Jacob" of Num 24:17 and linked to the person of Jesus is clear from Justin Martyr's discussion of the subject in Dial. 106; cf. the Zohar's flawed, but striking presentation of these matters (212b introducing "Phineas"). That "the Star" prophecy was 'in the air' in Justin's time is clear from the application of it to Bar Kochba in j. Taʿan 68a-b, which does not deny that R. Akiba interpreted Num 24:17 to refer to Bar Kochba, but rather turns it around (probably retrospectively) to read: "A liar has gone forth from Israel"; n.b. the typical juxtaposition of "liar" and "Star".

[136]The suggestion was first made by W. Weber in Josephus and Vespasian, Stuttgart, 1921, p. 43; Eisler, pp. 554-61, discusses the charade in detail. The point, of course, of all these messianic exercises, so lovingly detailed in the Gospels, is Isaiah's prophecy that "the lame would walk" and "the blind would see"; Is 35:5ff. and 42:16ff. Cf. Dio Cassius, Roman History, lxvi, 8 and lxxiv. 3.

[137]Ant. 19.8.1. Cf. his triumphal arrival in Alexandria after being appointed king by his friend Claudius (after similarly predicting Caligula's demise), where he is hailed by the Jewish crowds as "Lord" ("Maran"): Ant. 18.6.11 and Philo, In Flacc. 5ff. (2.521M). It is interesting that in the Slavonic Josephus' rendering of the world ruler quotation that most moved the Jews to revolt against Rome, it is stated in place of the usual pro forma ascription of it to Vespasian: "Some took this as a reference to Herod, others to the crucified miracle-worker Jesus, and others to Vespasian". For Herod's messianic claims, see the discussion of the priests around the time of the earthquake (i.e., 31 BCE) in the Slavonic

A succession of priestly *Zaddiks* had already been in existence for a century or two before the official appearance of this so-called "Zealot" movement: to identify at least four so indicated in the extant literature: Simeon, Onias, Judas, and Honi.[138] This sequence is, strictly speaking,

Josephus, secs. 373-79, though in fact the allusion is most likely to Agrippa I's pretensions. The whole question of Herodian family ambitions in the East, and the family's interest in "Messianic" matters tied to these, must be thoroughly investigated. Agrippa I is first suspected of plotting against Rome in *Ant.* 19.7.2ff., which appears to lead directly to his death. Antiochus of Commagene, one of his co-conspirators and co- ruler of Cilicia with Agrippa's brother, Herod of Chalcis, did ultimately revolt in 71 CE; cf. *War* 5.11.3f. and 7.7.1ff. and also the pro-Roman role of Herod's son Aristobulus here.

[138] As noted above, one should probably include John, Jesus, and James in the list. The all-important rain-making capacity adhering to the *Zaddik*-tradition seems to have been transmitted from HO7 to his daughter's son, Hanin or Hanan *ha-Nehba* (*i.e.,* Hanan the Hidden); *b. Ta*c*an* 23a-b. It was ascribed by tradition to Phineas and Elijah, and here also to *Habakkuk*. *N.b.* how the "rain-making" and the "hidden" traditions come together in the *Zohar's* description of the archetypical "rain-maker" Noah (63a and 67b). Note, too, Hanan the Hidden's outlook towards "the rabbis" (equivalent to "the Pharisees and Sadducees" of Mt 3:7), who send school children to ask him to make rain, obviously because they are afraid to approach him themselves. Not only does the "hidden" tradition attach itself to the person of Honi, Hanin's grandfather (*Ant.* 14.2.1), but it persists in clinging in Christian tradition to John (cf. Onias=Honi=Hanin=John), whose mother in Lk 1:24 "hid herself" for five months (fearing the authorities?); see *the Protoevangelum of,* 18.1, A. R. James, *Apocrypha of the New Testament,* Oxford, 1924, p. 46, where Elizabeth "hides" him in *a mountain cave* when Herod sought to destroy John (the basis of the similar tradition about Jesus?) and asks Zechariah: "Where have you *hidden* your son?" (italics mine); *n.b.* the typical note of cave-dwelling. See also al-Kirkisani's "Magharians", also associated with cave-dwelling and whom al-Kirkisani places between "Zadok and Boethus" and Jesus; pp. 326f. and 363f. The notice he gives in regard to their penalizing "guffawing" parallels 1QS, vii. 14 (the section of the Community Rule we have already identified as having been attached to the Zadokite Document in the Cairo *Genizah).* Syriac tradition actually identifies Elizabeth's father as *"Anon":* cf. Eisler, p. 244. B. Ta c an 23a-b tells of another grandson of Honi and the contemporary of James treated above, p. 32, "Abba Hilkiah". In the time of the drought, he was approached by "Rabbis", whom he treats quite gruffly, and asked to make rain. J. Ta c an 66b mentions yet another grandson of Honi (also named "Honi"), who drew circles and prayed for rain shortly before 70 CE (cf. our comments above about Honi/Onias and *"Oblias"* and the "Rip van Winkle" tradition adhering to Honi, above, pp. 27 and 32.

Jeremias, pp. 141ff., accepting Rabbinic tradition at face value, dates the first drought in Honi's time around 65 BCE Its end, despite Rabbinic hyperbole, appears to have been quite dramatic; M. Ta c an 3:8 and b. Ta c an 23a. The second was certainly around 48 CE and is referred to in the N.T. apocalypses mentioned above and in connection with Helen of Adiabene's famine-relief efforts; *Ant.* 20.5.2, itself sandwiched between references to the beheading of Theudas and the crucifixion of Judas the Galilean's two sons, James and Simon. It is also linked to a certain extent to Paul's activities; Acts 11:27ff. We have already noted James' rain-making activities in this period, and the very similar kinds of requests for aid by the Sadducees and Pharisees, reported in all traditions relating to him, anterior to "the Messianic". It undergoes a Messianic transformation once the Maccabean family, the last properly "Zadokite" line, is finally destroyed. Then a new variation of it is invoked for priestly and secular legitimacy. This is what Josephus is at pains to conceal in his Zealot-theorizing. What the movement in its new guise now anticipates is the coming of the Messianic Kingdom, *i.e.*, the Kingdom of the Messiah of Israel—"the Star".[139] The notion of a movement based on priestly "zeal" is not new, as 1 Macc corroborates in its portrayal of the Maccabean ancestor, Mattathias, and W. R. Farmer has shown in his much underrated book. The Zealot movement has effectively been in existence at least as long as the first Maccabean purveyors of it in the "Covenant of Phineas". What is new is the coupling of this movement with Israelite Messiahs in the wake of the demise of the Maccabean priest/kings. This is reflected in the literature of Qumran as we have it. It is preached by a teacher named "Saddouk" (as much a transliteration of "*Zaddik*" as "Zadok"), whom Josephus neglected to mention in his first account of this movement in *The Jewish War*, and Judas, the son of a former Messianic pretender and guerilla leader, Hezekiah.[140] Here is the first palpable manifestation (aside from Jesus ben Yehozedek and Zerubbabel long ago) of our Zadokite/Israelite

---

as those Rabbinic tradition reports regarding "Abba Hilkiah", Hanin *ha-Nehba*, and Honi. Beyond this, and the very real spiritual links between all these individuals (i.e., the *Zaddik*-tradition or "*Zaddikate*" they represent), there is also the possibility, should one choose to regard it, of a genealogical relationship as well. I should note that the tradition of "the Zealot" woes against the reigning high priesthood reproduced above, pp. 43f., is ascribed to one "*Abba Joseph b. Hanin*", identity otherwise unknown (as for that matter is Abba Hilkiah's, who appears to come from a village in Galilee). These "Abba" names in first century Rabbinic tradition should be carefully reviewed, as they often carry traditions related to our subject; cf., as well, N.T. confusion over names like "Barabbas", "Barsabbas", and "Barnabas", all linked to names with known counterparts in the "Messianic" family itself, e.g., "Justus", "Joses", "Judas", etc. (*N.b.* the curious parallel represented by the transliterations "Joses"/"Jesus".)

[139] *N.b.* the interesting seventy-year period that elapses from its first appearance in 4 BCE to the final stopping of sacrifice on behalf of non Jews in the Temple in 66 CE That Bar Kochba's followers were understood to have persecuted "Christians" (*E.H.* 4.8.4) is not particularly relevant, because one must first inquire what sort of "Christians" these were. Rabbinic Judaism also preserves a tradition that he was anti- Rabbinic; cf. his trampling of R. Eleazar of Modein and the Talmudic quotation from Zech 11:17 applied to him: "Woe to the worthless shepherd that leaves the flock ..."; j. Taʿan 68d.

[140] *Ant.* 18.1.1. Josephus' omissions from the *Jewish War*, which are corrected in Antiquities and the Vita, are extremely revealing; these include: Honi, Saddouk, John, Jesus, Banos, and James, i.e., all persons connected in some way with the inspirational or spiritual side of the Zadokite/Messianic movement (as Josephus himself was at least until his trip to Rome).

dual messiahship.[141] It is also preached by a mysterious Baptist named John, succeeded by Jesus, James, and others.[142] In the latter two we have the type of "the Messiah of Aaron and Israel" of the Zadokite Document, and there does appear to be a shift between the ideology of this document on this point and that of the Community Rule, though the Rule may imply *a series of,* not dual, Messiahs. The ideology on these points is not stationary. It is developing, as we have shown—the challenge is to be able to fit the appropriate ideology into its proper *sitz-im-leben* and not passively rely on the problematic results of archaeology and palaeography.

The settlement at Qumran is fed by waves of refugees from the corrupt Pharisaic/Sadducean regime of the procurators. The monastery is not suppressed in this period because the various governments are just not strong enough to do so; besides it employs an esoteric form of exegesis, the true meaning of which, to a certain extent, is difficult to pinpoint. For the moment, too, it seems to have adopted a quietist stance (cf. James counseling "patience" in the letter attributed to him "*until* the coming of the Lord", *i.e.,* "the second coming" or "return" of the Messiah).[143] Messianic disturbances are the rule from 4 BCE to 62 CE,

Even in the *Vita* and *Antiquities,* Josephus' references to these individuals are reticent and fragmentary. For the interesting links between Banus and James, see above, p. 53; for Saddouk and John, below, pp. 95f.

[141]Cf. the interesting imposition of Eleazar on Joshuah's activities in Joshuah 14:1, Jesus ben Yehozedek and Zerubbabel, John and Jesus, and Bar Kochba and Eleazar.

[142]R. Eisler, pp. 221-80, was the first to identify John as "Opposition" High priest, and he did this without the Scrolls to assist him, though the Zadokite Document was already known. Though he is generally held in contempt by modern scholars, his contentions about John (in contradistinction to those on the Slavonic Josephus) have never seriously been challenged. Anyone who doubts James' "revolutionary" sentiments, though they were discreetly covered in a veneer of patience, should examine his words to the assembled Passover crowd reported in early Church literature. Though these accounts conflate the two attacks on James, one by "the Enemy" Paul in the early 40's and one by Ananus in the early 60's, they are nevertheless informative. When asked to quiet the crowd's revolutionary fervor in the Temple, he rather fans the flames of Messianism; *E.H., lot cit.* That Jesus was seen as a revolutionary, at least by the Romans, needs no further elucidation. The manner of his death gives vivid confirmation as nothing else can, despite mythologizing and retrospective attempts to transform it, of what party and movement he adhered to. For a true picture of "Christian" revolutionary propaganda in this period, the reader would do well to turn to Revelation and the Sibylline Oracles. These might be the propaganda exercises of militant Shiʿism in Iran in our own time, which indeed, owes a debt, however indirect, to the Messianic/Zadokite movement.

[143]James 5:7ff.: "Now be patient, brothers, until the Lord's coming. Think of a farmer, how patiently he waits for the precious fruit of the ground until it has the autumn rains and spring rains" (cf. above "until the coming of the Messiahs of Aaron and Israel" of 1QS, xi, 11

mostly coming at Passover, and as a consequence usually involving some sort of "exodus" to the desert ("the land of Damascus") for a "New Covenant" (and revelation?) and presumable return.[144] There are innumerable crucifixions.[145] Aside from Jesus' (and the beheading of

and "until the rise" or "standing up of the Messiah of Aaron and Israel" of CD, viii, 24; xii, 23f.; xiv, 19). One cannot overemphasize, too, that the "rain" allusion, which continues in this section, and which we have already taken note of above, relates to James' proclamation of "the Son of Man coming on the clouds of Heaven" at Passover in n. 142. For the Karaites, the Messiah was even called "Anani" (*i.e.*, Anan ben David, and also "Cloudy One"), the last recorded scion of the family of David in 1 Ch 3:24. In Hebrew, the expression carries with it the additional connotation of "magician", which has interesting implications for this period.

[144]See, for instance, that of Theudas, *Ant.* 20.5.1 of 44-45 CE (mistakenly reported in Acts 5:36f. about 6-7 CE) What Luke has done, probably owing to an over-hasty reading of this passage in the *Antiquities,* to produce the anachronism, is to conserve the reference to "Judas the Galilean" and "at the time of the census", which immediately follows along with reference to Helen's famine relief effort in *Ant.* 20.5.2, but inadvertently (or otherwise) dropped the reference to Judas' two sons *"James and Simon".* Pursuant to these notices, Josephus then tells the story (*Ant.* 20.5.4) of the "Stephen a servant of Caesar" who was beaten (and perhaps killed) just outside Jerusalem by "robbers" (*i.e.*, "those who raised the tumult" in the Temple at Passover time over the legionnaire who scurrilously exposed himself to the assembled crowds). This is precisely the sequence of events followed in Acts 5-7. Schoeps in *Theologie and Geschichte des Judenchristentums,* Tübingen, 1949, pp. 441ff., has already suggested the basic interchangeability of Stephen and James, but he missed the error in "Stephen's" speech which provides the due to the speech's original provenance. Stephen claims (Acts 7:16) that *Abraham bought the ancestral tomb from the sons of Hamor in Shechem.* The whole speech is based upon Joshuah's farewell address in Josh 24; and the error arises, once again, from an over-hasty reading, this time of the notice with which the latter concludes, about *the ancestral tomb that Jacob bought and paid for* "from the sons of Hamor the father of Shechem" (Josh 24:32). This attack on "Stephen", anyhow, though presented as a stoning, textually rather takes the place of the 44 CE attack on James by Paul in Rec 1.70f.

Theudas who wants to part the Jordan and "the Egyptian" who assembles his followers on the Mt. of Olives (cf. *Ant.* 20.8.6 with Acts 21:38) function, in any event, as "Joshuah" *redivivuses.* In this context, one must review the whole question of "look-alikes" or "twins". That Paul is mistaken for this so-called "Egyptian" shows that in Roman eyes, anyhow, such agitators were indistinguishable from one another. *N.b.* the consistent pattern of ruthlessness and violent repression in the Roman response to these "imposters and deceivers". Cf. above, p. 36, and *War* 2.13.4f., where Josephus characterizes them as being "in *intent* more wicked even than the murderers" and desirous of "procuring *innovations* and change of government" (italics mine). The Felix who butchers them is the same man with whom Paul converses so felicitously in Acts ("who knows more about the Way than most people"). His alliance with the Herodian family through his illicit union with Drusilla should be carefully noted—a union connived at by a man who can be none other than *Simon Magus* (cf. Acts 8:9ff.). Simon convinces Drusilla to *divorce* her previous husband, a practice even Josephus admits "violated the laws of her forefathers"; *Ant.* 20.7.2).

[145]Where Felix was concerned, Josephus informs us that "the number of robbers whom he caused to be crucified ... were a multitude not to be enumerated"; *War* 2.13.2. In 5.11.1,

James, most probably along with his brother John, "the Sons of Thunder"), the most important are those of Jacob and Simon, the two sons of Judas the Galilean in anticipation of Passover in 48 CE at the hands of the Jewish collaborator, Tiberius Alexander (Philo's nephew), who along with Josephus was in a position to understand the significance of these individuals.[146] By the fifties the country is in chaos, fanned by

Josephus describes how the "poor people", who "made no supplications for mercy ... were first whipped, and then tormented with all sorts of tortures before they ... were crucified", concluding, "so great was their multitude that room was wanting for the crosses and crosses wanting for the bodies". See also *War* 7.6.4 for an additional example of the terrible effect of crucifixion on the people and *n.b.* the parallels with Gospel portraits.

[146] *Ant.* 20.5.1. In this episode one wonders if one does not have an echo of the "*Boanerges*", "the two Sons of Thunder"; *n.b.* the "rain" imagery again; Mk 3:17. "James" might well have been beheaded in the time of Agrippa, but neither he nor "his brother" drinks "the same cup" as Jesus (Mt 20:22 and Mk 10:38); however, James and Simon, the two sons of Judas the Galilean, did. At the beginning of this study, we noted how the problem of Jesus' brothers bedevils apostle lists and resurrection appearances. Josephus calls *Theudas* "*a magician*". Like "Judas Thomas", he is a Joshuah *redivivus* or Jesus "look-alike". His relationship with "Addai" (cf. "Thaddaeus" above, p. 51) and with Jesus' family is signaled at Nag Hammadi (cf. "Theuda the father of the Just One"—read "brother of"-2 Apoc Ja 5.44; for "Addai", 1 Apoc Ja 5.36). The additional phrase found there, "since he was a relative of his", shows the way towards sorting out all these confusing references to "brothers", "sons", and "fathers". What Acts has done is to substitute the beheading of "James *the brother of John*" for Theudas/ Thaddaeus/Judas (also Lebbaeus, "of James", and probably Judas *Thomas*) *the brother of Jesus*.

N.b. it is "the brother" theme which is the constant, and the whole fictional exercise of "John and James *the sons of Zebedee*" is part and parcel of the process of downplaying and eliminating Jesus' brothers (and successors in Palestine) from scripture. The central triad of the early Church in Palestine can now be definitively identified as "James (*the brother of Jesus*), Cephas, and John" of Ga 2:9, not the misleading "Peter, James, and John *his brother*" of Gospel portraits, and the bewildering proliferation of "Mary"s also evaporates. "Mary (*the sister* of Jesus' mother Mary) the wife of Clophas" (Jn 19:25), "the mother of James and Joses and the mother of the sons of Zebedee" of Mt 27:56 (of "James the less, Joses, and Salome" in Mk 15:40; of "James" in Lk 24:10), now simply becomes identifiable with Jesus' *mother*. This is, in any event, the implication of the Papias fragment 10 in *ANF,* which identifies *Thaddaeus as the son of Mary and Cleophas* and *the brother of James, Simon, and Joses* and, in the process, *affirms* the identification of Alphaeus and Cleophas. Even the "Mary the mother *of John Mark*", to whose house Simon goes in Acts 12:12 to leave *a* message for "James and *the brothers*" (*n.b.* the "brother" theme again), simply reduces to "Mary *the mother of James*" (*italics* mine).

We have already shown above that "Thaddaeus" in Mt 10:3/Mk 3:8 corresponds to "Judas the son of James" (read "brother") in Lu 6:16/Acts 1:13, and that two variant mss. of *Apost. Const.* 8.25 identify this same "Thaddaeus" as "Judas the Zealot who preached the truth to the Edessenes and the people of Mesopotamia when Agbarus ruled over Edessa". Once our comments about the relationship of Theudas to Judas Thomas and Addai are appreciated, we can now make almost a one-for-one correspondence between all the executions referred to in Josephus and their fictional counterparts in the N.T. Perhaps the incompetent, venal, and increasingly brutal administration of the procurators, and again as coin data attest, the monastery is in its most populous phase rising to a peak in the second year of the war against Rome.[147] Thereafter, it is downhill.

I will not at this point be drawn into the controversy over whether the monastery fell in 68 CE or thereafter, except to say that the destruction of its buildings would in no way make life untenable at the location in the conditions engendered by war. On the contrary; the site would have constituted an important forward outpost for the partisans at Masada even if its buildings had been burned, unless the Romans actually garrisoned it. This they would not necessarily have done in any serious manner as long as the partisans refrained from harassing the Jericho road before the commencement of actual operations against Masada *after the fall of the Temple* in 71/72 CE Any "token" garrison left on the spot of the kind most commentators propose could easily have been dealt with by the refugees themselves, by this time having found temporary sanctuary at Masada their ranks swelled by new recruits.

---

even more importantly, that "Agabus" who predicts the "famine" in Acts 11:28 is but a thinly disguised version of Helen's husband "Agbarus" (a title in any event). "Adiabene" now becomes Edessa (as it is anyhow in Syriac tradition), a rival center to the expansionist aims of Agrippa's brother (and Paul's probable "kinsman"; cf. Ro 16:11) Herod of Chalcis in "Asia"; cf. also Herod's son "Aristobulus" above, p. 63.

The preventive execution of James and Simon in the time of the great *drought* (both drought and census are mentioned in the same sentence; cf. "the *Boanerges*" above) gives vivid indication of the existing unrest, as does the visit that preceded it of "Simon" to Agrippa I in Caesarea with complaints similar to those of John the Baptist (above, p. 7; *n.b.* Herod of Chalcis had married Agrippa I's daughter Bernice, later mistress of Titus, and it is Agrippa's sister Herodias whose marital practices are the issue in the death of John the Baptist). Agrippa, as one would expect, handles the incident patronizingly, but diplomatically. That Simon would ultimately have been arrested by Agrippa (cf. Acts 12:1ff.) is a foregone conclusion; and that Luke, drawing also on the Agrippa II dining episode, would distort this into an episode where "Peter" learns to accept non Jews (and in doing so, unwittingly reveal that Jesus never taught *table fellowship* with Gentiles, other, wise why would Peter need a "Pauline" vision to reveal it?) is typical of the working method of these documents, as we have already expounded it.

[147]See above, p. 33.

Chapter Seven

PALAEOGRAPHIC PROBLEMS

The above reconstruction, I submit, is as good as any constructed around Essenes as such or so-called "Zealots" and unlike any of these, has the virtue of being able to give a plausible explanation to the whole expanse of "Zadokite" literature from the third century BCE to the second century CE. In addition, it does not resort to *unknown* or hypothetical individuals and/or teachers to do it. Everyone mentioned is *known*. As tempting as escapism might be, we have enough historical evidence from different sources in this period (even if some patently folkloric or mythological) to demand that scholars toe the line on making *historical* identifications.[148]

It is also in keeping with palaeographical finds, such as they are (as it is with archaeological, historical, and literary critical evidence). For instance, it very easily explains the archaizing Maccabean script so prominent among the scripts at Qumran, difficult to explain for those who see the group as being anti-Maccabean.[149] What is more, it does not resort to thinking that first century CE *peshers* of Biblical material give intimate explanations of events that occurred in the second century BCE.[150] This is as absurd as thinking that nowadays a preacher would

---

[148]Cross agrees, p. 72, n. 33: "The Qumran sect was not a small, ephemeral group. Its substantial community at Qumran persisted some two centuries or more ... Our task is to identify a major sect in Judaism. And to suppose that a major group in Judaism in this period went unnoticed in our sources is simply incredible". Having said this, he proceeds to make major identifications using unknown "Essene" teachers! De Vaux, p. 138, concurs: "This community, the life of which has been traced by archaeology over a period of two centuries and which has left behind a considerable literature is no small unknown sect"; he then proceeds to follow Cross in failing to grasp the import of his own statement.

[149]This archaizing "palaeo-Hebrew" Maccabean script, a characteristic of some Biblical manuscripts at Qumran and, for instance, writing the tetragrammaton in the Habakkuk *pesher,* was also used on the coinage, not only of the First, but also of the Second Jewish Revolt—another argument against the claim of anti-Maccabean feeling at Qumran and for the involvement of the sect at Qumran in what Brandon would call "Israel's national cause"; cf. R. S. Hanson, "Paleo-Hebrew Scripts in the Hasmonean Age", *BASOR,* 175, 1964, pp. 39 and 42, F. M. Cross, "The Oldest Manuscripts from Qumran", *SBL,* 74, 1955, pp. 147 and 159; "The Development of Jewish Scripts" in *The Bible and the Ancient Near East,* ed. G. E. Wright, 1961, p. 189, no. 4.; and S. A. Birnbaum, *The Hebrew Scripts,* Leiden, 1971, pp. 78 and 94ff.

[150]Cross, *The Ancient Library,* pp. 113-5 agrees: " ... virtually all commentaries and testimonia appear in manuscripts written in late hands ... duplication (or multiplication) of copies among the various caves is significantly absent in a single category of literature: the commentaries ... such works were rarely if ever copied, and hence are mostly original works ... the date of the script of a commentary will indicate normally its date of written composition." However having

interpret Biblical scripture in terms of the events surrounding the lives of George Washington, Napoleon, or the Duke of Wellington.[151] Indeed, this is the time span involved, since the homiletical/exegetical texts, known as *peshers,* are all from the first century CE Found only in single copies, they are not the "classical", but rather represent the "current" literature of the sect, which is why the Habakkuk Commentary found so *neatly* deposited in Cave I is so important. To think they relate to events in the Maccabean period or those covered by Daniel, except where this is expressly so stated for internal historiographical demands of the text itself, as already noted, is unrealistic.

These texts were very likely the quickly written records of weekly sabbath scripture sessions held by "the Teacher" ("Righteous" or "of

admitted these probably represent the "regular sessions of the sect" mentioned in our sources, where scripture was read and expounded, he draws the rather lame conclusion "that a corpus of traditional exegesis was put into writing only toward the end of the sect's life"; implying some oral transmission, but avoiding the question of why people would bother recording such intimate explanations of scripture (except in a fragmentary way as in the Talmud) 100-150 years after the fact, particularly when they did not judge them important enough to bother making more than single copies. As is so often the case in this research, Milik, p. 58, reproduces Cross' words almost precisely. For a description of the friendship of these three scholars, *i.e.,* Milik, Cross, and De Vaux, see Cross' description in "Scripts", p. 190, n. 9 on how he wavered back and forth between the other two on the matter of the bowl graffiti (relating to the problem of the wall and broken dishes), which Milik on palaeographic grounds dated to the second destruction and De Vaux true to his "earthquake" thesis claimed for period 1B. He was finally (against his original judgment) won over by De Vaux. That this would throw the chronology off perhaps one hundred years is passed off with the comment: "the possibility should be borne in mind that the minimal dates in our absolute chronology on shifts of certain letter forms ... *may be slightly low*" (*italics* mine). The matter of De Values obvious personal charm is commented on by R. North, *op. cit.,* pp. 433f.: "fortunately the trump- card (of direct exploration of the caves) eventually fell into the hands of De Vaux, whose loyal cooperation with the authorities has smoothed procedural details ever since." At the same time in n. 31, he notes "De Vaux's shrewdness in inducing the apprehensive Bedouin to cooperate with the Jordan government ..." I am quoting these remarks at length throughout this work because I have the distinct impression that most scholars leave the details of these matters to a few specialists. They assume rather in the manner Tolstoy reports of most Christians, when coming into his new pacifist stage he inquired of the disquieting tendency of Christians to serve in armies and Christian prelates to bless them, that "these matters were decided long ago". Upon further inquiry, Tolstoy never could find out by whom.

[151] See, for instance, Vermes' reconstructions, pp. 61ff., who remarks on p. 55 with the kind of discernment one has come to expect in Qumran research: "*No properly Judeo-Christian characteristic emerges from the scrolls, and unless we are much mistaken, the Zealots were scarcely a company of ascetics.* For the events reported in the Qumran literature *it therefore seems reasonable to* turn to the historical period prior to CE 66-70, and *more precisely ... to the epoch beginning with the accession of Antiochus Epiphanes* (175 BCE) and ending with the fall of Hyrcanus II (40 BCE)" (italics mine).

the *Yahad*" , whoever the current office-holder might have been) in his role as unique interpreter of the Bible.[152] It is inconceivable that the

[152]If Cross is correct in seeing the establishment at Qumran as something of "a library", then, of course, caves with massive hoards like IV would represent something of its storehouse and the literature in a cave like I, what was actually circulating at the time. If the location was abandoned in haste, as the helter-skelter condition of the materials in Cave IV suggests—not the most ideal hiding place as even Cross admits—then the finding of an all-important commentary like Habakkuk neatly placed in a jar along with the other materials in Cave I probably implies it was actually in use or being studied at the time of the fall of the monastery and represents the latest literature; an assessment with which palaeography, while offering uneven results, on the whole concurs.

As far as the textual content of Habukkuk is concerned, Driver's discussion is unrivalled for its development of war data. Since to any intelligent observer, Jerusalem's fall was a foregone conclusion once the main Roman army under Vespasian appeared, the allusions it and 4QpIs[a] appear to make to the fall of the city need not necessarily reflect a period of composition after 70 CE; though they could. For the *pesher,* the coming of and destruction inflicted by the *Kittim* are events in progress, not necessarily completed. The inexorable advance of the *Kittim,* as in other *pesharim* at Qumran, only forms the literary backdrop to the commentary, whose main foci are actually on the Wicked Priest. "who *defiled* the Temple of God" and "plundered *the Poor* of their belongings" (italics mine; xii, 2ff.), and on "the last priests of Jerusalem", who amassed wealth by plundering the people (ix, 4f.); as well as on the "Lying *Matif*" ("Spouter"), who *attacked* the Righteous Teacher and "denied the Law" in the midst of the whole congregation (v, 7ff.). In contrast to the right-guided exegesis of Is 53:11f. (see above, pp. 9 and 56), he "sets up a congregation of Lying", "leading *Many astray ... with works of Lying*" His eschatological "*'amal* (and that of his followers) *will count for nothing*" at the Last Judgment (x, 9ff.; *n.b.* in CD, i, 14ff. this "Scoffer" is described as "*pouring—hatif—over Israel the waters of Lying*", "*leading astray* without *a Way*", and abolishing the boundaries which the *Rishonim* had set up"—italics mine; cf. 4QpNah, ii, 8 on the *Tongue* "leading Many astray").

In such a context, the allusion to "building a worthless city with blood" (x, 10) is easily explained. Having regard for CD, iii, 6's "Noahic" horror of the eating "of blood", to which it ascribes the cutting off of "the children of Jacob" in the wilderness, and the comparable insistence in James' directives to overseas communities (so disingenuously discussed in 1 Co 6-10) to abstain from "blood"; the allusion can be seen as figurative, of the same genre as the allusion to "pouring over Israel the waters of lying" above, the figurative allusion to the central priestly triad as a spiritualized "Holy of Holies" in 1QS, viii, 8 and ix, 6, and the general play on the word "Zadok" itself. (Cf. Paul's use of precisely this kind of imagery in 1 Co 3:9ff., 8:1, etc., where he describes his community as "the building" and himself as "the architect", and actually uses extant Qumran language when referring to his followers as "the Temple", *i.e.* "laying the foundations" and the "Cornerstone", this in a letter that goes on to describe his idea of "the New Covenant in" and "communion with the blood of Christ"; 1 Co 10:16, 11:25, etc.). Again, attention to the methods of literary criticism would help specialists here. The much-labored reference to the *Kittim* sacrificing to their standards (vi. 3f.) is *generic,* not specific. Though Josephus pictures the Romans as doing this in the midst of the carnage on the Temple Mount (*War* 6.6.1), the reference need not be to this particular sacrifice (though it might be); but rather to others which no doubt occurred after each successful siege as the Romans made their bloody way down from Galilee (e.g., Yotapata, *War* 3.7.3ff., and Gamala, 4.1.1ff.). For the Habakkuk *pesher,* the booty and riches of the high priests would in the end be "delivered over to the army of the *Kittim*" (cf. above, p. 30,, on "Phineas the Temple Treasurer"—which was demonstrably not the case in 37 or 63 BCE), these last to be condemned with "sinners" and "idolatrous men" generally at "the Last Judgment" (xiii, 1ff.). This could have been written in 68 CE or 69 CE, as well as in 70 or thereafter.

In this context, it should not be overlooked that both so-called "Christians" and the extreme Zealot occupiers of Masada left Jerusalem on or before the year 67/68 CE, the first in response to a mysterious oracle; the second because of the killing of Menachem. The first reportedly fled to a location Christian tradition identifies as "Pella"; the second, to Masada. Brandon, pp. 208ff., G. Strecker, *Das Judenchrisientum in den Pseudoklementinen,* Berlin, 1958, pp. 229ff., and more recently, G. Lüdemann, "The Successors of pre-70 Jerusalem Christianity: A Critical Evaluation of the Pella-Tradition", *Jewish and Christian Self Definition,* i, Philadelphia, 1978, pp. 161-73 (recapitulating Strecker), have questioned the historicity of the "Pella"-flight tradition; but their doubts do not alter the fact of the basic resemblance between the two traditions, nor do they rule out the possibility of a "flight" to an alternative location (cf. below, p. 82, and James' similar flight to the Jericho region in the 40's and the precipitous rise in Qumran coin distribution in both these periods). For Christians, anyhow, once the *Zaddik James* was killed, the city of Jerusalem could no longer remain in existence. Both disassociated themselves from the further progress of the Revolt; and indeed, "the Zealots" on Masada do not seem to have undertaken any offensive action even up to its fall. Even their suicide was not an offensive action, though it robbed the Romans of the glory of triumph.

In palaeography, S. Birnbaum, whose work Albright regarded as "expert" ("On the Date of the Scrolls from Ain Feshka and the Nash Papyrus", *BASOR, 115,* 1948, p. 15) and Cross regarded as "a major contribution" ("Scripts", p. 135), in "How Old Are the Cave Manuscripts? A Palaeographical Discussion", *V. T.,* 2, 1951, p. 105, originally put both Habakkuk and the War Scroll sometime before the "Herodian" period. However, Cross, *op. cit.,* p. 198, nn. 118 and 123, calls Habakkuk "early Herodian", having already informed us, p. 173, that a relative chronology of the Herodian period is "easily worked out" because of the rapid development in scripts; cf. also "The Oldest Manuscripts from Qumran", *JBL,* 74, 1955, p. 163. Birnbaum subsequently changed his mind and in *BASOR,* 115, 1949, he placed it "about the middle of the first century". This he developed further in *The Hebrew Scripts,* Leiden, 1971, pp. 38-43, where using his peculiar form of mathematics, *i.e.,* a (the number of early characteristics): b (the number of late characteristics) as c (his artificial time span based on supposition and unexamined archaeology): x (his answer, the number of years above his starting point: 300 BCE), he ends up with a date (finally in agreement with Cross') of the last quarter of the first century BCE Here, it should be pointed out, for him c is always a constant equaling 368, *i.e.,* 300 plus his presumed *terminus ad quern,* 68 CE On p. 27, oblivious to hyperbole, Birnbaum states, echoing Cross above, it was "possible to build an unassailable basis for establishing order out of chaos" in this way and that he was "justified in applying the law of averages and *do not* run *much risk if, as a general rule,* we regard dated (*or datable documents*) as representative of their time" (italics mine). Presumably Birnbaum had never heard of - differential equations (more applicable to a situation involving multiple variables and limits). His archaeological assumptions, along with his rather superficial historical ones, which are not insignificant to his conclusions, I shall deal with separately, below, pp. 76-77f.

N. Avigad, who should perhaps be considered the most moderate of all these individuals, in "Palaeography of the Dead Sea Scrolls and Related Documents" in *Aspects of the Dead Sea Scrolls, Scripta Hierosolymitana,* Jerusalem, 1958, pp. 72 and 82, calls Habakkuk late, noting the presence of some very late characteristics in both it and Hymns, which almost everyone acknowledges as contemporary. Here, we are already speaking of a gap of some 120 years in these three

community as a whole had nothing new to say or no new reactions while one hundred and fifty years of the most vital and controversial history in Palestine passed before its eyes; that on the contrary it sat passively and piously by studying or penning texts relating to the period leading up to 63 BCE or before. It should be properly understood that this is what would be involved in following the general theories and yet acknowledging that the documents were deposited in the caves in 68 CE or thereafter (to which there are no serious objections). It should be also stated categorically that 68 CE is the *terminus a quo for the deposit of scrolls in the caves,* not the *terminus ad quern for the cessation of habitation* in the region of Qumran which it is generally taken to be.[153]

Only in the case of the Zadokite Document are there any real difficulties, palaeographically speaking, for the above theory. But for the

---

assessments. The following is an example of Avigad's moderation. "We shall refrain here from suggesting absolute dates far each of them (*i.e.,* the documents including Habakkuk under consideration) since the speed of development of the individual letters is a factor we cannot yet make out." Scholars have taken advantage of all of these considerations, especially De Vaux's imperfect archaeology and Birnbaum's sophomoric calculus, to claim that the Kittaean advance referred to and the fall of the Temple implied in the Habakkuk *pesher* must relate to earlier such events, *i.e.,* that of Herod's assault in 37 BCE or Pompey's of 63 BCE, despite the fact that the cult of the military standards does not seem to have begun until the Imperial period; cf. Driver, pp. 211-216 and North, p. 433. For my part, I shall state categorically, on the basis of internal criteria alone, Habakkuk *is* late. Aside from the numerous allusions to 50-60's-type events and the "falling of the cedars of Lebanon" imagery of Is 10:34 already expounded above, one should note the extremely important (and distinctly "Jamesian" as opposed to "Pauline") exegesis of Hab 2:4 certified by the extant Pauline corpus *as current* in the 50-60's.

[153]This De Vaux and Driver properly realize. De Vaux to his credit states, p. 41: "It is perfectly true that strictly speaking the coins only provide a *terminus post* quern", and on p. 103 in *NTS,* "I concluded that this year 68 *has a good chance* of representing the end of Period II and the beginning of Period III" (italics mine); but hardens this in his conclusion, p. 138 "... in all probability none of the manuscripts deposited in the caves is later than this date."; cf. Avigad, p. 72, with more caution designates "the end of the Qumran settlement at 70 C.E. as the fairly certain *terminus ante quern*" (*italics* mine); and Birnbaum, p. 27, who with customary obliviousness, states: "Archaeological evidence confirms the post-Christian era part, and even enables us to arrive at a precise *terminus ad quern:* the year 68 C.E., when the Romans put an end to the Qumran settlement." Typically, he then proceeds to use this date as a principal "peg" in every one of his scores of calculations. Fitzmyer in "The Qumran Scrolls, the Ebionites, and their Literature" in *Essays.* p. 446, follows him in this mistake: "The latest possible date for the deposit of the manuscripts is the destruction of Qumran in CE 68." Fitzmyer has turned it completely around. His sentence should read (however unpopular it might sound): "*the earliest* possible date for the deposit of manuscripts is 68-69 CE", the date of the last Jewish coins found before the Bar Kochba period. Cross' "Oldest Manuscripts", p. 163, realizes the "absolute *terminus ad quern* for Qumran script types" are the dated documents from the Wadi Murabba'at (though sometimes he behaves as if he doesn't).

moment we have made no claims concerning the date of this document. As to its "relative chronology", we would agree with the palaeographers who see it as being somewhat "later" than the Community Rule.[154] It is only when putting in "the pegs", as they are referred to by those in the field that real differences would emerge. But Milik himself says that palaeographic evidence can be considered accurate only within two generations, and De Vaux admits that such evidence cannot be taken as absolute in and of itself, but must be ranged alongside textual, historical, and other kinds of data.[155] The two-generation rule presupposes a correct

---

[154]See Milik, pp. 58 and 91, and Cross, *Library,* pp. 81-82, n. 46. See below, too, for our discussion of why a single "early" exemplar on such a crucial text cannot be considered definitive.

[155]Milik, p. 57: "Palaeography however enables us to establish, at least within two generations, the time in which our earliest exemplar of a book was copied." Cross understands this but typically tries to narrow it, "Scripts", p. 136: "the palaeographer can fix a characteristic book hand within fifty years in terms of absolute dates, or even a generation in terms of relative (typological) relationships" (a key escape word here is "characteristic"). Avigad, as usual, is more circumspect, pp. 86-87: "Far more problematic is the question of absolute chronology. Ancient Hebrew manuscripts and inscriptions are notorious for their lack of dating formulae. Comparative palaeography is doing its best with the help of a few absolute data at hand", and notes that while "Hebrew palaeography is rapidly advancing towards the status of a scientific discipline ... many *lacunae* still exist which need completion, and questions of overlapping and archaizing are to be settled." *Vis-a-vis* archaizing, Birnbaum, p. 138, admits that sometimes scripts "are frozen" for hundreds of years, but when faced with the persistence of palaeo-Hebrew, calls it "an artificial revival", p. 87 or an "isolated" rendering, p. 107, and when faced with its final revival in the Bar Kochba coinage, explains it by saying the "grandfathers" used the old coins and the "fathers" remembered them, p. 78, having already concluded elsewhere that because of poor workmanship in the First Revolt, "die- cutters were not familiar" with it. Actually, Birnbaum does not concern himself with such niceties as margins of error: "By working out a comprehensive system of measurement, letter by letter and age by age, it is possible to establish an unassailable palaeographical basis." Errors come from not having "a good eye, patience, and training" and from lacking "the necessary palaeographic equipment" (whatever this means); *V. T.,* p. 92 (echoed verbatim in *Hebrew Scripts,* p. 27). He sets out his method, such as it is, in detail, in *V. T.,* p. 105. De Vaux, p. 97, in responding to Driver's contention that "internal evidence ... must take precedence over external", makes perhaps his clearest allusion to the worth of tools like palaeography. Although referring primarily to archaeology, he is at least willing to admit: "other things being equal, there is no precedence between the two kinds of evidence; a correct solution must make use of both, must prove the worth of both." Cross, *Library,* p. 74, n. 33, also, berates Driver's "peculiar refusal to accept the validity and precision of these newer techniques" citing the existence of "a sufficient number of specimens of Hebrew script of assured dating *however narrowly the phrase is defined*" (*italics* mine). For him, in ,addition to materials dated by stratigraphic context (which afford *solute termini—sic!),* "there are documents of the first century CE which bear date formulae, and thus can be dated to the year, and in some instances to the day, month, and year of their writing." He means, of course, the Wadi Murabbaᶜat and Nahal Hever finds and one unpublished date

identification of the general chronological provenance of a given script in the first place, and barring this, the deviation could be much wider. Even where a document as crucial as the Nash Papyrus is concerned, where most scholarly opinion has ranged itself behind the religiously

---

formula from Cave IV. However, aside from these, the only absolutely secure "peg" he can come up with from 150 BCE to 100 CE are the funerary inscription of Queen Helen of Adiabene and the Bene Hezir inscription—hardly a precise tool (see below, p. 79).

In relation to the ossuaries he and Birnbaum so securely date in Herod's time, Albright, his mentor, "Scrolls from AM Feska", p. 17, only says "all antedate the year 70 CE and that the earliest of them are not later than the reign of Herod the Great." North, p. 435, at an early stage of Qumran research, lamented "the lack of an independent documented analysis with drawings and descriptions of pottery pieces from other sites giving ground for a chronological judgment". Citing the disquieting symptom on the part of other archaeologists "to leave everything to the decision of one judge, however skillful" and to accept De Vaux's numerous revisions with submissiveness; he also attacks Qumran stratigraphy and ceramic typology (in this he has since been backed up to a certain extent by Laperrousaz), which he contended were "not simple facts black and white", but had to be carefully evaluated on the basis of "many prudent judgments, aesthetic comparisons, and detached awareness of literary data." As against this, Cross, whose wavering over the issue of the hundred-year gap in stratigraphy between Milik and De Vaux has already been noted above, claims that "the rapid accumulation of discoveries ... provide additional data for fixing absolute dates within relative dating systems provided by typological analysis". Yet he has the temerity to rely on De Vaux's controversial 31 BCE date for the end of Period 1, while at the same time claiming this stratigraphy has made ostracon and ceramic dating more secure. Willing now to step out "boldly" in making use of the evidence of ossuary scripts, he claims that this "variety of archaeological and palaeographic advances" have made it possible to *peg* "a series of absolute datings at intervals throughout the Herodian Age and the subsequent era between the two Jewish Revolts against Rome". With considerable more modesty, however, he admitted that chronology for "proto-Jewish" scripts would be "less precise" and for Hasmonaean "more difficult to fix with precision than Herodian hands"; "Scripts", pp. 133-135.

The final insight, however, perhaps belongs to North. Despite Cross' attack on Driver and those dependent on him as "uninformed" (echoed later by De Vaux), he had some time before already cautioned in the manner of Avigad that "it must be admitted by a prudent observer that the materials at our disposal are simply not adequate" (*i.e.*, to make absolute chronological sequences). Noting Vermes' pronouncement that "the palaeographers acquitted themselves remarkably well of their task" given the materials at their disposal, North cautions, "he can mean only that they came to a relative agreement which however is far from being a genuine or independent scientific *consensus*"; pp. 430-1. For his part, Cross finally admits also that scholars in the medieval field "have expressed skepticism concerning the precision of dating claimed by workers in the early Jewish field." However, he brushes it aside with his usual brusqueness, saying it "is based on a fallacious transfer of problems occasioned by experience with a surpassingly conservativ̦e script to scripts of a radically different tradition." Still he concludes, contradicting his original contention above: "the dating of a script of Qumran to a single generation on typological grounds, in the case of individual manuscripts, cannot, of course, be convened into absolute dating"; "Scripts", p. 192, n. 29. All of these comments and polemics are quoted at length because earlier criticism of palaeographic methods have simply made no impression on the scholarly community.

conservative Albright (due in no small part to the successful efforts of his students), and upon which most subsequent data has been constructed, early voices, such as Idris Bell of the British Museum and F. C. Burkitt, initially represented a three or four century deviation from Albright.[156]

S. A. Birnbaum, who along with Cross has laid the foundations to this palaeographic structure, employs what in any other field would be considered the most pseudo-scientific and infantile methods in determining these "pegs".[157] In this way he adds new "pegs" to aid

[156]See Albright, "A Biblical Fragment from the Maccabean Age: the Nash Papyrus", *SBL*, 56, 1937, pp. 149ff. and 171ff. Sukenik originally placed Nash in the first century; *Megilloth Genuzoth*, i, Jerusalem, 1948, p. 14, but later in a letter to Albright, cited in "Ain Feshka", p. 19, n. 10, revised it back to the first century BCE; E. R. Lacheman put it in the second century CE. Under these pressures Albright in "Ain Feshka", p. 19, who first dated Nash at the start of the Maccabean age, now changed his estimate: "So far as the evidence goes, it thus supports a date for the Nash papyrus not later than the first half of the first century BCE" See also, p. 15, n. 5a and J. C. Trever's article, "A Palaeographic Study of the Jerusalem Scrolls", *BASOR*, 113, 1949, p. 18-22, who preceded him in this revision. Later, under Birnbaum's prodding, Albright was to revise it back again.

Cross, in "Oldest Manuscripts", p. 148, calls his mentor's original dating of the Nash Papyrus (if one can remember what it was after all the shifts) "definitive"; elsewhere in "Scripts", p, 135, he calls the analysis that produced it "exemplary" and notes, "his date in the Maccabean Period remains undisturbed. Indeed, his original preference for a date in the second half of the second century needs scant revision." His generosity to his mentor is understandable, as probably also under Birnbaum's pressuring (who in *BASOR,* 115, 1949, p. 22, had pressed for a date in the second quarter of the second century "very near the maximum figure 165 BCE—suggested by Albright in his masterly examination in ... 1937") he supports a date of 150 BCE; "Scripts", p. 166. Regardless of what the final truth is (which despite any claims to the contrary will never be known), we see here an outside range of some four hundred years and an inside one of one-two hundred years for one of the most important "pegs" in the structure. Birnbaum's system of reflecting this is particularly colorful; he uses square brackets when a document's dating is *practically certain* from external evidence; "broken brackets" when *certain from his own analysis* (italics mine), *Scripts,* p. 28. Perhaps the most perceptive insight into this sad spectacle of imprecision is once again North's, who obviously knew personally all the *dramatis personae; CBQ,* p. 430: "The fact should be faced that it is extremely difficult to divorce Albright's *arguments* from the considerable authority of his person; consequently his dating, ± 50 BCE, has attained a diffusion not strictly proportioned to the proofs ..."

[157]Cross, "Scripts", p. 135, called Birnbaum's *The Hebrew Scripts* (*even before its publication*), "a monumental attempt to deal with all periods of Hebrew writing ... which will remain for many years a standard handbook for student and scholar alike" (was this perhaps intended for the book jacket?). He excuses the author's "polemical tone" (hardly Birnbaum's principal flaw) in an earlier work with the comment that "it should be remembered that it was written by *a professional palaeographer* tried to the limit by the *Lilliputian* attacks of non-specialists" (italics mine); n. 20, p. 191.

The question of "pegs" is of course all-important. I have noted Birnbaum's mathematical procedure, which he repeats with single-minded obliviousness on virtually every page leaving the intelligent reader in speechless amazement. See, for instance, nos. 80' (4QSam[b]). 81 (1QIs.[a]). 82 (1QS). 84 (1QpHab), 87[a] (1Qh[b]). 87[b] (1QM). 87[d] (1QH[2]). 87[c] (1QH[2]), etc. His outside limits, based on general previous palaeographic estimates of the Edfu scripts and archaeological acceptance of 68 as the *terminus ad quern* for the deposit of the scrolls at Qumran, are 300 BCE and 68 CE For comparison purposes he uses the Edfu scripts to determine "early" characteristics: and "the ossuaries", by which he means 88 and 95-100', "late". But these ossuaries (including Uzziah. Beit Schur, Ein Roghel, Wadi Sali[c]a, and that of Queen Helen), which he himself dates anywhere from 50 BCE to about 70 CE, averaging about early first century, are themselves, except for Queen Helen of Adiabene (his only secure peg). hardly secure. In any case, his use of them as a measuring standard in one pole of his proportions, since they do not match the upper pole limit of his basic 368-year time span. vitiates even his school-boy mathematics before he starts. Take 4QSam[b], which he says has 45 features in common with the Egyptian scripts and 11 with the ossuaries. He, therefore, sets this up as: $(45/11 = 368/x)$ and subtracts x from 300 BCE to get a result of *228 B. C. (sic—the* computational error is Birnbaum's). "The result", he claims, "will be something like *the absolute date...*" (italics mine; p. 130), which is, of course, preposterous. Or on the other extreme, take 1QM, which he says has 52 features in common with the ossuaries and 1 with the Egyptian scripts, or $(52/1 = 368/x)$. He subtracts the result from 68 CE and gets 61 CE He is even willing to use this methodology on notoriously conservative scripts like Samaritan ones, *i.e.*, no. 70, the Abisha Scroll, choosing two *termini*, the 8th and 13th centuries, and finding that the characteristics point to the 11th century as the "not unlikely date", p. 117.

This is not a proper working methodology, Cross and Albright notwithstanding. He may end up, if he is lucky, with a rough relative chronology, but it does not take into consideration the multiple variables of the age of scribe, his school of training, his personal expertise, his conservatism, and the speed of evolution of individual letters (which Avigad rightly abstains from attempting to estimate and which Cross invariably assumes to be "rapid"), none of which can even be conceived of as straight-line functions. To obtain a proper working method, he would have to define separate functions for each of these variables and then plug them into a differential equation, the solution to which would tax even the abilities of a space engineer. To think that his errors simply cancel themselves out, as Birnbaum does, is in itself a good illustration of the unscientific nature of his methodology. What is worse he goes on to corroborate his "results" using results he previously obtained by the same method and with the same parameters, punctuating his discussion at various intervals with remarks like "results check", "tallies", "corroborated", which of course they cannot help but do. In reality, he might just as likely be compounding his errors and could be out one hundred years, or even more, depending on the mistakes he has compounded in his "pegs". It is pretentious to call such a methodology "unassailable", and what is more to use it to rule out credible solutions which can at least make sense of internal data (which Birnbaum doesn't even understand, no less make intelligible), which is what is being done by dutiful students of this technique at the present time. You cannot deal with your opponent's charges by calling them "Lilliputian", contemptuously dismissing them as "uninformed", or what is even worse, ignoring them, when you are using a methodology such as this. Certainly, you cannot claim you have cut your margin of error down to "one generation" even in relative chronology.

Before leaving this rather sad subject, let us set out a few of Birnbaum's "historical" assumptions. First, Birnbaum's answer to the lack of footnotes or bibliography in his work is simple: "The present study has not utilized any printed sources but ... the written documents themselves. For this reason no reference to previous work has been made in my book, and the compilation of a bibliography is not called for": p. 26. Where he does give references, they are usually either

in determining the provenance and date of the next manuscript, and so on down the line.[158] Far from homing in on the true dates of a manuscript by such a methodology, what he does, as any good student

from the Talmud or to make additional comments. In discussing Ezra, whom he credits *with introducing the Aramaic script,* he is completely unaware of questions concerning Ezra's own chronology and assumes without question he pre-dates Nehemiah. Claiming in a thinly disguised version of Wellhausen that such changes arc invariably religiously motivated, he explains: "When a nation adopts a new religion, it discards also the script of its former creed and adopts that of the new religion", pp. 69·75. Pointing out that John Hyrcanus issued the first coins (recently a massive amount of new coins have been found from the Persian period), he categorically asserts John was "a Hellenistic ruler", not "a nationalist". For him, on the other hand, "the Pharisees" were the "religious nationalists". John's war, therefore (since John was a Sadducee), against the Samaritans could not be "nationalistic"; he rather terms it "expansionistic". Pressing these historical insights further, he states that since John sided with the Sadducees, breaking with the Pharisees, the former "from what we know of their principles would have been the last people to dig out the old script" (*i.e.* the PalaeoHebrew)! He refers to this palaeo-Hebrew with endless scorn, as if he were personally antagonized by it, as "not a living script", "an artificial revival", "an isolated rendering", concluding—for whatever it's worth—with the observation that even now the State of Israel declined to use it, since it was "consigned to oblivion by the Jewish people"; pp. 77-79, 87, 94, and 103. Finally, he uncritically accepts De Vaux's archaeology. *Vis-a-vis* the 31 BCE date, he has this to say: "We know that there was a break in the settlement at Qumran during the last third of the first pre-Christian century and a renewed settlement at the beginning of the next century" and he completely misunderstands the import of the 68 CE date. He uses both dates without reservation and unquestioningly, and like Cross, finds them an "important help" in turning a "relative date into an absolute one", pp. 149 and 127ff.

[158]Cf. how he uses 115 and 151 to corroborate his dating for 80*. Obviously, they must corroborate since they have been arrived at on the basis of the same parameters. He uses 115 again in 81, corroborates 82 by 81, corroborates 84 (Habakkuk) with 87a, and actually makes a slight shift back from 25 to 50 BCE, saying he is more sure of 87a (1QIs^b-25 BCE). Then finding the difference between it and 81 (1QIs^a-150 BCE) "considerable", he says, results "check"; p. 143. Milik, p. 64, would rather put Habakkuk in the mid-first century and even later, saying it "could not come from any part of the first century BCE" Here we are out nearly 100 years on a key document. *Pace,* peace among palaeographers. Birnbaum's approach to 87a (1QIs^b) is classic. He invokes De Vaux's archaeology to show that the date for the temporary abandonment of Qumran corresponds with his own projection, *turning it into an absolute date,* and corroborates his dating by comparison with 84. But he has just used 87a to corroborate his results with 84. Nothing loath, he concludes: "Thus each of the two dates corroborates the other", p. 150; his logic could hardly be more circular. He then confidently proceeds to corroborate 87b (1QM) and 87e (Hand A of Hymns) by 87a again, commenting it "goes well" (they should), p. 155. Cross, too, is quite prepared to use his tenuous relative dates as "pegs" in the absolute chronology. He is even willing to "project backward" ("not as complicated as it sounds") along separate typological lines to achieve these. For his classic discussion of this in relation to Jewish, Palmyrene, and Nabataean scripts, see "Scripts", pp. 160-1; cf. also 196-7, n. 105.

of mathematics will realize, is to compound his errors increasing his margin of error exponentially. The methods of the other "palaeographers" working in the Second Temple period do not differ markedly from his (though they are not quite so forthcoming in their presentation of them). All involve a certain amount of subjective reckoning based on the assumptions and preconceptions I have been at pains to upset in this study.[159]

[159] I think we have covered these subjective preconceptions both in archaeology and other disciplines adequately for Birnbaum. Milik's were noted earlier above. Cross uses archaeology, as we have seen, for transforming relative to absolute chronologies; "Scripts' ", pp. 133ff. and "Oldest Manuscripts", pp. 147f. Here, while seeing relative chronology as secure, h$_e$ admits that, "Absolute dating of the documents poses a more complicated problem ..."; p. 163. He very definitely relies on De Vaux's "earthquake" hypothesis in dating "Herodian" script, *i.e.*, 30 BCE to 70 CE; but unlike Birnbaum. does not consider that the "abandonment" of Qumran produced any "equivalent lacuna in the typological sequence of manuscripts"; "Scripts", pp. 173 and 199, n. 127. Avigad, as we have noted, as always is more modest, but rarely stands against his peers. Cf. also Vermes, p. 55, quoted above. It is interesting, when one comes to investigate Cross' claims for "a series of absolute dating" pegs "at intervals throughout the Herodian Age", that, while protesting against Avigad's late dating of the Dominus Flevit ossuaries; he can only come up with the fact, citing Milik, that "the Herodian dating ("as Milik himself would insist") of the great mass ... is certain"—a range of some one-hundred twenty-five years. Actually, as stated above, he has only the Queen Helen of Adiabene inscription as really certain.

Another "peg" is, of course, the Bene Hezir inscription, which is of special interest to us, which he (Cross), Avigad, p. 174, and Albright, "Nash", p. 159, all seem to agree on a date of about the turn of the Christian era; "Scripts", pp. 174, 198, n. 123, and 199, n. 133. In "Oldest Manuscripts" Cross is so secure in this date (in his usual manner), that he even terms it "a *terminus ad quern*" for first century BCE scripts. Avigad in *Ancient Monuments in the Kidron Valley* (Hebrew), Jerusalem, 1954, pp. 62-64, originally sought an even earlier dating. The key analysis here is Albright's. Attributing the thesis to De Vogüé (cf. Klein, *Jüdisch-Palastinisches Corpus Inscriptionum*. Vienna, 1920, pp. 14ff.), he says the latter "is dearly right" in claiming "that the tomb of the Bene Hezir (popularly ascribed to St. James) belongs to the priestly family that contributed three high-priests during the reigns of Herod and Archelaus ... it would then date from the end of Herod's reign or a little later ..." There are, however, at least four names mentioned on the plaque, and Jeremias has shown with considerable more precision than De Vogüé that the Boethusians contributed at least eight high priests, the list probably being Joseph Cabi, 62 CE, "the son of the high priest Simon"; cf. Jeremias, pp. 94 and 194ff. and *Ant.* 19.6.2-4 and 20.8.11-9.1. It is not without interest, nor significance, that Joseph Cabi loses the high priesthood in the political machinations leading up to the judicial murder of James (see above, p. 43). There is, therefore, absolutely no proof (other than palaeographic; cf. Cross and Albright on the use of ligatures) that this tomb was built, nor the inscription made, before about the middle of the first century CE; and the unfinished condition of adjoining tombs, and to a certain extent its own, would argue for the later, not earlier, dating. Certainly, it cannot be considered a *secure terminus ad quern* for the first century BCE, as Cross would have it—at least not a precise one. This is to say nothing of the inherent imprecision of attempting to use lapidary work as a "*peg*" in dating manuscript sequences.

This is to say nothing of the other variables: for instance, that in a given community there might have been an archaizing conservative tradition (as, for instance, the Palaeo-Hebrew script at Qumran. Even today Samaritans use an archaizing script with roots going back perhaps some twenty centuries for biblical manuscripts).[160] Or, that one might have been dealing with older scribes. To posit for the purposes of argument the extreme case; let us suppose that an eighty-year-old scribe was sitting next to a twenty-five year-old scribe trained in a more "up-to-date" scribal school (whatever this might mean in such circumstances).[161] Here, of course, is where Milik's margin of error comes into play, but this is hardly very comforting when we are using one manuscript to date another, as Birnbaum does, none of which with

---

[160]Birnbaum, p. 138. Cf. his discussion of Palaeo-Hebrew, pp. 76ff.; of Samaritan, pp. 98ff.; and Cross, p. 189, n. 4.

[161]Cross is very much aware of this problem: "Despite the speed of evolution in this period, allowance must be made always for the extension of the professional life of a conservative scribe beyond his generation, or for the individualistic hand which holds out against the powerful current of scribal styles and fashions", p. 161. So is Avigad, who with typical caution, but considerably less élan, in the section where he asserts "the speed of development of individual letters is a factor we cannot yet make out", says, "It should, however, be kept in mind that various scribes are naturally inclined to conservatism in the case of formal styles"; pp. 72-3. Cf. also Laperrousaz defending his own theories, p. 98.

Cross' charm and aesthetic sensibility, evident throughout his work. undoubtedly help to win him many supporters; cf. p. 160 on "archaic semiformal", p. 173 on "Herodian (expressed even more sensitively on p. 192, n. 27 and p. 200, n. 141). and again on p 105, n. 4 on "Paleo-Hebrew" (though sometimes deteriorating into jargon or incomprehensibility as on p. 141 on the "Aramaic hand" or p. 153 on 4QExᶠ). Morton Smith has put the case well. In personal comments to me: he notes that originally Cross considered the greater part of Qumran documents to be in "private hands". He claims, only later, probably under Birnbaum's influence, did Cross begin to grasp the significance of and come to see them as being primarily in "book hands". Smith cites Mt. Athos and similar communities, where documents are datable. as verification of the proposition often several different book hands with widely differing dates of origin can be found simultaneously in the same community. He concludes that, even if accurate sequencing and dating of the original could be established—in themselves highly unlikely propositions—a given ms., written in a particularly durable hand, might in fact have been written years later than one written in a hand of more recent development.

Our purpose in criticizing the palaeographers is not to rule out a certain amount of value to such work *when taken within strict limits;* but to caution them to be more modest in their claims for precision: for instance, in the supposedly secure "Herodian" lapidary work and in the case of relative chronologies down to a single generation: (Birnbaum claims even more precision); and to open their admitted 50-year margin of error to one hundred years (in some instances even more), particularly where sectarian works are concerned. Even their own disagreements on mss. such as Habakkuk and Hymns exceed this. Cross, for instance, knows that all of Birnbaum's estimates are too early, but so probably, too, are many of his own; cf. "Oldest Manuscripts", p: 148.

an actual dating formula. What date would two manuscripts copied by these two scribes at exactly the same time appear to be? If the older scribe copied a manuscript using the script he learned when he was twenty, what date would we give a manuscript found in only one exemplar that was actually copied in 4 BCE? 63 BCE or before? Suppose the older scribe's teachers themselves were all old or very old-fashioned, what then would be the margin of error? Or suppose that a given student just had not learned his lessons very well and made errors which looked to palaeographers either like scriptual developments or regressions (there are many such confusing mixtures of innovative and regressive scripts at Qumran, depending of course on what is meant by "innovative" and "regressive").[162]

It is not possible to say on palaeographic grounds that a manuscript was written in 63 BCE and not, for instance, in 45 CE In particular, when one has only one exemplar of a given work (the case for instance of all the *pesharim* at Qumran and many other texts) or when one has one "older" copy as opposed to several or a cluster of "newer" ones (the actual case of the Zadokite Document), one must exercise extreme caution. The best one can hope for is a rough "relative chronology". Only when manuscripts begin to bunch up in a clearly discernible manner is one justified in thinking in terms of *possible* dates. In any event, it is certainly incautious to date it by its earliest exemplar, however tempting this may be, as all scholars in the field rush to do, but rather where the distribution peaks.[163] Yet Qumran scholars make these kinds

---

[162]See, for instance, Birnbaum's discussion of the earliest book hands at Qumran, in particular 1QLev and 1QEx, pp. 68-70 (nos. 28-32), where he says some features imply a later date for 1QLev and some, a later date for 1QEx. His conclusion is completely unscientific: "From this we cannot but conclude that both were written during .the same period, each of the scribes using some 'earlier' and some 'later' forms." But, of course, this is Birnbaum's method of dating every manuscript at Qumran; cf. his discussion of 4QSam[b] and Cross' general discussion of 4QEx[f], 4QSam[b], and 4QJer[a], pp. 140-58. Birnbaum's estimate of the mid-fifth century for these hands is based on the purest supposition having to do, as we have noted, with his preconceptions about Ezra's importance.

[163]Cross, p. 61, has signaled his awareness of this problem following up his caution concerning the longevity of a conservative scribe: "However, in the case of a group of scripts belonging typologically to a certain generation, we can assume methodologically that the majority of the group were copied in the normal span of a generation". The contrapositive, however, which he misses, involves exceptions to the "majority", either the case of a scribe whose longevity extends beyond the group or that of a single manuscript that "appears" substantially earlier than a given group.

This is exactly the situation of the "early" fragments of the Zadokite Document (4QD[b]) found in Cave IV. Fragments from at least seven other mss. of the Zadokite Document have been found in Cave IV, most of which appear to be "Herodian". Milik, pp. 38-9 and 57-8, gives

4QD[b] a date of between 75 and 50 BCE (cf. Cross, *Library*, p. 120), which palaeographically speaking probably presents the only serious stumbling block to the historical reconstruction we set forth above. Fitzmyer, prescient as ever in grasping the cruciality of this fragment in the scheme of Qumran origins, tried to push it even further back in time by attacking Starcky's "Pompeian" dating in "Theory of Qumran Messianic Development" (cf. Starcky, "Les Quatres Étapes du Messianism", *RB*, 70, 1963, pp. 496ff.) and asserting that this copy was ˉscarcely the original monograph": cf. his revision of "The Aramaic 'Elect of God' Text from Qumran Cave IV", *Essays*. pp. 138-9. Milik, however, parts company with him on this issue. citing 4QDb in a follow-up to his "two-generation" remark as an example of a Qumran text "more or less contemporary with the events to which they refer" (cf. Cross, p. 114, but also Cross' discussion, pp. 81-3, n. 46, where he rather agrees with Fitzmver). In the same context, Milik also discusses the general class of mss. called *pesharim, all* of which he places in "the last phase of the Qumran settlement"; see, also, Additional n. 3, pp. 151-2 and "*Milkī-sedq et Milkīreša[c]*", pp. 135f. Surely Fitzmyer is asking more from palaeography than it can scientifically sustain in attacking Starcky on the issue of such a palaeographically insignificant time differential (the same might be said for Cross, who agrees with Fitzmver on the matter of 4QD[b]).

A few pages earlier, pp. 132ff., Fitzmyer had already pointed to how 4QD[b] confirmed that the reference to a singular "Messiah of Aaron and Israel" in CD, xiv, 19 was not a medieval copyist's mistake, as has often been suggested, and, in addition, pointed out perhaps even more importantly that the same manuscript actually contained a reference to "the flight of the Essenes to their Damascus Camps". What could echo more the early Christian tradition of a flight by the Jerusalem Community to Pella (*i.e.*, "in the Damascus region" or perhaps as Acts 9:22 would have it "the Jewish settlement at Damascus"), since as Brandon points out, an actual flight to Pella in this period was probably precluded by the political and military situation? For the whole controversy, including the positions of Strecker, Munck, Filson, Schoeps, etc., see Brandon, pp. 208-214. One should also keep in mind the use of the allusion, "Damascus", as a codename (here Cross agrees with us, pp. 82f.; see, also, R. North, "The Damascus of Qumran Geography", *Palestine Exploration Quarterly,* 1955, pp. 34-48), and possibly too, even "Pella".

We have already noted above, p. 72, the similarity of the "Pella flight" tradition with the Masada flight of the *Sicarii,* both undertaken for similar reasons, *i.e.*, the stoning of their respective leaders. Both groups, too, appear to have withdrawn from further participation in the uprising against Rome, which was moving quickly into its "Jacobin" phase. We have, however, not mentioned the possible confusion of "a flight to Pella" with a "flight to Sela[c]", a name used both to refer to Petra (Paul's "Arabia" reference?) and an unidentified Dead Sea Valley location. Even Masada may have been known to the sectaries by such a codename (cf., for instance, the reference in Mur 45.6 to staying at the "*Mezad-Hassidin*", *i.e.*, "the Fortress of the *Hassidim*", which very likely refers to the area around Qumran, and which by implication identifies it as the original stronghold or location of "the Hassidaean" movement).

Here, I think, it may be possible to identify the actual scriptural passage containing "the mysterious oracle" referred to in Church tradition (cf. Eusebius, *E. H.* 3.5.2f. and Epiphanius, *Haeres.* 29.7 and 30.2; also *de Mens et Pond* 15) as the basis for this flight. Significantly, it comes in direct proximity to the famous passage which tradition tells us was actually used to arrive at an exegetical understanding of James' death (Is 3:10). I refer to Is 2:10ff. In considering it, one should try to visualize what a Qumran-style *posher* on the first four to five chapters of Isaiah would look like. The whole passage is addressed pointedly and several times to "*the House offacob*" and as in Habakkuk, the context is the imminent destruction of Jerusalem ("Jerusalem is ruined and Judea fallen"). Amid the telltale imagery of the Righteousness of "works" (cf. the use of

of assumptions regularly, claiming a precision that comes down in some cases to a handful of years, while dismissing better theories than the one on which their own methodological assumptions are based. I would like to state a rule of thumb that might be helpful. Palaeographic data cannot in and of itself be considered definitive. Scholars who use it to disqualify an otherwise convincing picture, which in most other ways fits the available evidence, do so at their own peril. At no time can it

---

maʿasim at Qumran, above, p. 6), allusion to "plundering the Meek" (3:14; cf. CD, vi, 16 and "plundering the Poor" in 1QpHab, xii, 10), "justifying the Wicked" (cf. 5:24 with CD, i, 19 in the context of an allusion to "assaulting *the soul of the Zaddik* and pursuing the Walkers in Perfection with the sword"). the imminent coming of "the Day of *Yahweh*". and the equally telltale overthrow of "*the cedars of Lebanon*" (2:12f.): the people are urged to throw away their gold and idols to the moles and the bats" (cf. Ja 5:2f. and 1QpHab, xi. 12tr) and "enter into the Rock ... for *the day of the Lord of Hosts* shall be upon every one that is proud and lofty (cf. Ja 4:611) ... and upon all *the cedars of Lebanon* that are high and lifted up (cf. 4QpIsᵃ and 1QpHab, xii, 2) ... *go into the holes of the Rocks* and *into the caves* of thₑ earth for fear of the Lord (cf. once more the allusion to cave-dwelling) ... go into *the clefts of the Rocks* and into the tops of the ragged *Rocks* (here "*Selaᶜim*" is actually used: anyone familiar with Qumran terrain will see the connection) for fear of the Lord and for the glory of his majesty when he arises to shake terribly the earth" (italics mine).

This is followed up at the beginning of Ch 3, leading up to the passage we know was applied to James' death, with the words (Is 3:1): "For behold, the Lord, the Lord of Hosts is taking away from Jerusalem and from Judah the stay and the staff, the whole stay of bread, and the whole stay of water." Anyone familiar with the techniques of Qumran exegesis would know the kinds of exegesis that would have been developed from such passages. In close proximity to this passage is also the famous "Zion shall be redeemed through Judgment (*Mishpat*) and her converts through Righteousness (*Zedakah*—in this context, more properly, "Justification") and the reference to the restored Jerusalem as "Faithful City" (*Kityah-Ne'ernanah*) and "City of Righteousness" (ᶜ*Ir ha-Zedek*), not to mention the well-known call to all peoples to come up "to the House of the God of Jacob", ending with: "0 House of Jacob, come ye and let us walk in the Light of the Lord" (Is 1:26-2:5; cf. "Ways of Light", "eternal Light", and "walking in the Ways of Light" imagery at Qumran generally, particularly in 1QS, iii, 7-23; iv, 2-7, etc.)

Here, therefore, one has considerable incentive to revive G. Margoliouth's original dating of the Zadokite Document when it was first discovered in 1896, trusting that the cautions I have outlined above, *vis-a-vis* a conservative use of palaeographic evidence and a healthy restraint on related preconceptions, will be taken seriously (*n.b.* we are not making any claims that this reference in 4QDᵇ is to the actual "Pella flight", only that it echoes and is representative of the flight traditions of this period). See also Milik, p. 117, who admits 4QDᵇ places the "ceremony of the renewal of the Covenant" at Pentecost, a festival of the greatest significance to the early "Church"; cf. Paul's rush to get to Jerusalem in time for the community's convocation at Pentecost, Acts 20:16 and the transformation of "the descent of the Law" implicit in the celebration of this festival into "the descent of the Pauline Holy Spirit" and its Gentile Mission accoutrements of "speaking in tongues", etc. (*n.b.* the ready-made scope for the additional possible extension of the "tongue" and "spouting" imagery at Qumran and in the Letter of James here).

be used to dismiss a theory which within these general parameters can make meaningful sense of internal textual evidence. Where "pegging" is so precarious and in the general absence of secure date formulae, "meaningful textual evidence" must be accorded precedence, as it is in any case by a majority of scholars (including even palaeographers as we have seen) albeit in a subconscious manner.

Ultimately, we shall probably have to admit that the situation regarding palaeography is much more chaotic and difficult to describe than was originally envisioned by Cross' and Birnbaum's assumptions of "rapid" *straight-line* development of scripts in the Second Temple period, which lie at the heart of their reconstructions and *equations* such as they are. Such a circumstance, anyhow, would be more in keeping with the reality of the historical *sitz-im-leben* of the period. Here, textual and historical studies will be able to play a role in helping to clarify the *true,* probably highly complex, character of palaeographic sequences, not *vice versa* as heretofore. On the basis of internal textual data alone (*i.e.*, the use of Hab 2:4, Is 40:3, Is 10:29f., Num 24:17, Deut 18:15ff., and the evocation of the terminology of Is 53:11f. in Qumran communal organization and in eschatological interpretations like those of Ez 44:15 and Hab 2:4, demonstrably all scriptural passages enjoying a vogue in first-century Palestine, but not before), one is entitled to conclude that almost all Qumran sectarian texts, are "late", *i.e.*, first century CE. Palaeography will have to accommodate itself to these results, not *vice versa*.

Such a conclusion where "sectarian" works are concerned, implying as it does the fact of *new* ideological departures, is completely in keeping with Josephus' repeated allusions to "innovations" and "innovators" since the appearance of Judas and. Saddouk at the beginning of the first century and the statements in the *ARN* and al-Kirkisani identifying the start of really destructive sectarian strife with the "split" between "Zadok and Boethus", as well as the parallel, albeit highly refracted, testimonies in the New Testament and Pseudoclementine Recognitions placing in conjunction "the division of the People into many parties", the birth of "the Sadducees" (who, "considering themselves more Righteous", "withdrew from the community"), and the coming of John.[164]

---

[164] Of the *two* "splits" or "withdrawals" we have discussed in this study (*i.e.*, that between "Zadokite Hassidaeans" and "Pharisee Hassidaeans" and that between "Messianic Sadducees"

and "Boethusian Sadducees"), we are speaking about the later one which triggers Josephus' descriptions of the "sects" in *Ant.* and *War*. For the early first century provenance of this and its connection with the split between Saddouk and Joezer b. Boethus, see above, pp. 11 and 41. For the basic interchangeability of John and "Saddouk", see below, p. 95. For the denouement of this split approximately 70 years later, see how "the Men of Power" (*i.e.*, "the Herodians"), "the high priests", "the principal of the Pharisees", and "all those desirous of peace"—principal among whom is one "Saulus of the king's kindred" (the descendant of the *Idumaean convert* "Costobarus" probably either through Agrippa I's sister Herodias or the family of Herod of Chalcis in Cilicia)—try to convince "the innovators" that the rejection of gifts from foreigners and sacrifices from Romans or Caesar was "impious" or "seditious". Thereupon *they invite* the Roman army into the city "to cut off the sedition before it became too hard to subdue"; *War* 2.17.2-6. *N.b.* it is these same innovators who ban Agrippa II from the Temple and all Jerusalem above, p. 7.

Chapter Eight
ARCHAEOLOGICAL PROBLEMS

The above caution about the precedence "meaningful textual evidence" must take over the claims of palaeography should be applied, as well, to claims in archaeology based on coin data, the use of which has gone so far as to convince the community at large that an absolute determination of the date of the destruction of the monastery can be made down to the year and month.[165] The reason this destruction, in particular, is so important is that the Habakkuk Commentary refers to the fall of Jerusalem including giving particulars that unmistakably point to the fall of 70 CE Yet our commentators use the archaeological data they have developed to contend this fall could not be that of 70 CE; but rather must be that of 40 BCE or 63 BCE (or even before), thereby pushing the provenance of all Qumran material back almost 150 years or more.[166] Nor do they worry in this regard what the sect might have been doing in the meantime until the deposit of the scrolls in the caves, expecting us rather to believe that it sat passively studying archaic scriptural exegesis and ignored 125 years of the most eventful Palestinian

---

[165]De Vaux proposes a date of June, 68; pp. 37-41 and "Fouilles", 1954, p. 233, echoed in Cross, p. 63. Despite noting quite a few additional coins of 68/69 found at Ein Feshka. Laperrousaz, pp. 85 and 90, agrees.

[166] Cross, p. 126: "Just as we cannot date the foundation of the sect in the Roman era because of *reference to Pompey's conquest of Jerusalem in the Habakkuk Commentary ...*" (*italics* mine). Cf. how he uses 4QD^b in the same way, pp. 81-3, n. 46. De Vaux is not slow to follow him, p. 122. While willing to utilize Pliny's testimony in *Hist Nat*. 5.17.4 about an "Essene" settlement near the shores of the Dead Sea between Jericho and EM Gedi to further their own theories (De Vaux, pp. 134ff., and Cross, pp. 15 and 70ff.), they ignore the clear implication it contains of continued habitation in the region (regardless of the condition of the permanent structures at Qumran), a circumstance also hinted at by Mur 45.6 as we have seen, because it doesn't suit their preconceptions or archaeological conclusions. For an opposing view, see Farmer, "The Economic Basis of the Qumran Community", *TZ*, 1955, pp. 295ff.

Here, one is obliged to point out that Simeon bar Cleophas, the man Eusebius appears to identify as "a Rechabite priest" and the successor to James and putative second brother of Jesus, martyred under Trajan sometime after 106 CE, while probably never going to "Pella", certainly subsisted with his followers somewhere in the environs of Jerusalem. *N.b.* the Qumran-style language *E. H.* 3.32, relying on Hegesippus, uses to describe his "end"—"like the Lord's" (*i.e.*, "until then the church remained a virgin ... then godless error began to take shape *through the deceit of false teachers* ... who preached against the *Truth*—"*Emet*" at Qumran—the counter-proclamation of "*false Knowledge*"—"*Da^c at sheker*"; italics mine). The passage, while obscure seems to include data, also based on Hegesippus, abOut the simultaneous executions of those descendants of Jesus' *third brother Judas*, who he attests *still* "presided over every church" because they belonged to "the Lord's family".

history.[167] To be sure, I, too, make use of coin data in this study, but only *in the most general way* to make comments about *general trends* and, in the process, to show of what acceptable usage of such data might consist.

For instance, no coins have yet been found in Qumran (though they have at Ein Feshka) from the fourth year of the Revolt, 69/70. A substantial number, though, have already been found from the third year of the Revolt, 68/69, the year De Vaux and his supporters claim the monastery fell. They go so far as to claim this as a *terminus ad quern* for the deposit of the scrolls in the caves, *i.e.*, that habitation ceased at the location and its surroundings, though it has been observed that the sectaries living in the caves probably did not carry money on their persons. Since no coins of any kind have been found in the caves and their environs, no judgment whatever can be made on this basis about the extent or lack of *Rechabite*-style habitation in the caves.[168] De Vaux

---

[167]Cross and Milik explain (in the view of the writer rather lamely) that *the traditions were preserved orally to be set down at a time close to the fall of the monastery,* yet they do not deny other mss. contain records of contemporary events; see Cross, pp. 94, 113-4, and 120, nn. 21, 24, 28, and Milik, pp. 57-9, 64, and 89 (with another slur on the Maccabees). That such intimate and intense commentaries could be thought to be the product of "oral transmission" (the generally fragmented and disoriented nature of which is well illustrated in the Talmud) is typical of the unreal world these specialists are permitted to inhabit by their peers.

[168]Sometimes De Vaux drops his diplomatic approach and categorically states, p. 112: "The community installed itself at Qumran in the second half of the second century BCE It abandoned the site for a period of some thirty years during the reign of Herod the Great, and *definitively left the area in CE 68*" (*italics* mine). No wonder some commentators have taken this for *a "terminus ad quern"* and not the *terminus post quem* he admits it is on p. 41 (however De Vaux is notorious for shifts of this kind; cf. North, "Archaeology", p. 430, who lists four retractions by De Vaux in the first three years of his work).
See Laperrousaz, p. 91, on the pottery found in many of these caves. De Vaux admits the caves were inhabited, though he tries to reduce the number; even so, he cannot get it down below forty; cf. pp. 44ff., 50f., and 57. On p. 107 he admits that some pottery even appears to be of a later date than the outside limit he set for the life of the settlement and that some of the repositories were hardly more than mere "depressions" in the cliff wall$_s$ (p. 57). In spite of this, though he acknowledges habitation took place in the Bar Kochba period, he still feels utterly secure in insisting, "The manuscripts of Qumran were certainly not deposited in the caves at the time of the Second Jewish War." The caves, of course, in the marl terrace (where Cross' "Library" is to be found, *i.e.*, Cave IV), while not inhabited, could certainly not have escaped notice in the Bar Kochba period; De Vaux, pp. 52ff. and 56f. The fact that Cave I shows dear signs of habitation and no money was found in any of these cave locations is important for our contention above that regardless of whether the buildings were destroyed or not in 68 CE, to claim an absolute abandonment of the "total site" on the basis of coin data is wishful thinking. De Vaux thinks he has proved the absolute abandonment of the site in 68 CE in his retort to Roth on p. 123, n. 1, but once more he has proved nothing, only a *terminus post quern* for th$_e$ abandonment of the site and that its buildings might have been burned. What no commentator has yet succeeded in explaining, if the site (and the caves) were clearly inhabited at various times up to 136 CE, is why

claims that minting must have begun in the spring of the year 68, which would have left enough time for this substantial number of coins to get to Qumran before its fall, which he places in June. But in the year 68 the siege of Jerusalem began, and it is surprising that as many coins got out to Qumran as did. It would be equally surprising if many more got out after that year and given the conditions in the city in 69 and 70, very few were likely to have been minted anyhow. In any event, Jewish coins would hardly have been very good tender in Jericho or similar outlying regions any longer.[169]

In this context De Vaux claims that Phoenician and other non-Jewish coins were found in the layer overlaying that of the presumed destruction in 68 CE Finding such foreign coins is taken as proof positive that a Roman contingent occupied the location from 68 CE onwards despite the fact that the number of such coins are few and finding coins in a given place says nothing about who the given individual was who happened to drop them there, or for that matter, when, only that he could not have dropped them there before the said date on the coin.[170] In particular,

---

the manuscripts survived at all in many of these locations, some of which were hardly more than "crevices", and in Cave IV itself which was hardly a hiding place at all.

[169]De Vaux, *NTS,* p. 102, cites five silver shekels from the year 4 found in a treasure near Jericho in 1874; but this is just the point. No one denies that with the fall of Jerusalem hoards of coins, big or small, would have *made* their way out of the city, but it is doubtful if these coins would have been very widespread in this area as popular tender, for they would have had no value. Take the counter example: no coins have yet been found either at Qumran or Ein Feshka from the year 1 of the Revolt, when such coins would have freely circulated. Do we, therefore, conclude there was no habitation in that year at Qumran? It is, therefore, textual evidence, of which there is a substantial amount, as De Vaux himself admits, p. 133, which must finally decide these questions. De Vaux counters: "this would be true if it were not for the fact that some Roman coins, the earliest of which belong to 67/68, had not been found in the level of reconstruction, and if this date did not coincide with the arrival of the Roman troops in the vicinity of Qumran"; *Archaeology,* p. 123, n. 1. But this proves absolutely nothing, as De Vaux well knows. For his explanation of how so many coins managed to appear at Qumran between April and June of the year, 68 CE, see p. 41.

[170]See pages 44ff. and 66ff., recapitulated in Laperrousaz, pp. 61ff. As has already been noted, De Vaux's stratigraphy is also cause for some concern. That he considers 68 to be the year "at which the two numismatic sequences meet" is hardly a scientific assessment. In any event, it would seem to be dubious in the extreme that De Vaux's archaeology was precise enough to determine the difference between a year or two in stratification. Evidences of destructions and earthquakes aside, we are talking here of small coins supposedly suspended between stratification layers. If he and Milik can't even agree on a one hundred year gap concerning a pile of broken dishes and the wall adjacent to them, what are we to conclude about such supposed coin data? Finally, that coins do persist at Qumran, including some seventeen or more coins from the reign of Agrippa II (78-95) at Ein Feshka, is evidence that habitation did continue in the area in a not insignificant manner until the period of Bar Kochba and beyond. That De Vaux and his colleagues

it says nothing about the precise date of the fall of the monastery. To counter some of the objections I raise, it has been pointed out that a hoard of coins from the fifth year of the Jewish Revolt was found in the Masada excavations.[171] This is true, but many refugees from Jerusalem undoubtedly fled in a straight line across the Bethlehem plain to Masada after the fall of Jerusalem. In these circumstances, they probably would not have fled to Qumran, which would have afforded little or no protection (particularly if De Vaux and his supporters are correct in believing that its *buildings* were destroyed in 68 CE by the Roman army on its way up from Jericho to the siege of Jerusalem).

I would like to offer a counter example: no coins have yet been found from the fifth year of the Revolt on the Temple Mount. Are we, therefore, to conclude using the kind of reasoning one finds in De Vaux's theorizing that Jerusalem fell in 69 CE—obviously an untenable thesis? [172] Suppose, for instance, that in his digging Father De Vaux happened to miss a single coin from the fourth year of the Revolt, or that he had gone on to dig a little further before propounding his thesis? As it is, we are well into the third year of the Revolt with the coin data he provides. Father De Vaux responds, "I think we can be pardoned for not having dug up the whole hillside outside the walls in search of others"; I

---

do not choose to analyze in any significant way the import of these coins has, of course, to do with their own peculiar preconceptions and somewhat lopsided interpretation of the texts; just as the fact that I do, has to do with my own. This is where the battle must be joined, and I submit the presentation I have set forth in the above pages is as or more credible than theirs. When a coin appears, for instance, that does not suit De Vaux's preconceived parameters: e.g., the "very worn coin of Aelia Capitolina from the reign of Antonius Pius, CE 138-61", he sets it aside with the remark: it "must have been lost by a passer-by", p. 67. Elsewhere, he calls it a "stray". For his comments on other ubiquitous passers-by, see p. 45: "The few surface finds of coins, the date of which extend from the third century CE to the Turkish period, indicate nothing more than the passing of chance travelers".. On the basis of the evidence he presents he certainly is not entitled to say: "No manuscript of the caves can be later than June CE 68", *NTS*, p. 104. For remarks on De Vaux's sensationalist discovery of a coin from the Tenth Roman Legion, see below, p. 92.

[171]See De Vaux, *NTS,* pp. 102f. and 126. and Yadin, *op. cit. ,* pp. 108f. and 170f.

[172]B. Mazar, "The Archaeological Excavations near the Temple Mount" in *Jerusalem Revealed: Archaeology in the Holy City 1968-1974,* ed. Y. Yadin, Jerusalem, 1976, p. 32, where it is also noted only one coin from the first year has so far been found. Even if more subsequently do turn up, this makes the number of coins at Qumran and its environs from 68-69 appear quite substantial—even too substantial for simply the first three months of minting, another example of preconceptions pressing more from the data than the data legitimately allows.

for one am tempted to respond in the negative.[173] The same father in his zeal for his dating theories let it be broadcast to the scholarly world that a coin from the 10th Roman Legion had been found at Qumran, thereby sending colleagues like Cross into a frenzy of activity to trace the movements of this legion, since previously it had been assumed it was quartered somewhere else at the time.[174] When it was subsequently

---

[173]Strictly speaking, he makes this remark in regard to his search for Roman arrowheads, but the mentality is illustrative; and the problem, analogous; *NTS*, p. 101. One should remember, here, the existence of a certain amount of unidentified coins which De Vaux, not uncharacteristically, usually neglects to mention. In questioning Ya ᶜacov Meshorer on the matter of De Vaux's numismatic evidence, I was told that he himself had never seen or checked De Vaux's coins, nor did he know anyone else in Israel who had. No doubt the members of De Vaux's "team" have, but apparently the coins are now locked up at the École Biblique. Some, perhaps, might harbor doubts of the kind expressed by J. Allegro in his description (necessarily personal, but not on that basis as fanciful as some of his other well-advertised ideas) of the machinations surrounding the publication of the Copper Scroll; *op. cit.,* pp. 28-38.

Where the Copper Scroll itself is concerned, it is hardly worthwhile commenting on the contortions some scholars are willing to go through in order either to divorce it from "the Essenes" or render it harmlessly "allegorical" (Domitian and Trajan would have been pleased; cf. *E.H.* 3.19 and 3.33 where they learn *for the first time that* the Kingdom of God "is not of this world", and either "despised" their informants "as simpletons" or Pilate- like "could find no harm in them"). It is not that "the Essenes" were not interested in money; rather like James' "Jerusalem Community" (from which they *are* hardly to be distinguished), they were against "Riches" and class distinctions, an antagonism they derived, as we have seen above, from their extension of the "all Righteousness" commandment into the realm of economic equality. Like the early "Christians" in Palestine, they kept a common purse, and as in the case of the keen interest taken both by Paul and in Jerusalem in overseas fund-raising activities, they were no doubt mindful of the economic necessities of administering a fair-sized community. As with the War Scroll, where specialists ignore the direct evocation of the coming of the Messiah and "the Heavenly Host" on the clouds of Heaven (as per Jamesian proclamation and Paul in 1 Thess 3:13ff.) and see only allegory; here, once again, one group of specialists see only "allegory"—yet when figurative allusion *is* intended, as with "Zadok" and the Community Council as a "Temple" or "sweet fragrance" (again as per Pauline allusion), it is very often ignored. The impetus behind such flights from reality should be gradually becoming clear.

[174]See (however futile) Cross' complete discussion of this matter, pp.62ff., particularly n. 18. At this point he refers to Roth's and Driver's attempt "to lower the date of the fall of Khirbet Qumran to CE 73", protesting that "archaeological data" cannot be manipulated so "cavalierly", though in the same breath, he himself refers to Josephus' description of the fanatic resistance of "the Essenes". See, also. De Vaux's own description of the movements of this legion (presumably now minus the coin), pp. 38f. For the opposing view, see C. Roth, "Did Vespasian Capture Qumran", *PEQ*, 1959, pp. 122-29. De Vaux is also tight-lipped on the existence at Qumran of what appears to be a good- sized forge presumably because it, too, does not fit his stereotype of the "peaceful" Essenes. Cross, p. 69, neatly skips over it.

pointed out to De Vaux that the "X" on the coin in question was not the quartermaster's mark of the 10th Roman Legion, he was forced to retract his claim, but his retraction was hardly ever heard and one still sees the original contention repeated in many quarters as fact.[175]

Milik, who in so many ways is closely identified with De Vaux, in addition to disagreeing with him on whether the fallen wall and "broken dishes" reflect the Herodian destruction or that of the Jewish Revolt, has on the basis of coin data queried the master's evidence for the absolute abandonment of the monastery in the Herodian period.[176] One is permitted on the basis of coin data to say certain kinds of general things. as Milik does, but one is not permitted to say that the monastery was destroyed in 31 BCE, any more than one is permitted to say *anything more than the monastery was not deserted before 68/69 CE.* Certainly not the opposite. When making a case for the absolute abandonment of the site, one must take into account all information from other habitable locations around Qumran, since the sectaries probably lived in caves, "Rechabite" booths, or slept outside; not in "the monastery", which was reserved for communal activities of one kind or another. On the basis of the available coin data, one is not even permitted to assert that it was abandoned until 136 CE (a distinct possibility, since little else can explain why such an obvious hiding place as Cave IV was not disturbed even more than it was between 70 and 136 CE when the site was

---

[175]On the matter of the existence of this coin. De Vaux is quite insistent in *RB*, 61, 1954, pp. 232f. (followed, as always, faithfully by Cross; e.g., his comment concerning Milik's *wall* hypothesis: "De Vaux has reviewed the archaeological evidence with the writer, notably the pottery typology, and appears to have the stronger case"; p. 65). In *RB*, 63, 1956, p. 567, De Vaux, once again, treats this as a proven fact and speaks without reservation of the Roman conquest and occupation "by the soldiers of the X[e] Legion"(typical of his working method). As against this, let us review his humble retraction in *Archaeology*, p. 40 (given only in a footnote). "Recent discussions refer to the existence of a coin with the countersign of the Tenth legion, which, so it is held (by us?), was found at Khirbet Qumran and which I have in fact recorded. ... The mention of this was unfortunate for this coin does not exist. Faced with a coin which was incomplete and much oxidized I believed that I could read the remains of an X, the countersign of the Tenth Legion. But Fr. Spijkerman has convinced me that it is the cruciform mark which appears on the stern of a galley in the designs of the coins of Ashkelon of CE 72/73." To such embarrassments will the injudicious use of evidence and the precipitous rush to judgment invariably lead.

[176]See Milik, pp. 51ff., particularly p. 55, n. 1, where the whole matter is discussed in detail, including De Vaux's non-existent "wall". See De Vaux's discussion of this pp. 24ff. (including his "wall", p. 25).

inhabited by several unspecified groups).[177] As far as this continuing habitation goes, there is to be sure a diminution of coins after about 75 CE, and these coins until the Bar Kochba period are all pagan. After the fall of Jerusalem, however, no one would be using anything but pagan coins until the time of Bar Kochba and, as I have noted, there is a substantial distribution of coins at other sites like Ein Feshka even after 75 CE. What then can be said archaeologically speaking about the deposit of the scrolls in the caves and the final abandonment of the site? Almost nothing, only that we have a *terminus a quo* of 68 CE and a *terminus ad quern* probably of 134-136 CE.

---

[177]For habitation in the caves, see De Vaux, p. 107. Cross agrees, p. 64, n. 20. While at times referring to Cave IV as "the library" of the sect (elsewhere, p. 25, n. 29, as "the remnants of the great collection originally housed in the community center"); he attests, p. 27, n. 32, that the materials in the cave were probably in great disorder and had already begun to decompose even before their abandonment. He refers to the manuscripts in the upper caves as individually owned, without seeing the implication of this in regard to the calendar from Cave IV citing the names of Aemilius Scaurus (62 BCE) and Shlomzion (Alexandra, 76-67 BCE—which, of course, again he wishes to use as proof positive for an early dating for the identification of historical personages), *i.e.*, that the cave was already being used as a repository (or according to some theories a *genizah*) even before the final abandonment of the site. For habitation in the caves, see De Vaux, pp. 51ff. and 107. There is, of course, even the possibility that the Romans simply burned the monastery and never bothered going after the people in the caves above, a difficult operation in the best of circumstances, for as high as a pursuer wished to go, one could always retreat back higher even to the Bethlehem plain (cf. the terrible modernday experiences of Mrs. Pike, who after leaving her husband, was able to negotiate such a passage even in the dead of night; *Search,* London, 1970).

To sum up: no member of the Maccabee family can be identified in any way with the "Wicked Priest" and/or "the Spouter of Lies", or for that matter any other pejorative title in Qumran literature, not even the infamous Alexander Jannaeus who is very probably referred to, albeit retrospectively, in the Nahum *pesher* (an expression like "the furious young lion" is not necessarily pejorative). On the contrary, the Qumran community flourished during his reign and probably even under his tutelage as a training ground for young priests (and others) adept at pseudepigraphic and apocalyptic literature and opposed to the Pharisaic "gathering of traditions". Judas Maccabee himself is very likely one of these Righteous Teacher/*Zaddik*-types closely akin to the *Hassidic* authors of Daniel and Enoch (and very probably Jubilees and the Testament of Levi). He is the prototype of the warrior priestly messiah of the War Scroll, as he is most probably of John the Baptist, who exhibits characteristics akin to such a warrior high priest (despite the highly stylized and doctrinaire presentation of John in the Gospels). Some exceptions to these statements are necessary in the cases of the "Phariseeizing" Simon, early John, and Hyrcanus II, the attitudes of whom, for instance, vitiate the historical accuracy of 1 Macc (as do similar ones the historical accuracy of the Phariseeizing Josephus); but not to the extent of defamatory characterizations of what was otherwise an extremely popular priesthood among "the people".

The monastery was destroyed during the struggles from 63 BCE to 37 BCE (*prior to the earthquake of 31 BCE*) that ended up in the assumption of rule by Herod in Palestine, probably in 37 BCE by Herod himself on his way, like Vespasian thereafter, to invest Jerusalem. It was destroyed, as it was around 70 CE, because it took the part of the "Zadokite" priest line, understood as much in its esoteric as its exoteric signification, *i.e.*, "the Righteous Priesthood" (the "Melchizedek Priesthood" being a further variation on this theme), and certainly not because it adopted anything even remotely smacking of Pharisaic-style collaboration with Herodians and Romans. Qumran gives ample evidence of an attitude of priestly "zeal for the Law", and with it a certain amount of xenophobia—an attitude also discernible in the relations of the Jamesian "Jerusalem Church" with the Pauline "Gentile Mission". This zeal was most notably expressed in the condemnation of "fornication", by which Qumran specifically denotes marriage with a niece and divorce (practices condoned by Phariseeism and widely indulged in by Herodians), as a result of which not a few of the movement's leaders were executed. Such a monastery so close to the Herodian summer palaces near Jericho, in whose swimming pool the last Maccabean high priestly claimant was drowned, *was intolerable*.

The outbreak of the "Zealot" movement in the disturbances of 4 BCE to 7 CE is a misnomer foisted on an uncomprehending public (including the modern) by Josephus, since there was always a "Zealot movement" (or orientation) as such ever since the events portrayed in 1 Macc, 2 Macc, and Ecclesiasticus, and even before. The orientation, including a preference for martyrdom and suicide, is also in evidence among the supporters of Aristobulus and Antigonus in their struggles with the Romans and the latter's Herodian protégés.

Here, it is important to realize that terminologies like "Zealots", "Essenes", and "Pharisees" are often being used generically, not specifically.For instance, both Paul and Josephus describe themselves as "Pharisees", which they are most certainly, but primarily in a *generic* sense, or part and parcel of what Qumran would group under the heading "Seekers after Smooth Things" (*i.e.*, *those seeking accommodation with foreigners*). Though Josephus only applies the "Zealot" terminology as a pejorative after the killing of the high priest Ananus, he hints at it earlier in his original description of the followers of Judas and Saddouk. The Gospels use this terminology (non-pejoratively) as a cognomen for one of Jesus' closest collaborators ("Simon the Zealot" probably interchangeable with "Simeon bar Cleophas") and evoke it also in regard to Jesus' own attitude towards "Temple service". Even more significantly, Paul shows his awareness of the currency of the terminology, particularly where his opponents within the early "Christian" movement itself were concerned, by repeatedly playing on it in Ga 1:14 (cf. Acts 22:3) and 4:17, Ro 10:2, 2 Co 7:11 and 9:2, Phil 3:6, etc.; and Acts 21:20 unerringly designates the vast majority of James' 'Jerusalem Church' followers as *"zealous for the Law"*. The attitude clearly expresses the approach of Qumran and parallels the well-known "not one jot or tittle" kinds of allusions in Ja 2:10, Matthew's Sermon on the Mount, and Lk 16:17).[178]

---

[178]*N.b.* how this proposition is reflected in 1QS, viii-ix in the same passage where the term "zealous for the Law" actually occurs. In the context of "Cornerstone" and "Foundation" imagery, allusion to the central council as a "sin offering" ("a sweet fragrance") or "Temple", and the Is 40:3 allusion tradition applies to the activities of John the Baptist; it is categorically stated that "anyone from the Holy Community ("the Walkers in Perfection of the Way") ... who transgresses one jot from the *Torah* of Moses either *overtly or covertly is* to be expelled

What is new in 4 BCE is the appearance of the "Messianic" variation of this "Zealot" movement, which fits in very well with the promise made by Simon at the time of his "election" to the high priesthood, that the Maccabees would only continue in that dignity until a "Prophet" arose who would make a new determination (1 Macc 14:41). That Prophet seems very likely to have been John the Baptist, from the time of whose coming "the Men of Violence have not ceased attempting to take the Kingdom of Heaven by storm."[179] He plays a parallel role to, and

---

from the community" (transgression through negligence is to be punished by denial of *'table fellowship'*—italics mine).

In the "not one jot or tittle" passage in Lk 16 many of these parallel, by now familiar, themes come together, *i.e.*, antagonism to the Rich (directed against "the Pharisees", who are called "lovers of money"), the "heart" and "justification" allusions, the *Zaddik* style allusion to "the passing away of Heaven and Earth", and the reference to violent strife coincident with John's preaching "the Kingdom of Heaven" ("the *Messianic* Kingdom"). The passage culminates with a reference to "fornication", in particular "divorce" and "marrying divorcees" so characteristic of Herodian family practices (substituting the word "nieces" here would bring about an absolutely perfect convergence of themes; cf. CD, iv, 15ff.). These same themes also come together in Ja 2: 1ff.on "the supreme law of scriptural Righteousness" culminating in allusion to "fornication" and "divorce", a passage which is clearly at the root of the parallel succession of themes (and their subtle deformation) in Mt 5:15-48. For Qumran parallels to the use of "Men of Violence", see 1QpHab, ii, 6, 1QH, ii, 21, and the *'Arizei-Go'im* who take vengeance for the Righteous Teacher in 4QpPs 37, ii, 19; iv, 10. These last definitely parallel our "Niger" (one of Josephus' "Idumaean" leaders), "Silas", Helen's son Monobazus, etc.

[179]The subject of John's dating is fraught with pitfalls. Certainly he appears to be a much more prestigious individual than Jesus at the time of the latter's appearance. This, of course, carries with it an implication of some seniority in age. Mt 11:12f./Lk 16:16f. leave little doubt that these evangelists, anyhow, considered John's appearance to have been simultaneous with that of the "Zealot" movement, *i.e.*, with that of the mysterious "Saddouk" of Josephus' portraits (Rec 1.54 considers it simultaneous with "those called *Sadducees*" who "*separated themselves* from the community"—cf. 1QS, viii-ix and the theme of "withdrawing" in *ARN's* treatment of "Zadok and Boethus" —because they were "*more Righteous* than the others"—italics mine); and that a considerable amount of time elapsed between his coming and the coming of Jesus. This is reinforced by Mt 2:22-3:1, where there is the definite implication (obscured in translation) that John came in *the time of ArMellow* , a notion stated categorically in the long passage about the confrontation between "the *Man*" (who came "*in the Way of the Law*" and called upon "the Jews to reclaim their *freedom*") and "Simon *a scribe of Essene* origin" in the Slavonic, which makes no sense as an interpolation (italics mine).

While Luke's narrative contains an echo of valuable historical data, where it signals a genealogical link between John and Jesus, and the latter's priestly blood, it can hardly be considered very historical where the chronology of this relationship is concerned. We have already commented on the relationship of the Honi/Hanan the Hidden material of Talmudic tradition and Josephus to the Lucan narrative. That Luke thinks John's father is named Zechariah may even reflect information relating to Honi's martyrdom; on the other hand, John's father, in fact, might have been called Zechariah, which leads to interesting questions regarding the tomb by that name in the Kedron Valley next to the one usually ascribed to James. That the traditions

is possibly identical with, the mysterious "Saddouk", mentioned by Josephus in the *Antiquities,* from whose first appearance and/or appointment of Judas, the "Messianic" agitation begins in earnest. It does not cease until the destruction of the Temple in 70 CE, only to break out sporadically again with the executions of Simeon bar Cleophas and Jesus' brother Judas' two sons and in the widespread 115/116 CE "Messianic" disturbances in the Roman Empire under Trajan until the last "Star" Simeon bar Kosiba (perhaps not just figuratively, but physically related to earlier "Stars").[180]

relating to John in Matthew and Luke and the fragmented one concerning "Saddouk" Josephus is ultimately willing to reproduce in the *Antiquities* imply that there is a relationship between the two individuals John and "Saddouk" (without saying what that relationship is) is inescapable,

It will be objected at this point that to claim a connection between John and "Saddouk" is absurd, since Josephus doesn't know of it. Strictly speaking, this is true, but Josephus' knowledge of even Judas the Galilean (the Gaulonite/Sepphoraeus) is extremely shaky. He reproduces the circumstances relating to a rabbi, "Judas", together with another rabbi encouraging the tearing down of the "Temple Eagle" in about 4 BCE and Judas and Saddouk preaching the tax uprising in 6-7 CE as different events. But Judas Sepphoraeus of the earlier event is quite clearly equivalent to Judas the Galilean who broke into the armory at Sepphoris. The teaching ascribed to both is identical, though Josephus thinks Judas Sepphoraeus was burned alive with his colleague by Herod while "Judas the Galilean" went on functioning. Here, too, one should note that the Slavonic Josephus (if authentic, it was written perhaps 20 or more years before the *Antiquities*) does not appear to know the name of "the Wild Man" it portrays as coming in the time of Archelaus; while at the same time, like the *War* and unlike the *Antiquities,* makes no mention of a "Saddouk" contemporary with him. However, the doctrine it ascribes to him is once again *exactly* equivalent to that attributed to Judas and Saddouk in the *Antiquities* and Judas Sepphoraeus in the *War*; cf. *War* 1.33.2 with *Ant.* 18.1.1.

[180]The whole question of the physical relationships of these "Messianic" families is something which remains to be investigated. The parallel developments of Judas' (also from Galilee) and Jesus' families, including even *preventive* (cf. Jn 11:50) and the almost contemporary crucifixions of "Jacob and Simon" (equivalent also to the names of two of Jesus' brothers—the second of whom, Eusebius insists, "won the prize of an end like that of the Lord") and the *stoning* of Menachem, an event both parnllel to and contemporary with the stoning of Jesus' brother James (not to mention the additional parallel crucifixions of the sons of Jesus' third brother Judas) must give historians some pause. That bar Kosiba, too, seems to come from the area of the Messianic villages, "Nazara" and "Chochaba" either in Galilee or Gaulonitus; *E. H.* 1.17.14 (cf. the modern city in Southern Lebanon of Kaukabe) must also present food for thought. That the documents at our disposal, characterized as they are by individual polemical aims, do not tell us of such a relationship is no reason for dismissing it *a priori.* We have already seen that Karaite documents with differing polemical aims do testify, not only that Jesus followed "Zadok" and was a "Righteous Man", but that their doctrines, and those of Anan *ben David's,* were identical. Others, while late, tell us of the identity of the Sadducees with the *Zaddikim* (or "Righteous Ones"), a term, they claim, the rabbis purposefully corrupted into *"Zaddukim".*

The "Messianic" movement, called in Antioch in the late 40's or early 50's "Christian" according to Luke in Acts, appears at precisely the moment one would expect it to, following Herod's total destruction of the Maccabean family including Miriamne and her two sons, her brother Aristobulus, and her grand uncle Hyrcanus II. Henceforward, secular rule will be accorded, at least on a popular level, only to Israelite messiahs or "sons of David" (Herod always one step ahead of his adversaries manages to equip himself with a relatively mild one from Babylon, the legendary Hillel). It also expresses itself in a series of "Messianic" pretenders from 4 BCE to 66 CE from Judas the Galilean to "the magician" Theudas, "the Egyptian" mistaken for Paul, and Menachem son or grandson of Judas, most of whom attempt to lead their followers out to the wilderness for a reaffirmation of the Deuteronomic Covenant of "Damascus", or purify the Temple in the manner of Judas Maccabee (and Ezra). The high-priestly messiah (for as in the days of Zerubbabel and Jesus ben Yehozedek and Joshuah and Eleazar, a dual Messiahship appears to have been envisioned) was to be elected by lot on the basis of *Perfect Righteousness.*

This process is probably to be seen reflected in the events centering about the lives of Jesus and his brother James (and Simeon bar Cleophas thereafter), as much as it is in those centering about Judas Maccabee and his predecessor Onias III two centuries earlier. This *election,* which was demanded in 4 BCE probably on the basis of Judas' earlier elections, was actually carried out in 68 CE with the selection, not insignificantly, of *Phineas the Stonecutter.*[181] Josephus rails against the meanness of the blood and social status of this man in a manner reminiscent of the way in which Eusebius rails against the "meanness" of the Christological conceptions of the *Ebionim* ("the Poor").[182] The reflection of such an

---

[181]We have developed this "Stone" and "Cornerstone" imagery above, pp. 30 and 71. It relates to the "Fortress", "Wall", "Protection", and "Pillar" imagery *vis-a-vis* the Righteous Teacher, the central priestly triad at Qumran, and James and the central three in early Church tradition. See, also, its development in the "Noah" and Phineas" chapters of the *Zohar* (including reference to both "Primal Adam" and "Pillar" ideologies; 59bff., 65a, 70aff., 76a, 213aff., 218a-b, 231a, and 241a). See, too, its further variation in both Paul's and Qumran's "laying the foundations" and "building" imagery, above, .p. 71. For a corresponding Pauline reference to "the Primal Adam" ideology, see 1 Co 15:45. For community as "city" imagery, see Mt 5:14 and Heb 11.

[182] Cf. *E. H.* 3.27.1 Observing that the Ebionites *"evince great zeal to observe every detail of the Law",* he complains that "they cherish low and mean opinions concerning Christ", whom they regard "as a *poor* and *common* man *justified through his advances in virtue, nothing* more" (italics mine).

election is probably, also, to be seen in "the Messianic acclamation" of Jesus upon his triumphal entry into Jerusalem, who in good Maccabean style proceeds directly to the business of purifying the Temple. It is also to be seen in the *election* of *the twelfth apostle* to replace "Judas Iscariot in Acts 1:15ff.—a probable Lucan counterfeit of James' episcopal election as successor to his brother. The confession of the sins of *the people* by such a priestly "Righteous One" in the Holy of Holies on *Yom Kippur,* a kind of "Noahic" atonement, could alone be considered soteriologically efficacious, particularly in eschatological anticipation of "the end of the last times" (*ha-kez ha-aharon*). It is the esoteric approach to "the Zadokite Priesthood", developed at Qumran in the context of "Righteous Teacher"/*Zaddik* "Zadok" theorizing, that provides us with the conceptuality necessary for understanding this process. It is at least one such "Zadokite" atonement (paralleled as well in the *somewhat obscure* notice in the Habakkuk *pesher* about difficulties between the Righteous Teacher and the Wicked Priest over events on *Yom Kippur*) which very likely ultimately leads to James' judicial murder on a charge of blasphemy (*i.e.*, pronouncing the ineffable name of God), the only recorded incidence of an execution of this kind (aside from that of the largely imaginary Stephen) since that of his predecessor—and putative forbear—Honi one hundred and twenty-five years before.[183]

---

[183]See, for instance *Zohar* 195a on "the prayer of the Poor Man" (including how "King David"—the Messiah—"placed himself among the Poor", considered coextensive with "the Pious" and designated as "those willing to sacrifice themselves and their lives for sanctification of the Name"). Cf. also Heb 7:26ff. and the Righteous Teacher as high priest in 1QpHab, ii,8, 4QpPs 37, ii, 18, iii, 15, and iv, 7, and probably 4QpHos[b], i, 3. Once the inherent fallacies in supposedly secure archaeological and palaeographic "results" are properly appreciated, it is a fairly straightforward matter to make a point-for-point link-up between the events of James' life and those of the Righteous Teacher's in CD, i and vii-viii, 1QpHab, and 4QpPs 37.

GLOSSARY OF HEBREW TERMS

I have preferred simple Hebrew transliterations and, therefore, have abjured diacritical markings. Beginning alephs also were not transliterated. In transliterating the Hebrew letter *tsadi*, I used "*z*", despite confusions in transliterating *zayin*, in order to conserve the common spelling, of expressions like *Zaddik*, Zadok, Nazoraean, etc. (there are several *tsadis*, but few *zayins*). I preferred the double "*s*" in *Hassidim*.

abeit-galuto, a defective expression in 1QpHab,xi.6 connected with the arrest/destruction of the Righteous Teacher. While obscure and usually translated "House of his Exile", it most likely has a different meaning altogether relating to the Wicked Priest's *judicial conspiracy to destroy* to Righteous Teacher, *i.e.*, "he pursued (after) the Righteous Teacher to destroy *him* in his hot anger in his *beit-galut*"—meaning, "his *beit-din*"/"*beit-mishpat*" or "*his* guilty trial" (italics mine).

Aharonim/*Dor ha-Aharon*, the Last/Last Generation; the opposite of *ha-Rishonim*, the First. Just as the first Covenant was associated with the *Rishonim*, the New Covenant was associated with the *Aharonim* of the Last Times; *n.b.*, how Paul refers to himself as "last" in I Co 15:8, a nuance not lost in N.T. parodies of the expression; cf. also *ha-kez ha-aharon* (the last end) and *aharit ha-yamim* (the last days).

ᶜam / *ᶜamim*, people/peoples. In the Habakkuk *Pesher* and Zadokite Document referring to people (primarily Gentiles) "led astray" by a guilty establishment and its "ways" (cf. CD.viii.8, 16, and 47 and 1QpHab,viii.5, 11, and ix.5). Particularly the plural has the sense of "Herodians," *i.e.*, "the Kings of the peoples" (CD,viii.10); cf. also *yeter ha-ᶜamim*—"other Gentiles"—for Romans below.

ᶜamal, works, *ᶜamalam*, their works; equivalent to "suffering works" or "works with soteriological force" as per the usage in Is 53:11f. (where it occurs in conjunction with other familiar Qumranisms such as *Daᶜat*, *Rabbim*, *nephesh*, *Zaddik*, etc.). In 1QpHab,viii.2 and x.12, used in relation to both " Jamesian" works and "Pauline" works, the former (with *amanatam* below) in the context of eschatological exegesis of Hab 2:4.; the latter, the "empty works" of "the Liar"/"Empty Man".

amanatam, their faith. A pregnant expression in 1QpHab,viii.2 found together with *ᶜamalam* in the exegesis of Hab 2:4's "the Righteous shall live by his faith" and interpreted to mean, their faith in the Righteous Teacher; in ii.1 and ii.4 the usage *he'eminu* ("believed"/"did not believe") is an ironic reference to the central focus of the teaching of the "Man of Lying"/"Jesting".

ᶜamod / ᶜomdim, stand up/standing; usually translated in Qumran texts as come/ coming, but evoking Ez 37:10's "they stood up" and carrying something of the connotation of "be resurrected"; cf. precisely this use in Dn 12:13 and its reflection in Lam.R,ii.3.6. Found in the Zadokite Document both in the context eschatological exegesis of the Zadokite Covenant and allusion to the Messianic return; for the latter, see also Lam.R, intro, xxiv, applying this usage to the "return of Moses and the Patriarchs."

ᶜAni (pl. *ᶜAniyyim / ᶜAnavim*), also *ᶜAnavei-Arez*, the Meek or Downtrodden; one of the sect's several interchangeable forms of self-designation. The equivalent of similar N.T. allusions; used synonymously with *Ebionim*, the Poor, and *Dallim*.

Anshei-(H)amas, Unruly Men or Men of Violence; a synonym of *ᶜArizim / ᶜArizei-Go'im* below and most likely "the Men of *War*" in CD,viii.37 ("who walked with the Man of Lying"). In 1QpHab,viii. 11 the allusion is to the guilty wealth which the Wicked Priest "collects" through them.

Anshei-Hesed, the Men of Piety or Pious Ones equivalent to the *Hassidim*; mistranslated as "Famous Men" in Ecclesiasticus.

Anshei Kodesh-Tamim, the Men of Perfect Holiness: equivalent to such other Qumran usages characterizing communal membership as the Men of the Perfection of Holiness (*Anshei-Tamim ha-Kodesh*), the Perfect of the Way (*Tamimei-Derech*), and the Poor Ones of Piety (*Ebionei-Hesed*); cf. "Perfection of Holiness" in 2 Co 7:1.

ᶜArizim, the Violent Ones; connected in 1QpHab,ii.6 and 10f. with "the Man of Lying", and "Covenant-Breakers"; cf. the parallel New Testament expression "Men of Violence" and the *Anshei-(H)amas / ᶜamim* above.

ᶜArizei-Go'im, "the Violent Ones of the Gentiles"; in 4QpPs 37,ii.20 and iv.10 they play an analogous role to Josephus' "Idumaeans" and pay back the Wicked Priest for his destruction of the Righteous Teacher.

ᶜAvlah, Evil or Sinning; sometimes translated as "Lying" as in "the town of Lying" erected by the Liar in 1QpHab,x.6 or the imagery of 1QS,iv,9-17.

ᶜavodah, work in the sense of "service" or "mission". To be distinguished from the more soteriological *ᶜamal* above and *maᶜaseh/maᶜasim* below. Often used when discussing the "mission" or "service" of the Liar (cf. *ᶜavodat-shavo*—worthless work; 1QpHab,x.11 and *ᶜavodat-tum'ah*—work of pollution; 1QS,iv.10) and those breaking off association with him in CD,viii.30, 1QS,viii.22, and ix.8; see also *lᶜ ovdam*, serving them (*i.e.,* serving idols) in 1QpHab,xii.14.

balla^c /Bela^c, as used in the Temple Scroll, varying the language of Nu 4:20 and Job 20:15 and playing on all the "swallowing" language at Qumran from Belial to *leval^{c}o/leval^{c}am/teval^{c}enu* below to produce "Bele^c", a circumlocution for Herodians; important for linking the notice in 11QT,xlvi.10 to its historical setting—*the Temple Wall incident directed against Agrippa II.* Cf. Bela^c an *Edomite King* in Ge 14:2ff. and 36:32f. and its variations "Belial" .(CD,iv.14f. and 1QH,iv.10) and "Balaam" (Re 2:14ff., 2 Pe 2:15, and Jude—the first three all making allusion to "nets" and "snares"; the last, "food sacrificed to idols"). One should also note the further adumbration of this terminology "Benjamin" and compare it to Paul's claims of "Benjaminite" ancestry.

Beit ha-Mishpat, "House of Judgment"; in 1QpHab,viii.2 used in conjunction with ^{c}*amalm, amanatam,* "doing *Torah*", and "being saved" in the eschatological exegesis of Hab 2:4. X.3 concretizes it as the actual *decision* of eschatological Judgment of "fire and brimstone" which God delivers through His Elect "in the midst of many nations" on all Gentiles and Jewish backsliders; cf. *Mishpatei-Esh* in x.13, 2 Pe 2:9, Jude 15, Re 20:4ff., etc., and *Mishpat, Yom ha-Mishpat* below.

Beit-Yehudah, the House of Judah or "Jews"; as used in 1QpHab,viii.2 to be distinguished from the Ephraim usage in 4QpNah, *i.e.,* Jews, as opposed to Gentile *nilvim* misled by a Lying teacher. Together with ^{c}*Osei-Torah*, it restricts the soteriological efficacy of the exegesis of Hab 2:4 in a two-fold manner, *i.e., only to Jews*, and of these, only to *Torah*-Doers; cf. too its use in the eschatological exegesis of Ez 44:15 in CD,iv.11.

be^{c}orot, "in skins" (also possibly beasts/burnt offerings); as used in 11QT,xlvii.13ff., always connected to "things" or "food sacrificed to idols", a key element in *James'* directives to overseas communities as conserved in Acts 15:29 and 21:25 (in Acts 15:20, "the pollutions of the idols") and reflected in 1 Co 8:1ff., 10:19ff., 2 Co 6:16 (*n.b.,* the specific reference to "Belial" and "light" and "dark" imagery), and Re 2:14ff. (*n.b.,* the attribution of the license to consume such "food" to "Balaam" and the allusions accompanying it to "snare" and "fornication" as in CD,iv.13ff. In regard to this last, one should note the possible play on "Be^{c}or", the father at once of both "Bela^c and "Balaam". This kind of word-play is known in b. San 105a).

beza^c, profiteered, as in 1QpHab,ix.5 on how "the last priests of Jerusalem profiteered from the spoils—or looting—of the peoples"(^{c}*amim, i.e.,* Herodians and "Violent Gentiles" generally); cf. the same usage in CD,viii.7.

Bnei-Zadok, the sons of Zadok; usually considered to imply genealogical descent, however as used at Qumran, particularly in the Zadokite Document, incorporating a play on the meaning of the root *Z-D-K* and carrying thereby a figurative sense; equivalent to many parallel usages like "sons of Light", "sons of Truth", "sons of Righteousness", etc.; when used eschatologically, also equivalent to N.T. expressions like "sons of the Resurrection"—even "sons of God".

Bogdim, Traitors, an important expression in the *pesharim* and the Zadokite Document, denoting those within the community who "departed from the Way" no longer following the Law (CD,i.12f.). In 1QpHab,ii.1ff. referred to with the Man of Lying as "Covenant-Breakers" and synonymous with "the House of Absalom and those of their persuasion" in v.8ff. These did not "believe" what they heard "*in the end of days*" from the Righteous Teacher. That these include "Violent Gentiles" is made clear from the *ᶜArirei-Goʾim* usage and a comparison of CD,viii.4f. with viii.16; cf. N.T. inversions/parodies.

Cohanei-Yerushalaim ha-Aharonim, in 1QpHab,ix.4f. "the last priests of Jerusalem" who "profiteered from the spoil of the peoples" and whose wealth would be given over in the last days to the army of the *Kittim*; probably reflective of first-century euphemisms like "high priests"/"chief priests".

Daᶜat, Knowledge, a basic concept at Qumran very much connected with the terminology of Is 53:11 and the process of justification generally; in some vocabularies *Gnosis*.

Dal (pl. *Dallim*), the Poor or the Meek, related to *ᶜAni* above and *Ebion* below.

Derech, "the Way", related. to 1QS,viii-ix's exegesis of Is 40:3, Noahic "Perfection" notation, "straightening" allusions, and New Testament "Way" allusions; often inverted when "the way of the people", the way "of the Kings of the peoples", and `` the Ways of the Traitors", "Abominations", "Uncleanness", "fornication", etc. are at issue.

Ebion (pl. *Ebionim*), the Poor; in 1QpHab,xii.3ff. related to the predatory activities of the Wicked Priest and his destruction of the community's leadership. Another of the sect's interchangeable forms of self-designation, as well as the name applied by the early Church to "Jewish Christians".

Ebionei-Hesed, the Poor Ones of Piety (1QH,v.23); another of the sect's interchangeable forms of self-designation combining, like such parallel usages as *Tamimei-Derech, Nimharei-Zedek, Anshei Kodesh-Tamim*, etc., two fundamental notations.

Emet, Truth, a basic concept at Qumran; together with *Hesed, Zedek*, and *Daᶜat* perhaps the most basic; often used in conjunction with *Derech*, Foundation and Cornerstone imagery, and *Daᶜat*. An expression like "sons of Your Truth" parallels formulations . like "sons of Light", "sons of Zadok", "sons of Hesed", and corresponding N.T. allusions.

ᶜezah / *ᶜAzat ha-Yahad*, council or Community Council, with interesting resonances with "the Jerusalem Council"; also having the connotation of "their approach" or "their persuasion" as *ᶜazatam* in 1QpHab,v.10.

ger-nilveh, resident alien. An important allusion playing on the sense of "joining" or "being attached to" of *nilveh*. Its use in 4QpNah,ii.9 prepares the way for a clearer understanding of the exegesis of "the Zadokite statement" in CD,iv and elucidation of "the *Peta 'ei*-Ephraim" in 4QpNah,iii.5f.; see *nilvu/nilvim* below.

geviot , sometimes translated "body", but actually "corpse"; a pivotal usage for correctly identifying the Wicked Priest in 1QpHab,ix.1f.'s "they inflicted the Judgments of Evil by committing on him the scandals of evil pollutions in taking vengeance on the *flesh of his corpse*" (italics mine).

hamato, his wrath; in 1QpHab,x1.5f., the "angry wrath" with which "the Wicked Priest pursued the Righteous Teacher." Though thought in xi.14f. to relate to his "drunkenness", the allusion, which plays on and inverts xi.6's imagery of "anger" and "consuming", is to that divine "cup of wrath" which would be "poured out" upon the Wicked Priest: Cf. Re 14:9f. in precisely this vein: "He shall drink the wine of God's wrath poured unmixed into the cup of his anger, and he shall be tormented in fire and brimstone..." For the latter image see 1QpHab,x.5 (also relating to the Wicked Priest): "He will judge him with fire and brimstone."

Hassidim, literally "the Pious Ones"; the original behind the expression Hassidaeans and probably the basis of the Greek transliteration "Essenes"; cf. *Anshei-Hesed* and the *Ebionei-Hesed* above.

Hesed, Piety; the first part of the *Hesed* and *Zedek* dichotomy, descriptive of man's relationship to the Deity, *i.e.*, "thou shalt love the Lord thy God". Taken with the second, "loving one's neighbor" or Righteousness towards one's fellow man, the two comprise the sum total of "the commands of *all Righteousness*" and epitomize the opposition ideological orientation; the root of the terminology *Hassidim*.

hittif, pouring out/spouting; as in CD,viii.13's "of Lying". For CD,i.14f. the Man of Jesting (or "the Comedian") "poured out on Israel the waters of Lying leading them astray in a void without a Way", which combines "Lying", "jesting", "spouting", and "leading astray" imageries with inverted allusion to "wilderness" and "Way" terminologies; see *Mattif/Mattif ha-Cazav*.

hok, statute or Law; at the heart of 1QS,viii-ix's exposition of Is 40:3's "Way in the wilderness", "the Way" being "the study of the Law". The phrase, "zealous for the Law", specifically occurs in ix.23 accompanied by reference to "the Day of Vengeance"; cf. *kin'at Mishpetei-Zedek* in iv.4. N. b. , CD,i.20's *yapheiru hok* to describe the "pursuit after" the *zaddik*—the synonym of 1QpHab,ii.6's *Mephirei ha-Brit* echoed too in 1QpHab,viii.17.

hon, Riches/wealth; one of CD,iv.17ff.'s "three nets of Belial"; in CD,vi.14ff. and viii.4ff. (including "fornication" imagery) directed against the establishment (probably Herodian); in 1QpHab,viii.10ff. and ix.4ff. related to the "gathering"/"robbing the Poor"/"profiteering from the Gentiles" activities of the Last Priests/Wicked Priest.

lechalah / lechalot, the language of destruction, applied in 1QpHab,xii.5f. to the conspiracy to destroy the Righteous Teacher and the Poor, *i.e.*, "as he plotted to destroy the Poor", so too would "God condemn him to destruction"; in this context synonymous with *leval^co/leval^cam*.

leval^co / leval^cam / teval^cenu, the language of "swallowing"/"destruction"; applied in 1QpHab,xi.5ff. to the confrontation between the Righteous Teacher and the Wicked Priest and the destruction of both. Its resonances with the Bela^c/Belial equivalence are purposeful, not to mention the "*hayil balla^c*" of 11QT,xlvi.10/Job 20:15 (*i.e.*, "swallowing wealth"). Cf. also "Balaam" as "swallower of the people" in b. San 105a. In this sense, all aspects of the *B-L-^c* usage were considered illustrative of the activity most characterizing the Herodian establishment, *i.e.*, "swallowing".

losif, the language of gathering, applied in 1QpHab,viii.12 to the Wicked Priest's/last-high priests' "gathering Riches" and "profiteering from the spoils of the Peoples" and a consonant harvest of blame.

ma'as, reject/deny/speak derogatorily about; a catchword for the legal posture of the Lying Spouter and those of his persuasion; in 1QpHab,v.11f. the former "rejected"/"spoke derogatorily about the Law in the midst of their entire congregation." Cf. the parallel, more general, use in i.10, 1QS,iii.51., and CD,vii.9, viii.18f., and 31f.

ma^casim / ma^caseihem, works/their works; generally works of the Law, paralleling the usage in the Letter of James and the use of *^camal* in 1QpHab and Is 53:11. Also used with inverted sense as in 1QpHab,x.11f.'s the Liar's "instructing them in Lying works" (*ma^casei-Sheker*) and 1QS,iv.23's *ma^casei-remiyyah*; also see *ma^casei-To^cevot* in 1QpHab,xii.8.

Ma‘oz, Protection or Shield; in 1QH,vii.8ff. and 23ff. related to Fortress, strengthening, building, Wall, Foundations, Stone, and Cornerstone imagery; probably the basis of the *Oblias*/"Protection"/"Bulwark" allusion applied to James in early Church testimony and related to "Stone" and "Pillar" imagery in the N.T. generally.

Mattif/Mattif ha-Cazan, the Spouter/Pourer Out of Lying; a variation of the *Ish ha-Cazav* (the Man of Lying) and the *Ish ha-Lazon* (the Man of Jesting/ Scoffing/Comedian) imagery at Qumran, incorporating plays on what appear to have been his characteristic activities, pouring out words or waters (even perhaps speaking with his "Tongue" or "in tongues") and Lying.

Mephirei ha-Brit, Covenant-Breakers; synonymous with the *Bogdim*/House of Absalom in 1Qp Hab,ii.1ff. and v.8ff., and related to the "breaking" charge in Ez 44:7ff. and Ja 2:10ff. The opposite of 1QS,v.2ff.'s "sons of Zadok" as "Covenant-Keepers".

Migdal, Tower/Fortress/Bulwark; in 1QH.vii.8ff. applied together with the language of "Strength", "Stone", "Wall", "Cornerstone", building and Foundations imagery to the person of the Righteous Teacher.

Mishpat, Judgment; used in 1QpHab,v.4ff. in conjunction with *Beit ha-Mishpat* above; expressive of that Judgment God would make "through the hands of His Elect" (*i.e.*, "the Bnei-Zadok" in CD,iv.3f.) on all Gentiles and backsliding Jews; cf. *Beit ha-Mishpat* above, *Yom ha-Mishpat* below, and 1QS,iv.4's *kin‘at Mishpetei-Zedek* ("zeal for the Judgments of Righteousness"—the opposite of 1QpHab.ix. 1's *Mishpetei-Rish‘ah*).

Moreh-Zedek/Moreh ha-Zedek, the Righteous Teacher or more literally, the Teacher of Righteousness.

nephesh-Zaddik (see also *nephesh-Ebion* and *nephesh-‘Ani,*), the soul of the *Zaddik*; terminology remounting to Is 53:11f. paralleling heart and body imagery generally at Qumran and in Ez 44:7ff., etc. Cf. CD,i,20 where *nephesh-Zaddik* is used synonymously with *Moreh ha-Zedek* and *nephesh-Ebion* and *nephesh-Ani* in 1QH,ii.32, iii.25, v.6, etc.

niddah / niddat, unclean/uncleanness; often used at Qumran in conjunction with the imagery of "*tum‘ah*" (pollution), as for instance in 1QpHab,viii.13, CD,xii.1f., 1QS,iv.10 ("*darchei-niddah*", replete with "lying" and "fornication" imagery), and the Temple Scroll generally.

nilvu / nilvim, joined/Joiners; evoked in 4QpNah,iii.5 in relation to the *Peta’ei*-Ephraim and in eschatological exegesis of Ez 44:15 in CD,iv.3 (also echoed in 4QpNah,ii.9's *gernilveh*). Es 9:27 concretizes it as connotative of *Gentiles* "attaching themselves" to the Jewish Community, which in turn helps elucidate the Ephraim/City of Ephraim/Simple Ones of Ephraim usages. Probably synonymous in other vocabularies with the terminology "God-Fearers".

Nozrei ha-Brit / Nozrei Brito, the Keepers of His Covenant; cf. Ps 25:8ff., and Ps 119, where the expression is used synonymously with *Shomrei ha-Brit*—the qualitatively precise definition of "the sons of Zadok" in 1QS,v.2ff.; also *britcha yinzor* in Deut 33:9 and 4QTest. The allusions *Nozrim* (Hebrew terminology denoting "Christians") and "Zadokites" can be viewed, therefore, as variations on a theme.

ᶜoseh ha-Torah / ᶜOsei ha-Torah, doing *Torah*/the Doers of the *Torah*; the expression *ᶜOsei ha-Torah* limits the soteriological scope of the exegeses of Hab 2:3 and 2:4 in 1QpHab,vii.11ff. to *Torah-Doers in the House of Judah*. "Doers"/ "doing"/"Breakers"/"keeping" usages are also reflected in the language of Ja 1:22ff. *ᶜOsei ha-Torah* defines xii.4f.'s "*Petaʾei*-Yehudah," distinguishing it from 4QpNah,iii's "*Petaʾei*-Ephraim" and tying it to the "Keepers of the Covenant" terminology. The root of *maᶜaseh/maᶜasim*.

Petaʾei-Yehudah / *Petaʾei*-Ephraim, the Simple Ones of Judah/Simple Ones of Ephraim; in 1QpHab,xii.4f. the former are the "*Torah*-doing" community rank and file. In 4QpNa,iii.5f. the latter must be associated with Gentile *nilvim*, who, it is hoped, "will once again join themselves to Israel" (cf. *ger-nilveh* in ii.9). In 8f. they are associated with being led astray by "Deceivers... teaching their Lies, a Tongue of their Lies, deceitful lips, and misleading the Many". Cf. also the use of "Little Ones" and "Samaritans" in the N.T.

Rabbim, the Many, used at Qumran to designate the rank and file of the community, who were presumably the beneficiaries of the justifying activities (whether via suffering works or imparted Knowledge) of the Righteous Teacher/Community Council; the usage goes back to the vocabulary of Is 53:11E—cf. also its use in the Dn 12 passage noted above. Its sense is reversed in 1QpHab,x.11's "wearing out Many with worthless work" and 4QpNah,ii.8's "leading Many astray" both relating to activities of the Liar.

Rashaᶜ / Reshaᶜim, Evil/Evil Ones; usually connected in the *pesharim* to the Wicked Priest, but sometimes, as in 1QpHab,v:9f., to the Man of Lying.

remiyyah, deceit; in 1QS,viii.22 and ix.8 tied to covert infractions of the Law and in 1QS,viii.22ff., ix.8ff. (reflected in CD,viii.30) to consonant bans on work, table fellowship, or common purse; cf. "deceit"/"deceitful works" in 1QS,iv.9 and 23 and "deceitful lips" in 4QpNah,ii.8.

Rishonim, the First; to be viewed in conjunction with allusions to "the Last" and resonating with N.T. parodies of both; in CD,i,4ff. and iv.9, specifically denoting the *Zaddikim* of old (or "the Forefathers") with whom God made the first Covenant.

Ruah-Emet, in 1QS,iv.21 (amid allusion to baptism, etc.), Spirit of Truth; a variation of the language of the Holy Spirit. In viii.12 this relationship to "the Holy Spirit" is made explicit. Also to be viewed in the context of several contraries more or less typifying "the Spirit" of the Lying Scoffer, *i.e.*, Lying, fornication, insults, Evil, Darkness, etc.; cf. 1QS,iv.9ff.

shavo, worthless; in 1QpHab,x.10f. used to characterize the community's perception of the Liar's activities, *i.e.*, "the worthless city" and the "worthless service with which he tires out Many" (cf. Ja 1:26 on his "worthless religion", "heart of deceit", and "Tongue").

Sheker/ma°asei-Sheker, Lying/works of Lying; the terminology is part and parcel of the lying/spouting/boasting imagery at Qumran. Often accompanied by allusion to "the Tongue" or "lips" and used in conjunction with reference to "works," baptismal imagery, or "leading astray".

Shomrei ha-Brit, Keepers of the Covenant, 1QS,iv.2ff.'s qualitatively precise definition of "the Sons of Zadok", harking back to allusions in Ez 44:6ff, and Psalms; *n.b.* , the parallel represented by *Nozrei-Brito* and the contrast represented by *Mephirei ha-Brit*.

Tamim/Tamimim, the Perfect; also sometimes, Perfection—a fundamental notion at Qumran based on references to Noah in Gn 6:9 as "Righteous and Perfect in his generation"; the relationship to parallel N.T. notation (cf. Mt 5:48, 19:21, Ja 1:4, 17, 25, 2:22, etc.) is intrinsic.

To°evot, Abominations—*darchei-To°evot* in 1QpHab,viii.12f. Here and in xii.8, those of the Wicked Priest, particularly his pollution of the Temple/Temple Treasure through violent tax-collecting and "robbing the Poor". Part and parcel of the language of "polluting the Temple"/"breaking the Covenant" in Ez 44:6ff.; in the Temple Scroll, related to forbidden foods (xlviii.6), marriage with nieces (lxvi.11ff.; also referred to as "*niddah*"), and Gentiles (lx.17ff. and lxii.16).

Tom, Perfect/Perfection; *Tom-Derech/Tamimei-Derech*. Perfection of the Way/the Perfect of the Way; also linked to expressions based on Is 40:3 like *Yisharei-Derech*, "the Straight" or "Upright of the Way".

tum'ah/teme' ha-Mikdash/yitame' et Mikdash-El, pollution/pollution of the Sanctuary of God, generally tied to a demand for "separation" (cf. 11QT,xlvi.9ff. and CD,iv.17ff.); with *To°evot* part and parcel of the charges relating to the admission of foreigners into the Temple in Ez 44:7, as well as in consonant "Zadokite"/"Zealot" ideologies. As used in 1QpHab,xii.8f., directed against the Wicked Priest who did not "circumcize the foreskin of his heart" (Ez 44:9), and in viii.13, 1QS,v.19f., and CD,xii.1f. linked to *niddah.*

yazdik-zaddik (*yazdik*u-*zaddikim*), the "justification" ideology at Qumran based on the terminology of Is 53:11 (and to a lesser extent, Is 5:23); cf. also its use in Dn 12:3 above and see *Zaddik* and *zedakah* below.

yazzilem/yazzilum, save them/be saved; the language of salvation, associated with the language of the "House of Judgment"/"Day of Judgment". The first in 1QpHab,viii.1f.'s exegesis of Hab 2:4 refers to the "salvation of the Righteous"; the second in xii.14ff., the condemnation of "the servants of idols (Gentile idolaters) and Evil Ones" (here backsliding Jews; cf. 2 Pe 2:9 and 3:7).

yehalluhu, pollute it. This plural usage is attached to the singular allusion to Belaᶜ in 11QT,xlvi.11 and forms the background to "the Zadokite Statement" in Ez 44:6ff., where the ban on "bringing strangers uncircumcized in heart and flesh into My Temple to pollute it" is enunciated.

yeter ha-ᶜamim, the other or additional ones of the Gentiles; in 1QpHab,ix.7 specifically identified with "the Army of the *Kittim*", *i.e.*, the Romans; see *ᶜamim.*

yikboz, gathering; in 1QpHab,viii.11 and ix.5 having to do with the *darchei-To'evot* or "gathering" activities of the Wicked Priest/Last Priests via the instrument of Unruly Gentiles; in this context "gathering" wealth—see also *losif.*

Yom ha-Mishpat, Day of Judgment, linking up with the usages *Mishpat/Beit ha-Mishpat* and *yazzilem/yazzilum* and used eschatologically in 1QpHab,xii.14 and xiii.2f., *i.e.*, on the Day of Judgment God would destroy all the Idolaters and Evil Ones from the Earth".

Zaddik/Zaddikim, the Righteous/the Righteous One(s); the terminology is highly developed in Jewish *Kabbalah* and Jewish resurrection theory. Via the Is 53:11 *yazdik-zaddik* conceptuality, the basis of "justification" theorizing, Qumran's esoteric exegesis of Ez 44:15, and the "purist Sadducee" movement.

zamam/zammu, conspired; in 1QpHab,xii.6 relating to the Wicked Priest's judicial conspiracy to destroy the Righteous Teacher/Poor/Simple of Judah doing *Torah*. In 1QH,iv.7ff. the usage applies to both "the sons of Belial" (Herodians) and their "nets", not to mention all "Scoffers of Deceit"/"Scoffers of Lying" (*Malizei-Chazav*) who lead the people astray "with Smooth Things", "give vinegar to the thirsty", and whose "works are boasting".

zanut, fornication, one of "the three nets of Belial"; in CD,iv.17ff. marrying nieces and divorce; in viii.5 tied to "Riches" and incest. Part and parcel of James' directives to overseas communities (cf. too Ja 1:14f., 4:1ff., and Re

2:14), the imagery of which pervades Qumran; e.g., 1QS,iv.10's "zeal for lustfulness, *ma^casei-To^cevot* in a spirit of *zanut*, and *darchei-niddah* in the service of pollution" and par contra 1QpHab,v.4ff.'s Elect of God "not lusting after their eyes" (cf. 2 Pe 2:13f.).

Zedek, Righteousness; with *Hesed*, the fundamental notation at Qumran. Taken together these two represent the basic ideological orientation of all opposition groups in the Second Temple period; the second of the two "all Righteousness" commandments, *i.e.*, "loving one's neighbor as oneself" or Righteousness towards one's fellow man, which moves easily into a consonant demand for economic equality and an insistence on poverty.

zedakah, also translated as Righteousness, but haying the form of a verbal noun implying something of the sense of "justification", *i.e.*, in place of sacrifice, one "was justified" by charity.

Robert Eisenman is the author of *The New Testament Code: The Cup of the Lord, the Damascus Covenant, and the Blood of Christ* (2006), *James the Brother of Jesus: The Key to Unlocking the Secrets of Early Christianity and the Dead Sea Scrolls* (1998), *The Dead Sea Scrolls and the First Christians* (1996), *Islamic Law in Palestine and Israel: A History of the Survival of Tanzimat and Shari'ah* (1978), and co-editor of *The Facsimile Edition of the Dead Sea Scrolls* (1989), *The Dead Sea Scrolls Uncovered* (1992), and *James the Brother of Jesus and the Dead Sea Scrolls Volumes I and II* (2012).

Robert is an Emeritus Professor of Middle East Religions and Archaeology and the former Director of the Institute for the Study of Judeo-Christian Origins at California State University Long Beach and Visiting Senior Member of Linacre College, Oxford. He holds a B.A. from Cornell University in Philosophy and Engineering Physics (1958), an M.A. from New York University in Near Eastern Studies (1966),

Author standing in Cave 4 mouth on first CSULB Radar Groundscan of Qumran marls, cliffs, and environs in 1989-90.

and a Ph.D from Columbia University in Middle East Languages and Cultures and Islamic Law (1971). He was a Senior Fellow at the Oxford Centre for Postgraduate Hebrew Studies and an American Endowment for the Humanities Fellow-in-Residence at the Albright Institute of Archaeological Research in Jerusalem, where the Dead Sea Scrolls were first examined.

In 1991-92, he was the Consultant to the Huntington Library in San Marino, California on its decision to open its archives and allow free access for all scholars to the previously unpublished Scrolls. In 2002, he was the first to publicly announce that the so-called 'James Ossuary', which so suddenly and 'miraculously' appeared, was fraudulent; and he did this on the very same day it was made public on the basis of the actual inscription itself and what it said without any 'scientific' or 'pseudo-scientific' aids.

Made in the USA
San Bernardino, CA
16 September 2013